STAGING CULTURAL ENCOUNTERS

PUBLIC CULTURES OF THE MIDDLE EAST AND NORTH AFRICA
Paul A. Silverstein, Susan Slyomovics, and Ted Swedenburg, editors

STAGING CULTURAL ENCOUNTERS

Algerian Actors Tour the United States

⸺〰⸺

JANE E. GOODMAN

INDIANA UNIVERSITY PRESS

This book is a publication of

Indiana University Press
Office of Scholarly Publishing
Herman B Wells Library 350
1320 East 10th Street
Bloomington, Indiana 47405 USA

iupress.org

Manufactured in the United States of America

Cataloging information is available from the Library of Congress.
ISBN 978-0-253-04961-2 (hardback)
ISBN 978-0-253-04962-9 (paperback)
ISBN 978-0-253-04963-6 (ebook)

First printing 2020

For Fanny Colonna, who first welcomed me to Algeria.
For Halima Belhandouz, who first welcomed me to Oran.
For Raja Alloula, who introduced me to Istijmam.

CONTENTS

ACKNOWLEDGMENTS

I AM GRATEFUL TO THE many people and organizations that helped make this project a reality. Without funding, this project would not have been possible. I was able to devote the entire 2017–2018 academic year to writing thanks to a Digital Publication Fellowship from the National Endowment for the Humanities and the Mellon Foundation. The digital components of this project, including video editing and website development, were generously supported by a New Frontiers of Creativity and Scholarship award from Indiana University. I spent two months conducting fieldwork with Istijmam in 2016 thanks to funding from a Mellon International Research Short-Term Faculty Fellowship and awards from various units at Indiana University, including the Institute for Digital Humanities, the College Arts and Humanities Institute, the New Frontiers in the Arts and Humanities program, the College of Arts and Sciences, and the Institute of Advanced Study. My research with Istijmam in 2008–2009, which informs chapter 4, was supported by the Fulbright-Hays Program, the American Institute for Maghrib Studies, Indiana University (particularly the New Frontiers in the Arts and Humanities program and the College Arts and Humanities Institute), and a joint international fellowship from the American Council of Learned Societies, the Social Science Research Council, and the National Endowment for the Humanities. My department administrators, Stephanie Odaffer and Amy Cornell, somehow managed to keep track of the finances.

Istijmam's visit to my home institution Indiana University in September 2016 was supported by a College Arts and Humanities Institute Workshop-Performance Grant alongside generous funding from twelve campus departments and programs. I am particularly grateful to the Department of Theater,

Drama, and Contemporary Dance for offering the use of the Wells-Metz Theater, where the video of *Apples* used in this book was filmed.

In Algeria, Dr. Robert Parks and Dr. Karim Ouaras of the Centre d'Études
Maghrébines en Algérie (CEMA) facilitated my travel and research in both
2008–2009 and 2016. I am beyond grateful for the support Bob and Karim offer
to researchers in Algeria, and I count myself fortunate to have their assistance
and friendship.

In Oran, Halima Belhandouz opened her lovely home to me and helped
make my stay in 2016 better than I could have imagined. As a scholar, she has
critically and generously engaged with my research since I began writing about
Algeria. As a friend, she has helped me to feel at home in Oran since she first
welcomed me to the city as a graduate student back in 1990.

Raja Alloula has generously supported my work on theater since I met her in
2008. She provided access to the archives of the Abdelkader Alloula Foundation and helped me set up interviews with theater practitioners whom I would
have been hard-pressed to reach on my own. Along with her friendship, I will
be forever grateful to Raja for introducing me to Istijmam.

Although this book focuses on Istijmam, my knowledge of theatrical practice in Algeria is informed by other troupes I have worked with over the years,
in particular the El Moudja troupe of Mostaganem and its director, Djilelli
Boudjemaa, who graciously shared his decades of experience with Algerian
theater. Theater expert Lakhdar Mansouri offered many hours of generous conversation. The actor Mohamed Yabdri helpfully responded to questions about
theater in Algeria as I was writing. I am also grateful to two former members
of Istijmam, Leila Bibouche and Meriem Medjkane, for generously responding
to my questions back in 2009 and for agreeing to appear in several photos and
videos in this work. Amo, my wonderful taxi driver and engaging conversa-
tionalist, helped me get around in Oran and the surrounding region for nearly
a decade.

My work with Istijmam in the United States would not have been possible
without the generosity of Lisa Booth and Deirdre Valente of Lisa Booth Management Inc., tour organizers for Center Stage. They allowed me to accompany
Istijmam in the United States: they gave me a seat in the tour van, they booked
my travel and accommodations, and they facilitated my introductions to the
various US presenters and hosts. Theresa Teague, tour manager and van driver
extraordinaire, was a wonderful road companion.

I am grateful to the US presenters and hosts who allowed me to video their
events for my research, including: Indiana University, University of St. Joseph,
Yale University's Pierson College, University of New Hampshire, Denmark

Arts Center, La MaMa Theater, Double Edge Theatre, and HartBeat Ensemble. After the tour, video screening events were hosted by Martha Rounds of New View Cohousing in Acton, Massachusetts; Reed College; and the following units at Indiana University: African Studies Program, Center for the Study of the Middle East, Arabic Flagship Program. Dr. Jennifer Goodlander hosted a screening for her graduate seminar in the IU Department of Theater, and the IU Department of Anthropology helped me host two additional screenings for Bloomington community members. My visit to Reed College was particularly energizing. Paul Silverstein organized a public screening and vibrant discussion of the play. Kate Bredeson invited me to her engaging theater studies class. Both of these events helped to inspire the epilogue.

Benameur Cherif Cheikh meticulously transcribed and, in some cases, translated hours of interviews, rehearsal sessions, and discussions in Darija and French. He also placed the subtitles in the video examples that appear in this book. Without his assistance, I would have been hard-pressed to develop this work. Jenny Parker transcribed postperformance and postscreening discussions in English and French. Lamia Djeldjel patiently tutored me in Darija and assisted with Arabic translation. Mohamed Khaled Sayed assisted with Darija transliteration. Ryan Feigenbaum was an extraordinary research assistant; he helped me develop systems for managing the many hours of video, he edited all the videos that appear in the book and on the website, and he always found the best solution for any problem. Priscilla Borges and David Ernst of Internet-Minded Design & Development created the website and were endlessly patient with this decidedly not-born-digital author.

A number of colleagues generously made time to read sections of this work while it was under development. Richard Bauman read the initial manuscript on short notice and helpfully pointed me in new directions. Ilana Gershon offered a timely reading of an early draft of the introduction. Jennifer Goodlander, Susan Lepselter, Anya Royce, and Susan Seizer participated in a book workshop at Indiana University that helped to guide my revision process. Three anonymous Press reviewers provided detailed and thoughtful comments that immeasurably improved the book. I am fortunate to have such generous colleagues and can only hope that I have done their readings justice. Any remaining errors of fact or interpretation are, of course, solely my own.

Many people kept me going through the various stages of this project. Rebecca Tolen was instrumental in helping me get the project off the ground, and I very much regret that she did not live to see it published. Wrye Sententia of Razor Writing helped me figure out where and how to start writing. Molly Mullin read my chapters as they were developing and provided thoughtful editorial feedback. Tristra Yeager Newyear read some of the early chapters and talked with me in Bloomingfoods as I tried to figure out what I wanted to say. My online faculty support group, Anne Foegen and Ann Marie Clark, helped make the writing process feel a little less solitary and always found just the right emojis. Dee Mortensen, my editor at Indiana University Press, believed in this project from the beginning. She, along with the Press's Ashante Thomas and Darja Malcolm-Clarke, did so much to bring this book into being. Jennifer Crane expertly guided the book through production.

The members of Istijmam are the ones who truly made this work possible. Words cannot convey what their generosity and friendship have meant to me over the years. They opened their rehearsals to me back in 2008, allowing someone they had just met to witness their daily practice. In 2016, they took me on tour with them, welcoming me in my triple role as a member of the project team, an ethnographer, and a videographer. To Jamil, Rihab, Lila, Mustapha, Moussa, and Djalel: Thank you. May this book do justice to your artistry in some small way.

NOTE ON TRANSLITERATION

THE TRANSLITERATION OF ARABIC TERMS largely follows the *International Journal of Middle East Studies* (IJMES) transliteration system. Most of the terms in this work come from Algerian Darija (spoken Algerian Arabic). In keeping with Darija pronunciation, I use *el-* rather than *al-* for the direct article.

Exceptions are made for well-known names, titles, and other terms that are generally represented through alternative transcription conventions. For example, I retain the conventional spelling of the playwright's name, Abdelkader Alloula. Similarly, terms such as *halqa* and *goual* are spelled as they have long appeared in the literature. When I retain conventional spellings, I provide proper transliterations in parentheses the first time the term appears. For example, the term *goual* (storyteller) is followed by (*guwwāl*) for the first usage only. Moreover, most transliterations refer to Darija terms. In Modern Standard Arabic, *guwwāl* would be transliterated *quwwāl*.

Titles of works are particularly challenging to represent because they have appeared in print in any number of forms, particularly those in Darija. I settled on the most conventional transliteration of titles of works. In most cases, I also indicated appropriate IJMES transliterations in parentheses, again using *el-* rather than *al-* for the article. A significant exception is the title of the play on which this work is based. It would be properly transliterated as *Al-Teffah*. However, the actors used *Et-Teffeh*, and that transliteration was employed throughout the tour on posters, programs, and other promotional materials. I therefore retain *Et-Teffeh* throughout.

I am grateful to Mohamed Khaled Sayed for his assistance with transliteration. Any errors are of course my own.

LIST OF VIDEOS

THIS BOOK IS DEVELOPED AROUND Istijmam's US tour of the play *Apples*. Two performances of the play may be viewed here: https://stagingcultural encounters.com/play/. The video of the performance at Indiana University (01:00:14) includes closed captioning in English.

Video	Length	Location and Notes	Page
02.05	01:24	University of New Hampshire, Durham, NH	86
03.01	02:14	La MaMa Theater, New York, NY	97
03.02	01:30	La MaMa Theater, New York, NY (with Sarah Lawrence College)	97
03.03	02:07	La MaMa Theater, New York, NY (with Sarah Lawrence College)	98
03.04	01:30	La MaMa Theater, New York, NY (with Sarah Lawrence College)	98
03.05	06:25	La MaMa Theater, New York, NY (with Sarah Lawrence College)	98
03.06	00:22	Indiana University, Bloomington, IN	108
03.07	01:50	University of New Hampshire, Durham, NH	116
03.08	01:40	La MaMa Theater, New York, NY (with Sarah Lawrence College)	117
03.09	02:14	Portland, ME	117
03.10	06:17	La MaMa Theater, New York, NY (with Sarah Lawrence College)	118
03.11	02:49	La MaMa Theater, New York, NY (with Sarah Lawrence College)	120
03.12	04:08	University of St. Joseph, West Hartford, CT (with HartBeat Ensemble)	124
03.13	01:34	University of St. Joseph, West Hartford, CT (with HartBeat Ensemble)	125
03.14	00:42	University of St. Joseph, West Hartford, CT (with HartBeat Ensemble)	125
03.15	02:55	University of St. Joseph, West Hartford, CT (with HartBeat Ensemble)	127
03.16	00:57	Forest Park, Springfield, MA (with Double Edge Theatre)	130
03.17	00:49	Forest Park, Springfield, MA (with Double Edge Theatre)	130
03.18	06:56	Forest Park, Springfield, MA (with Double Edge Theatre)	130
03.19	01:43	Forest Park, Springfield, MA (with Double Edge Theatre)	131
03.20	01:13	Forest Park, Springfield, MA (with Double Edge Theatre)	131

The excerpted scenes from the play *Apples* were filmed by James Krause of Tabletop Productions. All other videos were filmed by Jane Goodman unless otherwise noted.

To see additional footage from the tour, including photo and video galleries as well as actor profiles, please visit this book's companion website: https://stagingculturalencounters.com.

STAGING CULTURAL ENCOUNTERS

—✺—

INTRODUCTION

ON SEPTEMBER 2, 2016, YOU could have joined the virtual audience for the play *Apples* as it was live-streamed from the Kennedy Center in Washington, DC, where the Algerian theater troupe Istijmam was making their US debut.[1] The troupe had been selected to tour the United States by the Center Stage program, a cultural diplomacy initiative of the US State Department's Bureau of Educational and Cultural Affairs. They were putting on the play known in Algeria as *Et-Teffeh*, written by the country's renowned playwright Abdelkader Alloula. It was the first time his work would be seen in the United States and the first time it would be performed in English. The troupe's friends, families, and fans could tune into the broadcast, as could anyone with interest and an internet connection.

The Kennedy Center show would launch Istijmam on a monthlong US tour. Alongside eight performances of *Apples*, they would meet students, actors, and community members from Maine to New York, from Massachusetts to Indiana. If you were a student at the University of New Hampshire (UNH) or Sarah Lawrence College, you might have attended an improvisation workshop with the troupe. At UNH or Indiana University, you might have conversed with them in your French class or your theater class or at a luncheon. If you were in Hartford, Connecticut, or at Yale University, you might have heard them speak at a public panel about the kind of theater they practice. At all of these venues, you would have heard about how their theater is inspired by the traditional North African marketplace performance circle known as the *halqa* (*ḥalqa*) and its lead storyteller, the *goual* (*guwwāl*).

You might also have encountered the troupe on the streets of New York City or Bloomington, Indiana, or Bridgton, Maine, where, dressed in colorful

1

garb, they were singing and drumming traditional Algerian music and hand-
ing out flyers to publicize their show. Beyond the Kennedy Center, you could
have taken in the play itself in venues ranging from the rustic arts center in tiny
Denmark, Maine, to New York City's celebrated La MaMa Theater. You might
even have unwittingly run across the actors clustered around the latest MacAir
display in Best Buy or shopping for clothes and gifts in H&M or Macy's. You
could have logged in to the social media pages of Istijmam, Center Stage, the
individual actors, or my own page to follow Istijmam's travels from the Eastern
Seaboard to the Midwest.

Istijmam's journey began in June of 2015, when Lila, the troupe's administrator, opened her email as she did every morning. Istijmam's interview with
representatives of the Center Stage program some eight months prior was
not foremost in her mind. But there it was: Istijmam had been selected to
tour in the United States as part of Center Stage's 2016 season. They would be
performing Abdelkader Alloula's play *Apples*—which they would translate
into English—and would enter into various kinds of encounters with US students, theater troupes, and audiences. Lila immediately contacted the other
five members of the troupe. They were euphoric (and perhaps a bit incredu-
lous). Never had they imagined that they would one day be invited to perform
in the United States.

I was thrilled. I had begun doing ethnographic research with Istijmam in
Algeria when they were first getting started back in 2008. I had nominated
the troupe to the Center Stage program, but I was sure that dozens of other
groups would be applying from Algeria and Tanzania (the countries selected
for the 2016 season). I knew that Istijmam had the talent, the experience, and
the discipline that Center Stage was seeking, but presumably so did many other
applicants. I had been doing fieldwork with music and theater ensembles in Algeria since the early 1990s, but for the first time I would have the opportunity to
welcome an Algerian troupe to my own country. When Istijmam was selected,
I knew instantly that I wanted to write about the tour.

Istijmam's US tour tells a story of the encounters through which people and
products reach a global stage and what happens when they get there. Some products are designed for a world audience.[2] *Apples* was not. Its author, Abdelkader
Alloula, was a major Algerian playwright whose reputation extended across
North Africa, but this was one of his minor works, not widely known even in
his own country. Moreover, Alloula's aspiration was to write for his society.
He oriented his corpus of plays to his fellow Algerians and the dilemmas they
faced, not to Americans. But *Apples* had the good fortune of encountering a new
circulatory network. When *Apples* was added to the Center Stage repertoire,

it was turned from a play grounded in the Algeria of the early 1990s to one that could speak to neoliberal conundrums faced by people around the globe.

Similarly, Istijmam never could have anticipated that they would one day tour the United States. It was not on their "horizon of possibilities"—that implicit sense people have of which opportunities are available to them and which are foreclosed (Schielke 2015). On their own, some of the actors could not even have secured a tourist visa to the United States, let alone a permit allowing them to perform. When Istijmam was selected for the Center Stage program, the troupe's image would also be remade. They would become part of a scalar project—that is, a project that takes relatively small products and unknown groups and propels them to a larger arena. Center Stage "scaled up" both the play and the troupe, launching them into wider circulatory networks than they may otherwise have encountered.

Staging Cultural Encounters explores the performances and paradoxes of cultural exchange, translation, and scale that Istijmam and I encountered as we traveled with *Apples* from Algeria to the United States. Join us on the journey. Take a video trip to Oran, Algeria, where the troupe held a monthlong rehearsal residency in August 2016 to get the play ready for performance in the United States. Enter the daily rehearsals with us. See what kinds of dilemmas we faced in finalizing the translation of the script from Darija (Algerian Arabic) to English. Watch the troupe as they trained their bodies for a rigorous month of touring. Join them as they honed their skills in improvisation so they could be ready for anything on the road. Look over the actors' shoulders as they led workshops, spoke to classes, and staged the play at various venues across New England, New York, Indiana, and Washington, DC. If you are reading the e-book, click on the video links to join the tour. In hard copy, go to the website, where you will find the book videos by chapter (www.StagingCulturalEncounters.com /book). Also visit the Tour Galleries, where you will see additional footage of rehearsals and encounters on the road (www.StagingCulturalEncounters .com/tour).

The play *Apples* constitutes the centerpiece of this work. The book is designed to be read alongside the play. Watch the video of *Apples* before you go any further: www.StagingCulturalEncounters.com/play (or watch directly on YouTube here: https://www.youtube.com/watch?v=Qil7osS76GY).

CAST OF CHARACTERS

Istijmam Culturelle got its start in 2007, when a few friends asked Jamil Benhamamouch if he would guide them in theatrical exploration.[3] The troupe

Figure 0.1. The troupe and the author on the terrace of the apartment where Istijmam rehearsed, Oran, Algeria, August 2016. *Left to right*: Rihab, Moussa, Jane, Mustapha, Lila, Djalel, Jamil. Photo credit: Istijmam Culturelle.

chose the term Istijmam for their name because it indicates, in Arabic, what they collectively aspired to achieve: a space of relaxation after a period of hard work. Mostly, I saw their hard work: they were by far the most disciplined of the five troupes with which I worked. They coupled *Istijmam* with the French term *Culturelle* to signal that they were doing cultural work (as opposed to some other kind of labor), mixing Arabic and French to demonstrate their openness to exploring theater from a range of cultural and linguistic perspectives.[4]

Jamil Benhamamouch, the nephew of playwright Abdelkader Alloula, grew up surrounded by theater. As a young adult, he had lived for several years in Europe, where he was involved in both acting in and directing the plays of his uncle. He immersed himself in the works of twentieth-century theater theorists and took a formative workshop with Jean-Paul Denizon, actor, director, and associate of renowned director Peter Brook. He acted in Alloula's play *El-Lithem* (*The Veil*), under the direction of Kheireddine Lardjam. He has directed five of Abdelkader Alloula's plays, including *Et-Teffeh/Apples* (in both Arabic and English, with Istijmam), *El-Ajouad* (*The Generous Ones*, with Istijmam), *Qissas Nasin* (*The Stories of Aziz Nesin*), *Homq Salim* (adapted from Gogol's *Diary* *of a Madman*), and Alloula's unpublished script *L'Astuce* (*The Clever Trick*, in French, with Istijmam in collaboration with the Association Grande Maison of Tlemcen). He won the Best in Show award for his production of Alloula's play *El-Sha'ab Faq bi-l-Wajib* (*The People Became Aware of Their Duty*) at the Mostaganem Festival of Amateur Theater in 2006. Jamil has engaged in numerous collaborations with troupes from across Algeria and Europe, including, with Istijmam, the coproduction of *Yadra!* (*What's Up!*) with youth associations from Algeria, France, and Germany. He also led a seminar on the halqa and the goual for the International Academy of Acting in Rome. With Istijmam, he pioneered a series of improvisation workshops in Algeria called Improvizoo! At the time of the tour, Jamil was also working as an audio engineer in Paris.

Djalel Hadjel was among the founders of Istijmam. He had regularly acted in school plays from elementary school through high school, and he enjoyed it so much that he sought out opportunities to continue theatrical training on his own. His path led him to Jamil Benhamamouch, with whom he studied various aspects of theatrical production for over a decade. For the US tour, Djalel was the troupe's improvisation coach, road manager, stage manager, and lighting designer. He was previously involved in the troupe's productions of *L'Astuce* and *Yadra!* as well as in the Algerian performances of *Et-Teffeh*, and he was a lead coach in the troupe's Improvizoo! tournaments. Djalel also served as the troupe's *berrah* (*berrāḥ*), or town crier, in street performances announcing the show in both Algeria and the United States. In 2016, Djalel was working for a friend who owned a clothing store in Oran.

Mustapha Lakhdari joined Istijmam in 2008. With a background in martial arts and capoeira, he served initially as the troupe's physical trainer before becoming an actor himself. With Istijmam, he has appeared in *Apples, Yadra!*, and *Et-Teffeh*. In Berlin, he performed in *Medea* under the direction of Hannah Ehlers. He previously appeared in *El-Fanen*, written and directed by Ali Talbi, at the International Festival of Theater in Berkane, Morocco. He founded, directs, and performs with the music troupe Goudem in Marseilles, France. He has also sung and played percussion in troupes including Madjid Hadj Brahim and Diwanna, and he was a singer, storyteller, and dancer in K'nibla. His musical influences include Tamacheq (Tuareg) songs, Algerian diwan, blues, reggae, electronic music, and popular sung poetry. Mustapha holds a PhD in maritime engineering from the University of Science and Technology Mohamed Boudiaf in Oran, Algeria. At the time of the tour, he was working as an actor and singer in Berlin.

Rihab Alloula, daughter of the playwright Abdelkader Alloula, grew up in the theater world alongside her cousin Jamil. She was an actor in the troupe

El Ajouad, appearing in Alloula's *Jehloul Lefhaymi* (alongside actors from the French troupe La Mauvaise Graine). She toured with Alloula's play *El-Lithem* (*The Veil*) during the Year of Algeria in France in 2003. Her acting credits also include *Homq Salim* (with the Ibdaa Theater in Oran in collaboration with the Abdelkader Alloula Foundation), *El-Machina* (with El Gosto Theater), and *L'Astuce*. Rihab joined Istijmam in 2007 and has played lead roles in *Et-Teffeh/Apples* and *El-Ajouad*. Rihab holds a degree in translation studies, specializing in theatrical adaptations into Algerian Darija. She has worked as a researcher at the Center for Research in Social and Cultural Anthropology in Oran and teaches at the University of Oran 2.

Moussa Boukra earned a degree in dramatic arts at the University of Oran. He joined Istijmam in 2007 as it was forming. With Istijmam, he has had lead roles in *Et-Teffeh/Apples* and *El-Ajouad*, and he has also been featured in *Yadra!* and *L'Astuce*. Previously, he acted with Oran-based troupes including Ibdaa and El-Youm. In 2014, he moved to Marseilles, France, where he completed a degree in documentary film. His film directing credits include *Kouchet el-Djir*, *Temps de Pose*, and *Hamlet of Belsunce*.[5] Moussa is also the musical director for Istijmam's street performance called Living Communication. He cofounded and performs diwan-inspired fusion music with the troupe Jedba, with whom he also plays the guimbri (traditional string instrument) and is a lead vocalist and percussionist.

Lila Tahar Amar developed a passion for acting when her parents signed her up for children's theater, where she loved being able to imagine herself as different characters. She joined the troupe Nomads in 2004, acting in the musical comedy *The Prince of Corsaire* (by Francis Alfred Moerman) under the direction of Bouamer Yakhlef. She acted in a bilingual production of Alloula's *Djelloul Lefhaymi* and, with Istijmam, in *L'Astuce* and *Yadra!* Since 2009, Lila has been Istijmam's general manager and booking agent. She booked the troupe's tour of *Et-Teffeh* in North Africa from 2009 to 2011, and she has represented Algeria in numerous intercultural exchanges with troupes in France, Germany, Sweden, Iraq, and the United States. Lila holds degrees in Spanish language and literature and business management.

Abdelkader Alloula (1939–1994), the playwright, was born in the Algerian seaside town of Ghazaouet but spent most of his life in Oran. He acted in his first play in 1956, with the troupe Echabab. He joined the Theatrical Ensemble of Oran in 1962, the year that Algeria became independent, where he directed his first play, Plato's *Allegory of the Cave*. In 1963, he was hired as an actor with the Algerian National Theater (TNA). In 1964, he helped to create the National Institute of Dramatic Arts in Bordj el Kiffan, a primary center for actor training in Algeria, which he began directing in 1965.[6] In 1967, he began formal study of theater at the Sorbonne in Paris and was subsequently invited to the International Festival of Theater in Nancy. On returning to Algeria, he was hired by Ould Abderrahmane Kaki at what was then a regional branch of the Algerian National Theater, based in Oran. In 1968, he directed an adaptation of Cervantes's *Siege of Numantia*. Around the same time, he turned to writing, creating and producing *Laalague* (*El-'Alag, Les Sangsues*, or *The Leeches*) in 1969 and *El-Khobza* (*Bread*) in 1970. When theater in Algeria was decentralized in 1972, Alloula became the director of the Regional Theater of Oran (TRO), where he remained for a decade. There, he created his most famous works, known as the trilogy: *El-Agoual* (*el-Agwal, The Sayings*, 1980), *El-Ajouad* (*el-Ajwad, The Generous Ones*, 1984), and *El-Lithem* (*el-Litham, The Veil*, 1989), produced in 1980, 1985, and 1989, respectively.[7] In these works, he honed the style of halqa theater for which he became best known. He went on to found the May 1 Cooperative (Coopérative du 1er Mai) in 1990, a laboratory of theater makers focused on collaborative research, training, and critique (Belhadad 1989). His performance in *Homq Salim* in 1972 (his loose adaptation of Gogol's *Diary of a Mad Man*) at the Algerian National Theater was pathbreaking as the first single-actor monologue in Algeria. His use of storytelling techniques, intonation, and voicing to portray the character's descent into madness would become hallmarks of his theater. Throughout Alloula's career, he studied both canonical and avant-garde theatrical works and writings. He was influenced by the work of Erwin Piscator, Vsevolod Meyerhold, and particularly Bertolt Brecht, in whose approach he found numerous resonances with the Algerian halqa (see chap. 2). Alloula would call his work "a theater of social critique" (Kaouah 2014, 21), foregrounding stories and ways of speaking in which ordinary Algerians could recognize themselves. Abdelkader Alloula was shot outside his home in Oran on March 10, 1994, during the holy month of Ramadan, on his way to a conference on theater. Following his assassination, the city of Oran shut down in mourning.

I met Rihab over tea at the home of her aunt Soraya, who was a good friend of one of my Algerian friends. It was the fall of 2008, and I had just arrived in Oran with a Fulbright fellowship to do an ethnographic study of amateur theater troupes. Soraya knew I was seeking troupes to work with, and she graciously introduced me to Raja Alloula, spouse of playwright Abdelkader Alloula and mother of Rihab. Raja had dedicated her life to constituting the legacy of the playwright, founding the Abdelkader Alloula Foundation and supporting theatrical initiatives throughout the country. As Raja, Soraya, and I were talking, Rihab came in after spending the morning training with Istijmam.

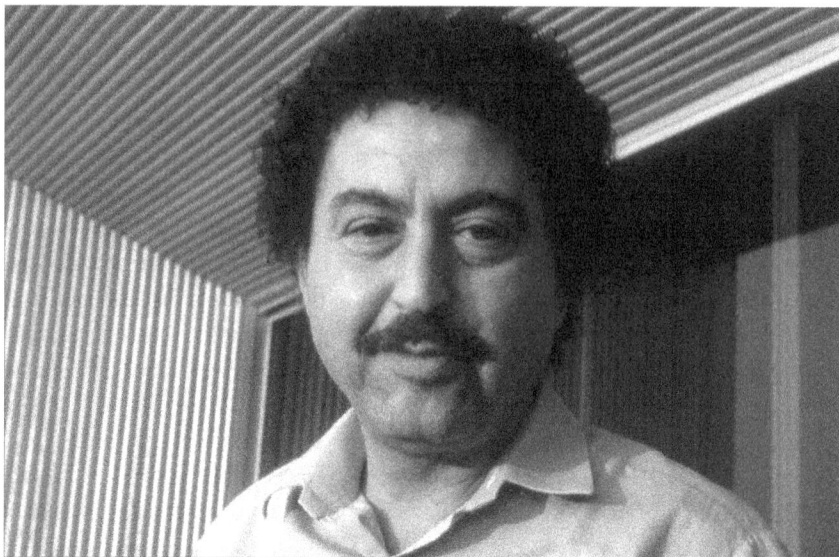

Figure 0.2. Abdelkader Alloula. Photo credit: Abdelkader Alloula Foundation.

She subsequently invited me to meet the troupe, and I was fortunate that they allowed me to attend their daily rehearsals.

Istijmam was billed in America as a "collaborative of theater makers."[8] In the United States, this sounds enterprising, entrepreneurial, and enticing. But in Algeria, the troupe had few choices about how to organize themselves. Professional theater companies are based in some of the seventeen state-supported theaters located in regional hubs across the country.[9] Most cities and large towns also have state-supported cultural centers that often sponsor local amateur troupes. Universities may have theater troupes attached to them. Outside of these networks, if a group of Algerian citizens wants to form a state-recognized theater company, they have two paths: either they form a cooperative or they create themselves as a cultural association (see chap. 4). Istijmam initially took the latter route. But when Algeria's law on associations became more restrictive in 2012, Istijmam chose not to renew its status.[10] This meant that they could not receive state subsidies, not even for their US tour. No private philanthropy network underwrites artistic activities in Algeria. Lack of state support means that a troupe must fall back on its own meager resources. Actors empty their pockets (and sometimes those of their friends and relatives) to pay for basic expenses. Unless they apply to compete in state-run festivals, they organize and self-finance their own performances.

There are no annual donors, no private foundations that underwrite the arts, no fundraising campaigns.[11]

Moreover, opportunities for formal theatrical training in Algeria are few. A graduate program in theater had been put in place at the University of Oran (where Moussa studied). But as Jamil repeatedly told me, most troupes tended to put people on stage with no training or *formation*—a French word referring to a practice-based training that "forms" people for a profession via both academic and hands-on skills. Under the guidance of Jamil, Istijmam would generate their own "formation" in theater, studying and practicing the approaches of the major theater theorists and practitioners from Konstantin Stanislavski to Bertolt Brecht, Peter Brook, Jerzy Grotowski, and beyond. Their goal was less to perform than to form themselves as theater makers. More than a theater troupe, they sought to constitute themselves as a research laboratory (*laboratoire de recherches*) in the experimental theater tradition. They developed their own training in theater theory and practice and engaged in extended critical conversations (which they called "debriefings") about every aspect of their performance. Constituting themselves as a laboratory became central to their identity on tour as well. As they saw it, they would continue research throughout their various encounters in the United States, using the performances, workshops, and presentations that Center Stage organized for them to further their development as actors.

All books start with their author, but I played an especially formative role in facilitating the tour on which this book is based. I nominated Istijmam to Center Stage and worked alongside the troupe in some capacity at almost every step of the way. About eight months before the tour, I reviewed and edited the English translation of *Apples* that they had commissioned. I subsequently audio-recorded the whole script for them so they could hear it pronounced in standard American English. The troupe graciously invited me to join them for their thirty-day rehearsal residency in Oran in August of 2016, where we worked on the play for up to nine hours a day, six days a week. Together, we polished the English translation, gathering around the table for an hour or more each morning to go over it line by line and word by word, coffee in hand and cyber dictionaries open on our phones. Most days, I was also asked to coach the actors individually on pronunciation and timing, drilling with them the rhythms and cadences of standard American English. I was present as the actors, under Jamil's direction, developed and rehearsed a new mise-en-scène. I alternately videoed and joined in from the sidelines as they rehearsed the traditional vocal and percussion music that they would play in the streets before every show—a practice they called Living Communication (using the English moniker even in Algeria). I sat watching as the actors resumed their rigorous physical training with the warm-up series developed by Polish theater maker Jerzy Grotowski (see chap. 4). Exercises that had seemed almost impossibly difficult back when I first saw them take up the Grotowski work in 2009 had now become second nature, essential to Istijmam's brand of physical theater.

We left Oran together on August 31, taking the train to Algiers. We stopped off at the American embassy for a reception and a short musical performance. On the second of September, we flew to Washington, DC, to begin a month of performances, workshops, and other events, both scheduled and impromptu. I flew with them to the Midwest for an engagement at my home institution Indiana University and then joined them in the black Mercedes Sprinter van that the Center Stage tour manager, Theresa Teague, drove up and down the East Coast. Sometimes, I was asked to introduce the troupe and to moderate or translate postperformance discussions. Occasionally, I helped translate during the workshops or panels. Always, I was there with my video camera, hoping to capture encounters as they emerged.

SCENARIOS OF ENCOUNTER

So far, I have cast the tour in largely positive terms, but neither Istijmam nor Center Stage considered it an unequivocal success. Istijmam members were sometimes disappointed and frustrated by what they experienced as fleeting and superficial encounters. They had hoped for something richer. The tour organizers for Center Stage—Lisa Booth and Deirdre Valente of Lisa Booth Management Inc. (LBMI)—also told me that they considered it less successful than some of their other tours. However, this shared sense that the tour did not quite measure up to expectations would not have been apparent to you had you attended any one of the scheduled events. The eight performances of *Apples* all went off flawlessly (aside from the failure of Kennedy Center technicians to turn on the microphones so that the audio of that first live-streamed performance could be adequately captured). The various workshops that Istijmam led for US students were animated and well organized, drawing on the troupe's long experience with theatrical improvisation. The classroom visits and panel discussions were similarly well put together. Audiences and workshop participants gave every indication that they enjoyed the events. Istijmam was unfailingly professional, showing up on time (not always the case with North African troupes) and delivering everything they were asked to do with polish and grace. The tour manager Theresa and the LBMI staff handled the organizational aspects of the tour beautifully, responding immediately to any glitches or concerns. Everyone was well meaning. Everyone came through. What was it, then, that made this tour feel less "successful" than it might have been? What accounts for the sense that it somehow fell short of expectations?

I take up these questions through the nested encounters, both structured and informal, that unfolded during and around the tour. These encounters were bound up in what Diana Taylor calls scenarios, or paradigms that "structure social environments, behaviors, and potential outcomes" (2003, 28). Cultural diplomacy tours like Istijmam's are part of a well-rehearsed, decades-old script that promotes cultural exchange around artistic heritage and looks to structured interpersonal encounters as a key medium of exchange. Like all scenarios, cultural diplomacy tours operate through both narrative and embodied dimensions. As narratives, these tours are scripted around forms of heritage that can be attractively packaged and easily displayed for global audiences. In Istijmam's case, the halqa and the goual—the North African marketplace performance space and its lead storyteller—constituted palatable and intriguing cultural figures that Center Stage could readily market in the United States. They represented the right kind of difference: difference that could be held up for North Americans as a unique North African contribution to the world's theatrical traditions. As embodied performances, scenarios are recognizable because they are built around repeated repertoires. For instance, cultural diplomacy tours unfold through familiar genres of encounter such as meet-and-greet events; educational or experiential workshops; audience Q&A sessions; artistic exchanges; "get-to-know-you" luncheons, dinners, and teas; a sprinkling of tourism; seemingly informal (but generally preplanned) encounters such as street performances; and of course the main performance event itself. Such genres of encounter are built around implicitly scripted roles in which the visiting artists act as the cultural ambassadors while the US participants are the welcoming hosts.

The familiarity of the cultural exchange scenario creates a sense among participants that they have seen it all before. Indeed, the strength of the scenario can work to "promote certain views while helping to disappear others" (Taylor 2003, 28). Taylor's term *percepticide*—a "partial blinding" to what a scenario hides from view—may be too strong to characterize the relatively benign and arguably mostly positive impacts of cultural diplomacy tours (Taylor uses the term to discuss the "displacement and disappearance of native peoples" in scenarios of colonial discovery [28]). But the contemporary cultural encounter scenario does put certain kinds of events and behaviors on center stage (pun partially intended) while obscuring others. This disappearance, however, is never total. If scenarios are structured around certain kinds of social roles, human beings—with their own reflexive capacities and unique histories—are the ones enacting these roles. Like actors on stage, social actors need not fully identify with their assigned role. A space of critique can open up between actor and role, allowing for the possibility of "resistance and tension" (30). These points of tension can be fleeting flashes of discomfort or unease, surfacing, as they sometimes did on tour, in awkward questions or comments. They can manifest as "gestures, attitudes, and tones" that are sensed but not made explicit (28). But if scenarios "predispose certain outcomes" (31), they do not guarantee them. Varying "degrees of critical detachment and cultural agency" can open up between the role itself and the person who is charged with enacting it (29). Still, the strength of the scenario often precludes further exploration of tensions or frictions, relegating critique to backstage grumblings.

This book critically engages with the scenarios and performances of encounter through which cultural diplomacy tours are fashioned. Groups like Istijmam are selected by organizations like Center Stage because they fit the scenario. That is, they offer an artistic product that can be easily packaged for travel and that has recognizable, attractive, and readily marketable elements of vernacular heritage. Groups are also selected because they know how to engage with the genres or repertoires of encounter that make up such a tour. Yet the very familiarity of the cultural exchange scenario can result, paradoxically, in "no-culture shock"—that is, "the disorienting feeling of having traveled in search of novelty only to be confronted with sameness" (Scher 2014, 103).

In approaching the tour as part of a wider scenario, I draw on a conceptual toolkit developed in linguistic and cultural anthropology. The encounters themselves are clearly part of what Taylor would call a repertoire—an embodied set of learned behaviors through which a scenario may be reactivated. Linguistic anthropologists would say that the repertoire is made up of *genres of encounter*—that is, structured and structuring communicative forms that orient the ways people interact. Genres furnish expectations and norms that strongly promote certain ways of communicating while discouraging others (Briggs and Bauman 1992). Genres of encounter like those that structured the tour depend first and foremost on the ability of participants to establish and maintain connections. The idea of phaticity speaks to the ways channels of communication are opened, maintained, threatened, and sometimes foreclosed (Jakobson 1960). Moments of phatic friction can result when connections are threatened. On tour, participants almost always worked to smooth these moments over. In some cases, frictions arose from different horizons of possibility, or the uneven historical and political-economic formations that shape the ways people can imagine their future opportunities and challenges

(Schielke 2015). Divergent horizons of possibility could not be easily acknowledged or addressed within a cultural diplomacy scenario, but they do help to account for the penumbra of discomfort surrounding what was on the surface a successful tour. Cultural differences were more readily available through figures of celebratory otherness (Stasch 2009) such as the goual or the street performances that Istijmam called Living Communication.

Translation is central to the entire enterprise of cultural diplomacy and cultural exchange. Istijmam's tour was the first one organized by Center Stage that involved a scripted play that had to be translated before it could be presented in the United States. It was the first tour for which the invited artists performed in a language that none of them spoke fluently. The translation effort, which took place entirely behind the scenes, entailed recontextualizing and then reentextualizing the play, turning it from a work that spoke primarily to Algeria in the early 1990s to one that could resonate with neoliberal dilemmas on a more global scale (Bauman and Briggs 1990). The work was scaled up, in other words, to speak to wider contexts (Bauman 2016; Carr and Lempert 2016a; Lempert 2016). In translating the play for US audiences, Istijmam also encountered their own heritage and history in novel ways.

As focal points through which to approach the various kinds of encounters that made up the tour, these conceptual tools are threaded throughout this work. Just as the encounters themselves were emergent, developing in relation to each day's agenda and activities, so too have been the ideas through which I approach these encounters. They come to the foreground at some points and recede at others, mirroring the ways that different aspects of the tour itself would alternately move into and out of focus. Moreover, the cultural encounter scenario was not the sole lens through which this tour unfolded. When Istijmam was preparing the play for presentation in the United States, they were not seeing themselves as cultural diplomats but rather as actors engaged in a process of growth and professionalization. This book also makes visible some of Istijmam's behind-the-scenes labor, which was largely invisible to US audiences.

FIRST ENCOUNTERS

That the Center Stage tour was based around the primacy of encounter was apparent from Istijmam's first meeting with personnel from the Bureau of Educational and Cultural Affairs (ECA), the arm of the US State Department that sponsored the tour. It was the Tuesday after the long Labor Day weekend in September 2016. We had flown from Algiers to Washington, DC, the previous

Saturday. We had already walked to the White House, seen the Lincoln Memorial and the Washington Mall, outfitted Djalel (Istijmam's road manager) with a US SIM card for his cell phone so he could stay in touch with the Center Stage tour manager Theresa, and spent several balmy evenings people-watching on the sidewalk terrace of the Whole Foods Market near our hotel. On the morning of September 6, we walked several long blocks from our hotel to the State Department in the scorching late-summer heat and humidity for which Washington, DC, is known. After clearing security, we gathered around a long oval table in a windowless conference room, along with ECA administrators and representatives of the two private partners working with Center Stage— the Lisa Booth Management company, which organized the tour, and the New England Foundation for the Arts, one of the tour's major underwriters. Julia Gómez-Nelson, ECA program officer, opened the meeting by outlining the Center Stage program's history and objectives. As Center Stage artists, the six Istijmam members, she said, were among some three hundred thousand foreigners that the ECA had brought to the US via some one hundred forty programs.[12] Most of these "in-bound" programs were educational and professional initiatives. Center Stage was the first, Julia told us, to be explicitly focused on the arts. The ECA's hope was not only that Istijmam would provide Americans with opportunities to engage with world-class foreign artists but also that the actors would experience America for themselves, disseminating stories and images of their trip to their friends and family back in Algeria through the lens of social media. Clearly, for the ECA Istijmam's tour was only partly about the play they would present. It was also a node through which wider connections between Algerians and Americans could be forged. The US government would not have been funding a tour for six young actors from Algeria without these larger objectives in mind.

Julia voiced these aspirations at the first meeting, encouraging Istijmam members to engage in "frank discussions" and find opportunities to "talk from the heart" with their American counterparts. Ideally, she said, the tour would be the start of "long-lasting relationships." Ideally, Istijmam would take their (hopefully positive) experiences home with them and share them with their networks, using social media and personal accounts to shore up the image of the United States in a place where there were few opportunities to meet Americans and where views of the United States (or at least of US government policy) tended to be more negative than positive. Center Stage, Julia told us at that first meeting, sought to go beyond governments, getting at human connection, at "the flesh and blood of what makes people tick." Her words echo text found on the Center Stage website: "Center Stage supports cultural understanding

Figure 0.3. Selfies in front of the White House, September 2016. *Left to right*: Mustapha, Lila, Rihab, Moussa. Author's collection.

Figure 0.4. Looking from the Lincoln Memorial to the Washington monument, September 2016. *Left to right*: Djalel, Mustapha, Moussa. Author's collection.

between American and international communities. . . . Participating artists experience the U.S. first hand and cultivate lasting relationships."

Part of what brought Istijmam to Center Stage's attention was not only their considerable artistry but also the fact that they fit the profile of cultural diplomats. In the post–September 11 and post–Arab Spring United States, fostering connections with citizens of Arab countries was of particular interest. Moreover, Istijmam had two women in their troupe, including one of the lead actors, in a part of the world where men are perceived as dominant in the public sphere. The other two groups selected from Algeria, Democratoz (Officiel) and Ifrikiya Spirit, were all-male musical ensembles. Furthermore, Istijmam was already versed in cultural exchange. They had just finished a multiyear project with youth groups from France and Germany, culminating in the trilingual coproduction *Yadra! Remembering in Order to Construct [the Future]* (the title has a better ring in French: *Se Souvenir pour Construire*). They had toured successfully with *Et-Teffeh* for nearly two years in North Africa. Most of them were university-educated, and all had some form of postsecondary education. Most spoke some English, and one—the lead actress Rihab—spoke it with reasonable fluency (Center Stage requires working knowledge of English from at least one ensemble member). They had all traveled in Europe. Three of them had been living in Europe (two in France and one in Germany) when Istijmam was selected. In short, Istijmam fit the model of the kind of cosmopolitan group for which Center Stage was looking.

I also fit the profile. My research in Algeria had been funded twice by Fulbright (another government-funded international exchange program, this one for students and scholars). Earlier in my career, I had lived between France and Algeria for five years. For more than two decades, I had performed with US ensembles focusing on women's music from around the world. I knew the kind of group Center Stage wanted and was able to recommend Istijmam. I also knew that my background would attract funding for me to accompany Istijmam on the tour. Our experiences aligned beautifully with a profile of citizen diplomats.

CULTURAL DIPLOMACY: A BRIEF HISTORY

Istijmam's US tour was informed by a scenario of cultural diplomacy through the arts that had been in place for decades. This scenario was in evidence in the United States as early as the 1930s, when Franklin D. Roosevelt's Good Neighbor Policy was put in place to strengthen not only trade but also cultural relationships within the western hemisphere (Campbell 2012). Over the course of the twentieth century, cultural diplomacy through the arts was envisioned as being able to nurture desire for American cultural products, generate respect and admiration for the arts in America, build working relationships with arts organizations and organizers in the target countries, and "creat[e] imagined connections across vast distances" (Fossler-Lussier 2012, 63). But its goals could also be more nefarious. During the Cold War, tours were intended "to enhance the reputation of American culture, create a positive impression of the United States and its foreign policy, and compete with the many Soviet and Chinese performers who traveled for similar propaganda purposes" (Fossler-Lussier 2012, 53).[13] As Jennifer Campbell reports, President Eisenhower "viewed music as a psychological tool" and argued for including "the singing of a beautiful hymn" as part of his plan for "psychological warfare" (Campbell 2012, 41). National Security Council executive officer Elmer Staats went so far as to call music a "secret weapon" (Campbell 2012, 41).

"Reciprocity," or the act of bringing artists to the United States, was the flip side of the "push-pull" dynamic that shaped cultural diplomacy initiatives. Rather than "pushing" US culture abroad, the government would "pull" into the country musicians and artists from other places to share their work with Americans. The Office of Inter-American Affairs had begun bringing ensembles to the United States in the early 1940s (Campbell 2012). This accelerated under the current ECA, founded under the Mutual Educational and Cultural Exchange Act of 1961[14] (more popularly known as the Fulbright-Hays Act after the two congressmen who sponsored it).[15] Its stated purpose was to "increase mutual understanding between the people of the US and the people of other countries" by means of educational and cultural exchange. The ECA staff who met with Istijmam located Center Stage's roots in the Fulbright-Hays Act.[16]

As with Istijmam's tour, government-sponsored artistic exchange programs have long centered around the performance of interpersonal encounters. The US performers selected for overseas tours were expected to be not only artists but also citizen ambassadors who could offer a friendly, accessible, and positive impression of the United States. They were supposed to generate "new sympathies" for both the traveling Americans and their audiences (Fossler-Lussier 2012, 56). As early as the 1940s, the members of the Yale Glee Club were lauded for "exemplary" conduct during their tour of Chile, which entailed "being quiet" and "refrain[ing] from getting stinko [drunk] in public" (Campbell 2012, 36). Their good behavior led them to be characterized as "the best ad the US had had in a long time" (Campbell 2012, 37n31). As Jennifer Campbell put it, "Being a good ambassador would become as important as being a good musician—perhaps even more important," so much so that "by 1961, it became official policy to require appropriate 'off-stage' activities" (Campbell 2012, 36).

As with the Center Stage tour, the success of these earlier encounters was gauged in part by the amount of "meaningful personal contact" that was generated (Fosler-Lussier 2012, 55). Sometimes, encounters were deliberately staged to appear informal or spontaneous, such as when Finnish musicians were recruited to what they were told was an impromptu jam session with the Americans that in fact had been carefully programmed (Fosler-Lussier 2012). Members of the New York Pro Musica, who visited the USSR in 1964, were reported to have made "'soul to soul' contacts with about 20 Soviet citizens" alongside "[s]ignificant contacts" (numbering around 300) "on a medium-depth basis, involving friendly conversations of 30 minutes or more" (Fosler-Lussier 2012, 56, citing the liaison officer).

By the time Center Stage welcomed its first artists in 2012, then, the channels for citizen diplomacy through the arts had been in place in the United States for some eight decades. Center Stage was created under the George W. Bush administration (though the first tour did not occur until the Obama era). President Bush had talked about countries as "friends" or "enemies" of the United States. The three countries he perceived to be the ultimate enemies of the United States anchored his so-called axis of evil: Iran, Iraq, and North Korea. In these terms, Center Stage could be understood as a modest effort to nudge people living in countries on the borderline into the "friends" category. In 2013, with a decade of war and terror largely behind it thanks to a strongly anti-Islamist military-backed government, Algeria was emerging as a prime candidate to be a closer "friend."

In the early years, cultural diplomacy programs were more invested in sending US groups abroad than in bringing foreign groups into the country. But by the 2000s, the prevalence of social media alongside expanded worldwide connectivity may have made it increasingly attractive to bring groups to the United States from abroad. Through social media, these groups could disseminate images of their travel to their home country networks in real time. People in Algeria could follow the Istijmam actors on Facebook or Instagram, watching them engaging in workshops with Americans, experiencing with them the pride of seeing their own country's music and theater troupes on prestigious stages in the United States, and vicariously enjoying their daily adventures. By following the travels of their performing friends on social media, Algerians would perhaps come to see the United States as a bit less distant and forbidding, a bit more humane and more attractive. They could see the actors encountering Americans, sharing meals, and sharing conversation. The mediated images of violence that often shape people's notions of the United States could be countered with photos and videos of performers eating ice cream in Connecticut, or playing Algerian music on the streets of small-town New England, or being welcomed as professional performers on the stages of world-renowned arts institutions and universities.

If artistic exchange programs are rooted in policy initiatives, this does not make them less appealing for performers and audiences. Performers of all stripes generally welcome new opportunities to share their work and to broaden their horizons. Moreover, by and large, performers do not experience themselves as carriers of a particular ideology or as fulfilling any sort of governmental mission. To the contrary, they may even work hard to present themselves as opposed to the foreign policy initiatives of a government sponsor. Audiences, too, know how to differentiate between a government's policies and the citizens of that country. If performances are supposed to be a "hidden weapon," their danger is also hidden to the artists and audiences almost to the point of vanishing.

I write as a global performer myself. In 2013, I toured Morocco with the Boston-based women's world music ensemble Libana.[17] Though this was not a government initiative, our tour was partially supported by the US Embassy in Morocco and included a concert on embassy grounds in Rabat. Libana did use a language of diplomacy on its website: "Never have we experienced the power of cultural diplomacy so personally and deeply as in the living rooms of Morocco—one song, one rhythm, one dance at a time."[18] Yet it is hard to see how sharing drumming and tea with Sufi women in a private home in the city of Fes or engaging in a trance dance with Gnawa women in Essaouira served diplomatic ends. It felt more like we were working to make connections despite—not in support of—government policy objectives. If this is how soft diplomacy is supposed to work, it is hard to see for whom and how it is working. Indeed, a language of cultural diplomacy has been appropriated by artists to describe a shared humanity that transcends state boundaries.

SCALAR LOGICS

The primacy of "first hand" interpersonal connections around which programs like Center Stage are built points to what Richard Bauman calls "the auratic power of 'being there'" (2016, 25): a power grounded in the ideological conviction that face-to-face interaction impacts people in a way that mediated forms of communication do not.[19] Yet face-to-face interaction is not an end in itself. Instead, it speaks to the conviction that interpersonal connections through the arts can "scale up" to serve diplomatic ends. At a micro or "scaled down" level, interpersonal relationships between visiting artists and in-country hosts can be experienced as (hopefully) pleasant moments: perhaps fleeting, perhaps leading to more durable connections that manifest through exchanging emails, following each other on social media, and maybe even making plans to meet again. At a macro level, images and narratives generated from these on-the-ground connections "scale up" to become signs of diplomacy and good will between nations. At this level, they might be broadcast on the sponsoring organization's website, written up in the local press of the places the artists visit, or included in a post-tour report. The touring groups themselves may have their own ways of scaling up, presenting their encounters abroad as evidence, for instance, of the universality of their own country's traditions. When a practice is scaled up, then, it is made to speak to more encompassing global connections; when it is scaled down, focus is on the particulars of the encounter itself.

Scenarios are themselves "scale-making endeavor[s]" (Carr and Lempert 2016a, 5) in that they make purportedly small-scale events represent something larger. The scalar dimensions of the Center Stage tour were readily apparent. Istijmam would encounter Americans not only through the play *Apples* but also via classroom presentations, workshops, panel discussions, and exchanges. At most of these face-to-face events, participants all shared their names and a bit about themselves. But if Center Stage was going to bring six young Algerians to America, it was not only so they could speak in a few classes. It was also to create encounters between the troupe members and their US interlocutors that could radiate beyond the tour itself. The face-to-face encounters on the road would scale up to become examples of the program's larger goal of "build[ing] mutual understanding through shared cultures and values."[20] The encounters would presumably generate a "multiplier effect" (Bauman 2016, 30), moving out to larger constituencies via social media feeds, press accounts, and the participants' own stories. In so doing, they would align with the many government-sponsored cultural heritage events that had long been in place.[21]

GENRES OF ENCOUNTER

If the scalar logic of the tour turned the encounters between Istijmam and their US interlocutors into vehicles for anticipated cultural exchanges, that expectation was undermined (at least for the actors) by the very familiarity of what they were doing. For years, Istijmam had been leading improvisation workshops in Algeria and Europe. They had enacted a presentation that resembled what they did in college classes only a few weeks earlier at a pretour press conference in Algeria. As genres of encounter, workshops and presentations feature organizations of participation that govern the ways people interact with each other.[22] They orient participants toward certain topics and ways of speaking. If Istijmam had come to speak in your class, both you and they would have known precisely how to act: where to sit, when to speak, what kinds of questions to ask, what to do when the event ended. As a genre of encounter, the classroom presentation by a visiting guest is one you have practiced for most of your life. Because of the strength of genre frameworks, the very occasions that were meant as moments of cultural exchange worked instead to smooth out cultural differences. Whereas encounters in anthropology have long been understood through a presumption of difference (Faier and Rofel 2014), Istijmam's tour pointed instead to similarities between the actors and their US interlocutors.

PHATIC FRICTIONS AND PHATIC CONNECTIONS

Phatic forms of communication emphasize the work of opening, maintaining, and closing the channel through which communication takes place (Jakobson 1960). No encounter is possible without such an opening. It can be as simple as

"Let's get started"—a phrase that, uttered in the right way by the right person, will generally put an end to small talk and focus attention on the one running the event. To begin workshops, Istijmam used a familiar phatic device: they would have participants sit in a circle and introduce themselves in turn. Paying attention to phatic connections—to how and when they are threatened and how they are maintained and restored—can point to moments of friction (Tsing 2005) where the success of the encounter may be at risk. Looking at phatic connection also points to the stakes of encounters, in that the effort that goes into creating connection sometimes becomes the most salient feature of the exchange.

Consider what happened at an event with students from Sarah Lawrence College. At the end of an improvisation workshop that Istijmam led, students had the opportunity to ask the actors questions. One student wanted to know when the troupe would be back in the States so she could continue to work with them. Istijmam members all knew that there was virtually no way they could make this happen. The Sarah Lawrence student, herself from Italy, could innocently assume that she could work with other international actors. But as an Algerian troupe, Istijmam knew that they did not have the funds or the institutional backing that would allow them to return. They lacked access to administrative and financial structures that could help them envision and plan such a trip. Securing permission to perform in the United States without the help of a program like Center Stage would be all but impossible. But the actors nevertheless gathered student emails and promised to be in touch if they were back. The offer to collect emails worked as a phatic device, maintaining connection between actors and participants. It also enabled the actors to smooth over the moment without articulating the uneven and potentially uncomfortable histories to which it pointed. It enabled them to gloss over the fact that their "lifeworlds"—the "underlying practical knowledge" about how the world worked and what their place was in it—were not the same (Schielke 2015, 15). During the workshop, this disparity was not visible. Istijmam members and the workshop attendees came together in a shared temporality of the present (Stasch 2009): that is, they were in the room together, participating in the same activities as equal or coeval subjects. But possibilities for trans-Atlantic travel that were available to many of the workshop participants were not as readily available to the Algerians. They had a different sense of "futurity" (Muñoz 2009). This "otherness of expected future" (Stasch 2009, 10) could leak out in ways that sometimes felt awkward or uncomfortable.[23]

The Sarah Lawrence student's question may have brought into relief for Istijmam the fact that they did not share the orientation to the future that her question presupposed. But the troupe's phatic response of smoothing it over also did not allow the students to understand how their own possibilities were shaped by their positioning in a wider international order.[24] On all sides, the desire to perform connection was more easily accomplished by foregrounding similarities than by raising differences. Phatic "performances of connection" like the offer to collect email addresses held in abeyance some of the potential "disconnections of performance" (Feld 2012, 204) that might otherwise have surfaced.

On tour, establishing and maintaining a phatic connection—an opening between Istijmam and their interlocutors—was perhaps the most critical dimension of every encounter. In part, this was due to the lack of a shared language in which everyone was equally fluent. Translation was needed for many of the encounters, making the maintenance of connection itself more prominent than it would ordinarily be. The encounters took on metalingual dimensions as participants figured out how to converse with each other in a mix of English, French, and occasionally Arabic. After each event, both the tour manager Theresa and Istijmam posted to social media photos of the troupe engaging with US hosts. These posts arguably became the most lasting part of every encounter. The images display an archive of phatic connections: Istijmam and their US hosts gathered together, always smiling, at a luncheon, in a classroom, or in a workshop. The images show people in intimate and friendly settings, coming together across and despite different histories, different languages, different nationalities, or (presumably) different religions.

It was perhaps in social media images—more than in the encounters themselves—where the scenario of a cosmopolitan world of cross-cultural encounters was most convincing. Such images are by now so commonplace that they have almost become simulacra, taking on more reality than the events themselves.[25] The images work as performatives that, "in creating a representation of an ongoing act, also enact [. . .] it" (Lee and LiPuma 2002, 195, cited in Scher 2014, 106). In Istijmam's case, social media posts of the smiling actors with their US counterparts came to stand for an imagined intercultural relationship that was only imperfectly realized on the ground.

HORIZONS OF POSSIBILITY: ALGERIA'S DARK DECADE

When I started doing research with Istijmam in the fall of 2008, they would occasionally talk about coming to see me in the United States. But we all knew that this would be almost impossible. At the time, the United States might as well have been as far away as the moon. Not only was travel prohibitively expensive for young people like these six actors, but securing a visa to the United States from a country like Algeria had become extremely difficult.

Part of what made travel so hard to imagine is that in the 2000s, Algeria was emerging from what is now called the Dark Decade or the Black Decade (1992–2000)—an extended period of violent conflict alternately termed a civil war, an Islamist insurgency, a war on terror, or a factionalized "dirty war" sponsored by the military regime (see chap. 1). The six Istijmam actors came of age during a period in which as many as two hundred thousand Algerians lost their lives through violent and unpredictable guerrilla attacks.[26] They had grown up in an Algeria that was virtually cut off from the world. They came of age when to drive almost anywhere meant being stopped multiple times at police, national guard, or insurgent-run ("false") checkpoints. They came of age with nightly curfews, part of an extended "state of emergency" that would not be lifted until the Arab Spring in 2011. They came of age when rural populations were pouring into the cities to escape the violence in the countryside, where armed groups of all stripes launched attacks from the forested mountains. In the kind of civil war taking place in Algeria in the 1990s, there were no armies moving against each other. You didn't always know who was your friend and who was your enemy. Your life went on normally, until it didn't. You often didn't even know who the killers were. As James McDougall notes, the lack of an agreed-upon way to frame the events of the 1990s is part of the ambiguous nature of the events themselves. It was a decade of "contradictory stories . . . in which Algerians themselves sought to make sense of what was happening to them and their country" (McDougall 2017, 294). But there is no doubt that the Algeria of the 1990s was "a broken polity" (Roberts 2003).[27]

Algerian artists and intellectuals were particularly hard hit. When Abdelkader Alloula was writing *Apples* in the early 1990s, Algerians were witnessing the opening fury of what has since been called a "culturicide" (Bennoune 2013) that would see the murders of more than 150 intellectuals, writers, artists, musicians, and reporters.[28] Most of them belonged to the secular intelligentsia, which early on was targeted by what were reportedly Islamist insurgent groups, ostensibly because they did not share a vision of an Islamic state that would operate through sharia law. Perhaps more to the point, killing high-profile cultural figures made for an easy headline that would make an international impact.

On March 10, 1994, the playwright Abdelkader Alloula was gunned down in front of his home in Oran, leaving the Regional Theater of Oran without its director and Algeria mourning one of its most significant playwrights. As a longtime member of the oppositional communist party and its successor, the

Parti de l'Avant-Garde Socialiste (PAGS), as well as a beloved cultural figure, Alloula was an obvious target. Alloula's assassination shut down the city as tens of thousands converged on the streets of Oran in collective grief and outrage. He was the most renowned playwright of his generation, developing a halqa-style theater that spoke to contemporary Algerian society (see chap. 2). His tragic assassination left the Alloula household without its head, Rihab (then eleven) without her father, and Jamil (then fourteen) without his uncle.

When the Istijmam actors were coming of age in the 1990s, almost anyone who could leave Algeria legally was doing so. But securing a visa to get out of Algeria had become next to impossible. Even as I write in 2019, it is difficult for young visa applicants to demonstrate the stability and resources that all but guarantee to consular officials that they will return to Algeria, such as marriage and children, property ownership, strong business interests, and a comfortable balance in their bank account. During the Dark Decade, it was exceedingly difficult for Algerians to make a convincing case for why they would return to their violence-torn country rather than try their luck somewhere else. In 1994, even neighboring Morocco expelled Algerian nationals.[29] Some of the thousands of Algerians with no shot at a visa were choosing to go *harraga*: they burned (*haraq*) their documents and climbed by the dozens into small boats on Algeria's Mediterranean coast, trying to get across to Spain, France, or Italy. When the Istijmam actors were growing up, the United States was largely a place Algerians visited in movies and TV shows—not one that most thought they would see.

By 2016, the political-economic situation in Algeria had improved. The actors were older, with increasingly stable lives. By then, two of them had European residency papers. Most of the others had professional careers. All of them had already traveled in Europe both with Istijmam and in other contexts. They could all marshal evidence for consular officers of a history of returning to Algeria from the Schengen area.[30] By 2016, some members of Istijmam could probably have secured a tourist visa to the United States on their own. But even with the Center Stage endorsement, one actor initially saw his visa application refused (see chap. 1). And such a journey was still almost unimaginable for the troupe itself. There were few channels in place through which an Algerian troupe of limited means and no institutional backing could travel to the United States. A US tour was simply not part of what the actors even dreamed about. As Thomas Serres notes, the low-level state of "permanent crisis" that has characterized the Algerian regime in the twenty-first century "alters the [. . .] capacity to think the future (*penser le futur*)" (Serres 2019, 42). Until Center Stage announced that they were seeking troupes from Algeria, touring in the United States was not on Istijmam's horizon of possibility.

As evidenced by the Sarah Lawrence exchange, different horizons of possibility emerged as one of the unspoken but palpable differences on the tour.[31] The historical and political-economic imbalances between countries in the global north and their counterparts in the global south mean that the expectations people hold about the future as well as the concrete possibilities to realize those expectations do not necessarily align. On tour, these asymmetries were largely erased by the scenario of cultural exchange that, if anything, valorized the Algerians and situated them as the experts and leaders. Indeed, Center Stage was arguably formed to right some of the historical imbalances that had led to significant inequalities among the world's populations. But Center Stage would not be inviting groups from the global south to the United States if they did not recognize on some level the ongoing disparities that led to the need for such encounters in the first place. These disparities lurked beneath the surface.

CELEBRATORY OTHERNESS: HALQA AND GOUAL

If differences in anticipated futures were not discussed, one area of cultural difference was foregrounded at almost every encounter: the halqa and the goual as foundational figures for Istijmam's theater. These figures helped to anchor the cultural exchange scenario because they could slide easily between scales. Oriented in one direction, they pointed to a locally rooted vernacular culture centered in the intimacy of the neighborhood market. Oriented in another, they could take their place in a slot already opened up by other popular cultural figures that have made the leap to the global stage, such as Morocco's Gnawa musicians (Kapchan 2007, 2008, 2014), Senegal's Wolof griots (Tang 2012), or Nigeria's Yorùbá Bàtá performers (Klein 2007). At the North African weekly market, or suq (sūq), the goual is described as a bearer of tales for the marketgoers gathered in a halqa (circle) around him. At this scale, he could readily improvise, adapting his stories to the particulars of his audience and their own histories. At a national level, the goual could be imagined as a bearer of cultural heritage transmitted through the ages, a carrier of the unique repertoire of culture that contemporary nation-states are expected to be able to call upon and display as evidence of their own historical rootedness. At an international level, the goual would be scaled up still further, where he would be cast as "part of a global economic agenda that relies on the consumption of culture" (Scher 2014, 106). All of these associations were in play when Istijmam brought the goual with them to North America.

   Halqa and goual carried none of the sticky residue evoked by different horizons of possibility. Center Stage advertised Istijmam as "repopulat[ing] the halqa, Algeria's town square" by sharing this "populist" form of theater with US audiences.[32] For US audiences, halqa and goual were evoked as signs of an indigenous North African theatrical tradition. As heritage figures, they constituted an attractive and readily recognizable form of cultural difference. This sense of difference was generated in part through the use of the Arabic terms without translation: *goual* sounds both more enticing and more foreign than *storyteller*. For US audiences, halqa and goual could constitute figures of what Rupert Stasch has called "celebratory otherness" (Stasch 2009)—figures of difference that can be lifted out of one setting and celebrated in another. In other words, they created opportunities for "pleasurable encounters with otherness" (Bigenho 2012, 29).

Another component of Istijmam's repertoire came to signal celebratory or pleasurable otherness in the United States: the street performance that they called Living Communication.

LIVING COMMUNICATION

In August 2016, a week away from our departure, we gathered around a table on the terrace in Istijmam's rehearsal space in Oran. A large blue tarp stretched above our heads, shielding us from the intense Mediterranean sun. Lila had just received word from the US Embassy in Algiers: whereas they had previously asked the troupe to perform *Apples* at the embassy before leaving for the States, this was not going to be possible. Embassy staff had planned a lovely outdoor reception for the troupe at the home of then ambassador Joan Polaschik. But there was no seating that could accommodate the dozens of invited guests, and the embassy couldn't ask their invitees to stand for an hour-long performance. Could Istijmam perform only a few excerpts from the play? The troupe was not happy. They had been hoping to use that performance as a trial run, performing for an English-speaking audience in Algeria before their US debut at the Kennedy Center. They had been looking forward to sharing their work with the consular staff who had given them so much logistical support. But more critically, they were upset at being asked to rip apart a play that to them was of a piece, a work of art in its own right. They could not just pull out an excerpt. Though they didn't say this directly, I sensed that they resented being turned into a kind of advertisement for the embassy's work, when they had been working so hard to try to make *Apples* accessible to Americans. They decided against a performance. Then someone raised the possibility that perhaps they could instead perform the music from what they called their Living Communication set.

Figure 0.5. Living Communication, Elmer's Store Restaurant, Ashfield, Massachusetts, September 2016. *Left to right*: Rihab, Mustapha, Moussa, Jamil, Lila, Djalel. Photo credit: Travis Coe.

Figure 0.6. Living Communication, Elmer's Store Restaurant, Ashfield, Massachusetts, September 2016. *Left to right*: Mustapha, Jamil, Lila, Moussa, Djalel. Photo credit: Travis Coe.

Istijmam had created Living Communication back in 2009, when they began touring in Algeria with *Et-Teffeh*. Although the Dark Decade and its violent nights had largely ended, Algerians were reluctant to resume any nonessential activities that would put them on the streets after dark. So the troupe decided to invite people by adopting the performance practices of the traditional *berrah*, or town crier. Historically, the berrah would walk the streets of a town to share news of current events or issue invitations, often accompanied by street musicians. Istijmam took up this form. When they arrived in a new city or town, they would parade through the streets playing traditional Algerian music until they gathered a crowd. Then Djalel—their berrah—would announce the evening's performance and invite people to attend. Istijmam wanted to bring this to the United States, so Center Stage scheduled time for Living Communication whenever they showed up in a new town. The troupe would don colorful garb, take up their instruments (bendir drums, the stringed guimbri, and guitar), and start to sing and play as they walked, periodically inviting those gathered to attend that night's performance and passing out flyers that Center Stage had supplied.[33]

In the United States, Living Communication took on a dimension that it did not have in Algeria. Alongside announcing the troupe's theatrical performances, it became a performance in its own right: a way for Istijmam to display their artistry in contexts where *Apples* was not on the agenda. At Double Edge Theatre in Ashfield, Massachusetts, for instance, Istijmam was overheard rehearsing their music and was invited to give a concert at the local café the next evening. It turned out to be an animated event that performers and audience members thoroughly enjoyed. {**Video Introduction 01**} Similarly, when Istijmam played in front of the White House during their first days in the United States, troupe members and tourists alike seemed to have a good time. {**Video Introduction 02**}

But the performance at the US Embassy in Algiers was more problematic. In agreeing to play their music at the embassy, Istijmam avoided potential friction that may have resulted had they refused to perform at all. They were diplomatic. They kept the channel of communication open. It was, from this perspective, a successful performance. Yet it came at a cost for Istijmam. Rather than a collective engagement with an English-speaking audience around an Algerian play that had much to say about the neoliberal economy in which both Algeria and America were caught up, the event became instead a moment of connection around celebratory otherness. Istijmam was visually attractive, acoustically compelling, and energetically dynamic, but they were performing a traditional repertoire that was clearly marked as other. This is not to say that it was not enjoyable for performers and audiences alike. It was a terrific moment. The ambassador herself joined the crowd dancing in the Mediterranean-tiled gardens as Istijmam played. The performance was followed by a raucous after-party in the ambassador's home, where Istijmam and other embassy guests continued to play, sing, and dance together into the wee hours. But it was not *Apples*.

I had not yet understood that in the United States, Living Communication was potentially working as a form of celebratory otherness when we arrived at the University of New Hampshire and found that the evening's production of *Apples* was already sold out. Should they still do Living Communication? troupe members wondered. I said I hoped that they would. From my perspective, Living Communication was a lively cultural performance in its own right. It would still be an unexpected and enjoyable encounter with Algerian culture for those who saw it. But as with other "heritage events" (Kapchan 2014a), or contemporary performances of traditional repertoires, the potential pleasure of Living Communication came with a darker underside. So-called folk traditions have long been used within colonial and nationalist projects to build scenarios based on representations and performances of a supposedly premodern past.[34] Jamil pushed back. He didn't want to folklorize Istijmam, he said. He was attuned to how heritage could be "mummified" (Kapchan 2014a, 14), or frozen into a colorful display located outside the contemporary world. Jamil seems to have sensed the ways that "the right to be cultural easily slips into the obligation to be cultural" (Noyes 2014, 61). He would have viscerally understood the words of Ghanaian musician Ghanaba: "Why celebrate us as where something else came from?" (Feld 2012, 55). The troupe had come to the United States to share their theater, not to present a bit of traditional culture to Americans. In the end, they chose not to play their music in the streets of Durham or the pathways of UNH. For the troupe, Living Communication was a marketing device—and there was no need to market a sold-out show. If the street performance of the berrah was going to be commodified, it would be to advertise the play, not to stage a performance of otherness, no matter how celebratory.

Discussions of horizons of possibility, phatic frictions, and celebratory otherness point beyond interpersonal moments of tension to more structural differences in how people sense their relative possibilities in the world—and to which world one belongs. When performances like Living Communication get scaled up for a US tour, these kinds of differences tend to be erased or smoothed over. Yet they surge up at unexpected moments, sensed affectively as "resonances that circulate about, between, and sometimes stick to bodies and worlds" (Seigworth and Gregg 2010, 1). Individuals do not encounter an abstract force called political economy. They do not encounter a "postcolonial formation." They do not encounter a "global order." Instead, they encounter difficulties in securing a visa or gaining access to financing that would allow them to travel outside their country. The knowledge in one's bones of what opportunities can even be imagined may be historically shaped, but it is affectively experienced.

Finally, if the tour was framed in terms of cultural encounters, for Istijmam, these encounters were not only with US interlocutors. The usual cultural exchange scenario presumes that a troupe from abroad comes loaded up with their culture, as if it lives in them already. Yet in preparing *Apples* for the United States, Istijmam had to encounter aspects of their culture that they had previously taken for granted. They had to hold up what to them was so familiar that it passed almost unnoticed, making it strange for themselves so that they could make it intelligible for US audiences (Marcus and Fisher 1986). This encounter with their own culture took place primarily through the process of translating the Arabic play *Et-Teffeh* to the English play *Apples*.

TRANSLATION

Each morning of the rehearsal residency, the actors and I gathered around a table in what I call the translation sessions. We were reworking the English translation that they had commissioned from local experts Malik Bourbia and Nabil Taibi (see chap. 5). Reworking the script in translation constituted a process of entextualization, a term that directs attention to the social process of making a text rather than to the finished product (Bauman and Briggs 1990). We were also recontextualizing the play, or reworking it in a new language and in relation to a new context (Bauman and Briggs 1990). We wanted to ensure that it would make sense in English to US audiences. The capacity of text to point beyond itself, simultaneously responding to earlier contexts and addressing anticipated futures, is part of what Mikhail Bakhtin called its dialogism. From a dialogical perspective, a text is not static but emergent: that is, it is born in dialogue with previous texts as well as with the contexts of its creation while also anticipating potentially new audiences and horizons.[35]

Of course, recontextualization happens at every level. Even an apparently fixed script can take on different meanings in new contexts of performance. But here, we were reconstituting the text in a new language and for a substantially different audience and purpose than what the playwright had initially conceived. On the one hand, we looked back to the early 1990s when the play was written. We tried to see it from the playwright's perspective, talking about the play as his response to a particularly challenging set of cultural and political-economic concerns. From the vantage point of 2016, it was readily apparent that in the early 1990s, Algeria was not only at the beginning of the Dark Decade but also in the opening years of the country's turn from a socialist to a neoliberal economy whose effects the characters in the play were just starting to sense. In looking back at that period, the actors also encountered their own histories and memories as children and young teens. On the other hand, developing the English script invited us to imagine what the play might mean to anticipated US audiences. Here, we looked forward, recontextualizing the script in relation to how we thought it would play in the United States. In short, we had to figure out how to make the play both feel Algerian and speak to contemporary US audiences. But our translation process was not readily apparent on the tour itself. This book makes available some of the behind-the-scenes labor of translation that Center Stage audiences did not have the opportunity to see, aside from in short talk-backs after a few shows.

INTERCULTURAL EXCHANGE IN
THEATER AND SCHOLARSHIP

The strength of scenarios results in part from the fact that they can be activated across different disciplines and domains of practice. A scenario of cultural exchange has informed not only government initiatives but also practitioners and scholars of the arts. In the 1960s, around the time the Fulbright Program was launched by the US State Department, academics and theater makers alike began seeking inspiration in performance forms and theatrical works outside the Euro-American canon and cultivating relationships with theater companies across the world.[36] Among the most prominent figures who brought theater into a scenario of intercultural exchange was Richard Schechner, an internationally known director who was also one of the founders of the discipline of performance studies in the academy. The work of Schechner and his colleagues helped set the stage for the kind of exchange that, decades later, would inform programs like Center Stage. Indeed, Schechner and his troupe arguably accomplished the very kinds of cross-cultural exchanges to which Istijmam aspired. Throughout his career, Schechner traveled the world to seek out new performance forms and to cultivate "cultural intersections" (Jiancun and Yongwen 2011, 108). Sometimes, this meant reworking plays of the Western canon in relation to theatrical norms and practices of the host country (such as producing *Hamlet* in China; see Jiancun and Yongwen 2011, 108). Often, it entailed developing relationships with foreign theatrical ensembles and laboratories, as when Schechner's troupe trained with Jerzy Grotowski's theater company (The

Polish Laboratory) in their home base of Wroclaw, Poland. Schechner would go on to study ceremonial and ritual practices in India, Asia, and beyond. At one point, he even took up the path of the anthropologist Margaret Mead: he followed her tracks up the Sepik River in Papua New Guinea, stayed in the houses the villagers built for her, and reported viewing ceremonial performances "that even anthropologists couldn't get to see" (Rosenthal 2011, 204).[37]

Schechner and his colleagues were hardly alone in seeking out encounters that were simultaneously intercultural and experiential. Participant observation as a hallmark research method in anthropology has long meant that scholars take part in the activities about which they write. But the study of performance seems to draw an unusual number of performer-scholars who entered into scholarship through their own performance. I am among them. Although I do not practice theater, I am a singer of world music, and I wrote about my experience as a backup singer in an Algerian concert in Paris (Goodman 2005). I would occasionally join in on vocals with Istijmam during their Living Communication rehearsals, unable to resist the music. After seeing me rocking out on the sidelines while they sang at a farmer's market in Bridgton, Maine, Jamil insisted that I formally join Istijmam for the next performance (I declined). And though I could not have acted with Istijmam, they frequently told me that they considered me a member of the troupe (like their three nonacting members) and that we were fully engaged together in the project of bringing *Apples* to the United States.

Many other scholar-performers have both accompanied and (in some cases) performed with the artists they write about in ways that resonate with my experiences with Istijmam. These scholars similarly highlight encounters as pivotal for both performance and scholarship. The anthropologist Johannes Fabian, who worked with the theater troupe Groupe Mufwankolo (in then Zaire, now the Democratic Republic of the Congo), focused, as we did, on the talk surrounding the performance, approaching the work as an ongoing oscillation between "doing the play and talking about it" (Fabian 1990, 161). Karin Barber, who accompanied and sometimes performed with the Yorùbá Oyìn Adéjọbí Theater in Ghana, was able to see how the troupe "generated" plays out of the context of their "lives, practices, and knowledge" not as fixed works but as coming into being "from the ground up" (Barber 2000, 7). In a similar vein, Laurie Frederik (2012) traveled (and occasionally performed) with La Cruzada Teatral, a troupe that devised plays in and for rural Cuban communities. She both participated in and documented the encounters between the actors (who, she says, also acted like ethnographers) and the campesinos (local rural inhabitants) in continuing conversations about how to translate their lives to the stage. Beyond focusing on the artistic works themselves, scholar-performers have attended to the social organization of performing groups. Catherine Cole, who entered into the Ghanaian theater scene through her own performances with the troupe Jaguar Jokers, sought to develop "insight into the concert party creation and rehearsal process and the dynamics of troupe organization" (Cole 2001, 10). Debra Klein (2007) apprenticed as a dancer with a Yorùbá troupe, foregrounding both the collaborative relationships and the discords that emerged in the process of creation. These scholars joined performing troupes in their own contexts.

Michelle Bigenho and Steven Feld are among the scholars whose work articulates with some of the conundrums I take up in this book. Bigenho performed for decades in Bolivia with the Bolivian orchestra Música de Maestros. But when she toured Japan with the troupe, playing indigenous Andean music that was native to none of them, she saw how the desire for "intimacy across nations" through music could simultaneously evoke pleasurable encounters with otherness and hold potential for "global friction" (a reference to Tsing 2005)—here, around racialized expectations about Andean indigeneity (Bigenho 2012, 26). Steven Feld found his "lives as musician and scholar ... fusing" as he played and conversed with Ghanaian jazz musicians in both Accra and the United States (Feld 2012, 4). Feld's collaboration deliberately decentered the usual scenario: the musical creation and production between him and his Ghanaian counterparts was fully collaborative from the beginning and was never self-consciously marked or marketed as cultural exchange. But in telling his own "stories about encounters" (2), Feld could not escape their "global pre- and after-lives"— including the "place of race in musical history" (6) and "how cosmopolitanism, mine, others', is embodied, lived, uneven, complicated" (7). Still, Feld's work stands out for its attempts to grapple in experimental and unconventional ways with the "poetics and politics of irony" that infuse the encounter stories as well as for its inclusion of extensive video footage (8).

In casting the Center Stage tour as a scenario that paradoxically both calls for and constrains possibilities for exchange, can I offer more than a jaded critique based in a "romance of negativity" (Muñoz 2009, 12)? Can such tours allow for forms of cultural exchange that move beyond awkward or uncomfortable forms of encounter and spectatorship? Cultural exchange, for many of us who are engaged in it as either scholars or performers (or both), has also been informed by what José Esteban Muñoz calls a "utopian potentiality" (2009, 6) or a "futurity" (7)—that is, a hopeful possibility that is sensed but "not quite here." It is grounded in what Jacques Derrida has called "the promise of translation," or (as Deborah Kapchan reframes it) "the idea of an ultimate albeit imperfect communicability" (Kapchan 2020, 27). The possibility, promise, and practice of cultural exchange have passionately informed and enriched my own life as a scholar and performer, along with many scholars, performers, and scholar-performers before me. Perhaps performance holds forth the possibility for finding hope because it offers what Jill Dolan calls "utopian performativity" (Dolan 2005, 8): "a processual, momentary feeling of affinity" (14) that "lifts everyone slightly above the present, into a hopeful feeling of what the world might be like if every moment of our lives were as emotionally voluminous, aesthetically striking, and intersubjectively intense" as it can be during a performance (5). Perhaps the sense of unfulfilled hope that Istijmam, Lisa Booth Management, and I all sensed came from simultaneously anticipating and failing to fully realize the "restructured sociality" (Muñoz 2009, 7) on which this hope rests.

OVERVIEW OF CHAPTERS

This book invites you to follow Istijmam and me through a range of encounters as we prepared for and embarked on our tour of the United States. The play *Apples* itself is structured around two encounters that take place in a public Restroom—a place to let go of what is too nasty to be released in public. A place of leveling, where everyone has the same needs. A place for the foul by-products of living that bodies can no longer contain. A place—to put it bluntly—for all the shit. Frustrations, fears, and hopes come out in encounters between the Restroom Attendant and his two clients, the Customer and the Actor.

Chapter 1 takes up the Customer's dilemmas of desire, disappearance, and disenfranchisement, all located around his search for an apple. The encounters between the Customer and the Restroom Attendant provide a lens into the Algeria of the late 1980s and early 1990s, when the Customer was written into being—a time of political and economic transition that was starting to go terribly awry for people like him. The chapter also considers how these dilemmas resonated for the actors in 2016, as apples gave way to Apple. In making what occurred in the Algeria of the 1990s also speak to the present-day United States, the actors had to reinterpret the play in their own imaginations. In essence, they reencountered the play as they prepared to perform it for US audiences.

Chapter 2 turns to Istijmam's engagement with the halqa as a traditional form of North African street theater. Following the lead of earlier Algerian playwrights and directors, Istijmam drew the dialogic storytelling techniques of the halqa into their mise-en-scène, finding resonances with Brechtian styles of narration in which a single actor creates various characters through different kinds of voicing. But they went further, putting into practice the rigorous physical training program developed by Polish director Jerzy Grotowski to create their halqa as an embodied, sensory experience that would generate an energetic connection between the actors and the audience. They also sought to create their performance of *Apples* as a halqa by leaving aspects of the mise-en-scène intentionally ambiguous and open to discussion and debate—as might have been the case for a story told in the marketplace. If for US audiences, the halqa represented a space of cultural difference, for the troupe, the halqa was refashioned as a form of embodied encounter that was creative and open-ended, always evolving, and highly participatory. In short, the halqa as Istijmam envisioned it was precisely the kind of encounter they were seeking (but did not often find) in the United States.

Chapter 3 takes up Istijmam's travels in the United States, highlighting the workshops, panel discussions, and class presentations they led as part of the tour. The classes, workshops, and panels were polished, professional, and generally fun. But the familiarity of these genres of encounter to all concerned tended to elide and even constrain the very kinds of cultural exchange that the tour might have addressed. Cosmopolitan expectations about particular kinds of cultural exchange were undermined by familiar performance genres that worked either to downplay differences or to contain them in predictable ways. Everyone involved with the tour—from the US hosts to audiences to the Algerian actors—was already well versed in what it meant to attend a theatrical performance, to participate in a class presentation, or to take part in a hands-on workshop. Repeatedly, the workshops and presentations fueled desire for cross-cultural connection while being structured in ways that put it always out of reach. Instead, phatic communication—or communication concerned with establishing and maintaining channels of connection—became a dominant feature of these events.

Chapter 4 accompanies Istijmam into their rehearsal space in Algeria, looking at how the troupe developed in a country with limited resources for actor training. It draws on research with the troupe I conducted in 2008–2009, before we had any inkling that they would one day travel to the United States. The labor that Istijmam undertook behind the scenes in rehearsal was not visible on tour, but it points to some of the most significant differences in orientation and approach between the troupe and their US interlocutors. Two texts emerged as foundations of their largely autodidactic work: Jerzy Grotowski's *Actor Training* and Christophe Tournier's *Manual of Theatrical Improvisation*. Istijmam took up these training methods through a metapragmatic frame that emphasized zealous discipline, conformity, and submission to the authority of the text. This culturally informed pedagogical orientation was visible only behind the scenes, however. In the United States, differences in training methodologies did not enter into either the workshops or the wider conversations.

While cultural translation was part and parcel of the entire tour, chapter 5 takes up the textual translation of *Et-Teffeh* into *Apples*. The actors sought to create what they called a "bilingual" script that would simultaneously speak to US audiences while retaining an Algerian "feel." In translation studies terms, we were trying to simultaneously "domesticate" and "foreignize" the text (Venuti 2012, 2013), making it sound both familiar and strange to US audiences. As we worked through the script, we encountered various kinds of "cultural matter" (Silverstein 2003, 75), or implicit understandings about context and usage that did not readily translate. We ran into "indexical penumbras" (Silverstein 2003, 89), or culturally specific associations surrounding a word in one language that were not present in the other language. We also had to reimagine what the play might mean to US audiences in 2016, scaling it up from an account of Algeria in the early 1990s to a story of neoliberal transformation that people in the United States might relate to. The translation sessions yielded some of the richest encounters in cultural exchange, but—as with the disciplines of rehearsal—these encounters remained behind the scenes, not visible on the tour.

Istijmam envisioned the halqa as a model for the kinds of theatrical encounters that they hoped to have in the United States. An epilogue connects the responses of various US audiences to the play in a kind of meta-halqa, joining together commentary around common topics of discussion in a series of tableaux that point to some of the ways *Apples* has continued to speak to the contemporary United States. In the spirit of the halqa, the epilogue does not provide an overarching conclusion to this book. Instead, you are invited—as in a halqa—to continue the conversation.

In the spirit of the halqa, Istijmam would ask you to watch the video of the play and see what you make of it before you read the rest of this book. But those who have not had the opportunity to see the video may find a synopsis helpful.

Apples revolves around the stories of two clients who successively enter a public restroom that is managed by an Attendant. (In Algeria, which was long subject to strict water rationing, a restroom attendant is often employed to maintain the stalls in working order and fill buckets of water that clients need for flushing and hygiene.) The first client is called simply the Customer. He sets out on a quest to find an apple to satisfy his pregnant wife's cravings. Apples were a luxury product in Algeria when they could be found at all, and they were utterly inaccessible to someone of his socioeconomic status. But his wife is sure she can smell them, so he sets out to follow the smell. It leads him to a grocer

who has the shiny red fruits out—but for display only, not for sale. As the Customer searches the city for apples, he also discovers that the factory where he
had long worked had been torn down overnight. Seeking justice, he complains
to the courts, requests an audience with the attorney general, and tells his story
to a policeman. But he gets nowhere. So he stumbles into the Restroom desperate for release. He begs the Attendant to let him scream, holler, stomp his
feet, and release the pain. The Attendant, a former labor union representative,
is initially resistant: release of that nature is not part of the house rules. But
after hearing the Customer's anguished stories, he is won over, and he sends
the Customer into a stall where he can holler and scream to his heart's content.

As the Customer is releasing his pain, a second client enters the Restroom
dressed in a Roman toga. He turns out to be an actor in the state theater, but he
was marginalized, given meaningless bit parts like playing a closet and saying
"zeet, zeet" as his door (made by his arms) was opened. Seeking a place to pur-
sue his own creative projects, he is entranced by the Restroom's acoustics and
bursts into a vocal exercise. Then he starts to recite Brutus's famous speech to
the Romans after Julius Caesar was stabbed to death: "Had you rather Caesar
were living and die all slaves, than that Caesar were dead, to live all free men?"
He goes on to sketch the kind of play he would like to put on, a play that gives
such a spot-on critique of the corrupt nature of power that the Attendant fears
for his own job. But despite his initial reservations, the Attendant ends up being
drawn into the stories of his two clients. At the play's end, the Attendant comes
up with a vision for their collective futures: they will work together to make the
Restroom an entrepreneurial space by offering a cultural experience—music
and theater—alongside its more visceral function. "Let's get to work," he exhorts them. "Customers will be coming in soon."

NOTES

1. The play as staged at the Kennedy Center on September 5, 2016, including
the ECA introduction, may be viewed here: https://www.kennedy-center
.org/video/index/M60531, accessed July 25, 2018. Both the Kennedy Center
performance and the play as staged at Indiana University on September 9,
2016 (with optional English closed captioning) may be viewed here: https://
stagingculturalencounters.com/play/.

2. I trace the history of one such product in my book *Berber Culture on the
World Stage: From Village to Video* (Goodman 2005).

3. For more on the current activities and members of Istijmam, visit their
website at https://www.cie-istijmam.com, accessed July 13, 2018.

4. Personal communication via Messenger with Lila Tahar Amar, the troupe's administrator, on January 21, 2019.

5. *Kouchet el-Djir* is the name of a neighborhood in Marseilles, France. *Temps de Pose* may be translated "Time to Pose" (i.e., for a picture).

6. It operated under the auspices of the Algerian National Theater (Théâtre National Algérien, TNA) until 1970, when it was renamed the National Institute of Dramatic and Choreographic Arts (Institut National des Arts Dramatique et Choréographique, INADC) and became administratively and fiscally autonomous. In 2004, it was renamed the Higher Institute for Training in the Theatrical and Visual Arts (Institut Supérieur des Métiers des Arts du Spectacle et de l'Audiovisuel, ISMAS). See Amine and Carlson 2012, 143.

7. Alloula's play *El-Lithem* (*The Veil*) was translated into English by Marvin Carlson (Carlson 2008). French translations of *El-Ajouad, El-Agoual,* and *El-Lithem* are found in Alloula 1995. French translations of *Laalague, Homq Salim, El-Khobza,* and *Hammam Rabi* are found in Alloula 2002. Messaoud Benyoucef was the translator for both books.

8. https://centerstageus.org/artists/istijmam, accessed July 26, 2018.

9. See chapter 4, note 16, for a list of state-supported theaters.

10. Loi n° 12-06 du 18 Safar 1433 correspondant au 12 janvier 2012 relative aux associations.

11. In 2018, Istijmam used the online crowdfunding platform KissKissBankBank.com, based in Europe, to finance their next project, but this had not been common practice in Algeria.

12. Programs and initiatives of the Bureau of Educational and Cultural Affairs (ECA) can be found here: https://eca.state.gov/programs-and-initiatives /initiatives/cultural-diplomacy, accessed June 5, 2018. All of Center Stage's events can be found here: https://centerstageus.org/about/numbers, accessed June 5, 2018.

13. A fascinating diagram released by the International Information Administration in 1953 assesses the "basic attitude in Country X" toward the United States, the USSR, and "others" alongside "other determining factors in Country X" such as aspirations, Soviet activities, other foreign interests, other US programs, nongovernmental activities, and means of communication. "Information objectives" are depicted as flowing into the targeted countries through the United States Information Service (USIS), which operated on the ground to organize artistic activities and select audiences (Fosler-Lussier 2012). Performing groups were presumably selected to disseminate these "information objectives" in ways that were at once more subtle and more enjoyable than overt propaganda, though there is little evidence to demonstrate whether the strategy worked (Gienow-Hecht 2012).

14. For a history of the ECA, see https://eca.state.gov/about-bureau, accessed June 22, 2018.

15. The Fulbright-Hays Act was sponsored by Senator J. William Fulbright in the Senate and Representative Wayne Hays in the House.

16. A history of the Fulbright Program can be found here: https://eca.state.gov /fulbright/about-fulbright/history/early-years, accessed June 22, 2018.

17. Images from Libana's trip to Morocco may be viewed here: https://libana .com/morocco-2013, accessed February 6, 2020.

18. www.libana.com, accessed June 22, 2018.

19. Richard Bauman developed the notion of auratic power from the work of Walter Benjamin (1969) on aura and Cormac Power (2008) on auratic presence.

20. https://centerstageus.org/about, accessed July 24, 2018.

21. Of particular relevance here is Richard Kurin's account of the cultural presentations offered through the Smithsonian Institution (Kurin 1997). See also Kurin 1998 on the Smithsonian Folklife Festival.

22. The approach I draw on here is rooted in the work of Roman Jakobson (1960) on the pragmatic structure of communicative events, as developed by Dell Hymes (1989) and significantly redeveloped and refined within the field of linguistic anthropology. On genre and performance, see especially Bauman 2004, 2012; Bauman and Sherzer 1989; Briggs and Bauman 1992; Goodman 2005; Kapchan 1996; among others.

23. Rupert Stasch (2009) develops the proposition that one inhabits multiple temporalities simultaneously from the work of Johannes Fabian (1983) and Alfred Schutz (1944, 1967).

24. I owe this point to Ilana Gershon, personal communication.

25. On simulacra, see Baudrillard 1994; on simulacra and postmodernity, see Harvey 1990, 300–303. On heritage as a "simulacrum of value," see Kapchan 2014, 11.

26. Lack of clarity about death toll "expresses both the enormity and the unaccountability of the violence" (McDougall 2017, 291). A figure of 250,000 was most frequently cited to me by the Algerians with whom I spoke.

27. For accounts of this period, see Hannoum 2010, ch. 5; Martinez 2000; McDougall 2017, ch. 7; Rahal 2017. See also Serres 2019.

28. Information is drawn from https://www.alaraby.co.uk/english/features /2015/2/2/silencing-the-scribes-of-algeria, accessed August 29, 2017, and http:// www.nytimes.com/1993/09/07/opinion/the-war-on-arab-intellectuals.html, accessed August 30, 2017.

29. Visa controls between Algeria and Morocco had been lifted in 1989 as part of an anticipated Maghreb Arab Union, leading to a brief period of reconciliation between the two countries. In 1994, when a bomb went off in the Moroccan city of Marrakesh, Morocco's King Hassan blamed it on Algeria and expelled Algerians. In response, Algeria closed the border. See https://www.economist .com/middle-east-and-africa/2017/07/27/morocco-and-algeria-keep-building -more-barriers, accessed May 24, 2019.

30. The Schengen area includes twenty-six European states (at the time of this writing) that functions as a single jurisdiction for border control. Securing a visa into the Schengen area gives travelers access to all twenty-six countries.

31. See also Schielke 2015 on the lack of hope for a better future among Egyptian youth.

32. https://centerstageus.org/artists/istijmam, accessed July 16, 2018.

33. Istijmam's practice of Living Communication can be compared with what Karin Barber has described for the Adéjọbí theater in Nigeria, which "parade[s]" around town in a pink lorry, announcing its performance over a megaphone (Barber 2000, 1).

34. Of the many works on the use of folk traditions for colonial and nationalist projects, see especially Bauman and Briggs 2003; Bendix 1997; Briggs 1993; Goodman 2002; Herzfeld 1996; Ivy 1995.

35. For a succinct account of Bakhtinian dialogism, see in particular Holquist 2002. Key texts on Bakhtinian dialogism are excerpted in Morris 1994. For ethnographies of text and performance that develop a Bakhtinian dialogical perspective, see Barber 2007; Bauman 2004; Goodman 2005; Kapchan 1996, among others.

36. For more on this moment, see especially Harding and Rosenthal 2006, 2011.

37. On Schechner's ensemble The Performance Group, see also Puchner 2006.

THE CUSTOMER AND THE ATTENDANT

Desire, Disappearance, and Disenfranchisement in Neoliberalizing Algeria

The Customer is desperate. He can barely keep it together. He enters the Restroom groaning, his hand plastered over his mouth, straining to hold in the words that he knows will spew out if he lets down his guard. The Attendant is puzzled: Who is this new client? What does he need? Unable to get the Customer to respond, he at first takes him for hearing impaired and tries to direct him to the School for the Deaf. Finally, the Customer takes his hand off his mouth and begs the Attendant to let him "jump, stomp, holler, release the pain." The Attendant is put off. After all, he's trying to run a business. His house rules don't allow for stomping and screaming. But the Customer is persistent. He starts telling the Attendant his story.

—ᶮᵛᵛ—

When Abdelkader Alloula started writing *Et-Teffeh* in 1991, he and his characters were living through the most significant social and political upheaval in independent Algeria's history. The short version is often told like this: On October 5, 1988, Algerians took to the streets to protest a variety of ills: skyrocketing unemployment, severe housing shortages, soaring prices, scarcity of basic goods, and a general sense of dissatisfaction with their lives and their government. During six days of street riots, army tanks fired on the crowds, killing several hundred and injuring many more.[1] The government regained control by promising political reforms. Then-president Chadli Bendjedid rapidly put through a new constitution in February 1989 that permitted the creation of independent political parties and paved the way for democratic elections. Seemingly overnight, Algeria went from a single-party socialist stronghold governed since independence by the National Liberation Front (Front National de Libération, FLN) to a fluid electoral field featuring some sixty new parties, including the burgeoning Islamic Salvation Front (Front Islamique de Salut, FIS).[2] In 1991, Algeria appeared to be on a path to democracy.[3]

When the Customer and the Attendant were born of Alloula's pen in 1991, Algeria was also on the brink of the Dark Decade. The Islamic Salvation Front, having won municipal elections in June of 1990, was poised to take over the national parliament in December of 1991. The FIS had swept the first round of national elections, but their victory was short-lived. In a military-backed coup on January 3, 1992, the second round of elections was canceled and President Bendjedid was forced to resign. A small group of cadres calling themselves the High Council of State (Haut Comité d'Etat, HCE) took the reins, calling revolutionary war figure Mohamed Boudiaf back from exile in Morocco to head the state. The FIS, made illegal, formed a military wing (the Armée Islamique de Salut, AIS) and entered into what became a widespread civil war that would claim between one hundred thousand and two hundred thousand lives over the next eight years.[4] On June 29, 1992, Boudiaf was assassinated.

Just after I arrived in the country to begin my dissertation fieldwork in August 1992, the international airport in Algiers was bombed, killing 9 and injuring 128 (McDougall 2017, 307). First police and government officials became targets of violence, followed by reporters and writers, artists and singers, intellectuals, foreigners, and ordinary Algerians. I left the country in December 1993, four days after a "foreigners: leave or die" fatwa (religious opinion) went into effect.[5] Abdelkader Alloula tragically succumbed to an assassin's bullet four days after he was shot outside his home on March 10, 1994.

The intense years from the riots of 1988 to the coup d'état in 1992 and its tragic aftermath can be readily incorporated into a scenario of populist uprising like that often marshalled in popular discourse surrounding the Arab Spring. In this scenario, the people, fed up with their authoritarian rulers, rise up against them, experience a brief but exhilarating surge of democratic aspiration, but are quelled in the end. Such an account, however, obscures the ways that Algeria had already been moving toward political pluralism and economic liberalization before 1988 and would continue to do so during the Dark Decade. On the ground, the process was not linear but contingent, stemming more from internecine, factionalized power struggles than from any centrally orchestrated plan. These struggles show that Algeria's transition was motivated not by an altruistic demand for liberty and justice that exploded onto the scene in 1988, but by a more implosive process that saw pressures for liberalization mounting from any number of sectors.[6]

From the vantage point of the Center Stage tour, the stories of the Customer and the Attendant convey an "intimate" and "gritty" sense[7] of what it can feel like to live into the kinds of precarity often associated with neoliberal transformation.[8] These characters (like many of the Algerians they are meant to represent) did not experience neoliberalism as a named political-economic formation but as an "atmosphere" (Anderson 2016) that was as much affective as economic. Affect, writes Kathleen Stewart, "is the common-place, labor-intensive process of sensing modes of living as they come into being" (2010, 34). As an atmosphere, neoliberalism could be sensed but not seen, encountered but not identified. It was one of those "barely coherent, amorphous backgrounds that people adjust to, live with and dwell in" (Anderson 2016, 8). It was like the air: present but invisible, permeating everything but barely palpable. It emerged in fragmented, momentary encounters. It came into people's lives almost the way a dream does: People sense something that they can't quite articulate but that lingers with them, sometimes troubling and sometimes hopeful, unfolding in unpredictable sequences that often do not make sense until later (or just as often, never at all).

In 1991, the Customer was not yet experiencing the violence to come, but he was living the kinds of explosive frustrations that would leave him begging for a place to holler and shout, to stomp his feet, to release his pain. The hopeful prospect of being able to buy an apple became the point at which his life started to unravel. In the Restroom, the Customer vomited up the bile accumulated by his generation: of those who could no longer provide for their families, who saw their jobs vanish overnight, who could find no justice, who could not purchase a simple apple. The Customer's stories speak of tantalizing desire that is just out of reach, of apples that can be seen and smelled but not consumed. They speak of jobs and entire factories that disappear overnight without warning or explanation. They speak of the Customer's initial sense of hope as he goes to the courts only to be dashed when he finds a system stacked against him. They speak of desire, disappearance, and disenfranchisement. The Attendant's story offers a counterpoint. Formerly a labor union steward, he lost his job and had to start over from scratch, becoming an entrepreneur who set up a new business in the Restroom.

The Istijmam actors, as gouals or storytellers, animated the stories of the Customer and the Attendant some twenty-five years later, using the play and the tales it tells as a springboard to revisit memories of that era and critically evaluate their own present. Fragmented recollections of the years when the play was written inform Istijmam's 2016 encounter with the play as the actors (born between 1979 and 1987) came to see Algeria's present through the shards of events and memories from their childhood and adolescence. The actors could use their own present, informed by their knowledge of what had happened to

Figure 1.1. Talking about the play in rehearsal, Oran, Algeria, August 2016. *Left to right*: Mustapha, Jamil, Moussa, Jane, Rihab. Photo credit: Istijmam Culturelle.

Algeria since the early 1990s, to talk about Algeria's past in ways that were inaccessible to the Customer and the Attendant.

This chapter moves between the encounters in the Restroom between the Customer and the Attendant and the encounters of the Istijmam actors with these characters in 2016. Stories of desire, disappearance, and disenfranchisement emerge from both the characters in the play and the actors as they talked about the play. The stories the Customer and Attendant told each other in the Restroom speak of the Algeria of the late 1980s and early 1990s in which Alloula was writing. These stories are told not as linear arcs but as fragments. From the perspectives of the Customer and the Attendant, Algeria's transition to neoliberalism took shape in episodic and uneven ways. It was through messy, inchoate encounters like theirs that most Algerians began to feel their way into new economic times. The experiences of the Istijmam actors as they got to know the play's characters were likewise conveyed to me in fragments—sometimes as we discussed the play together in rehearsal, other times in one-on-one interviews. Alloula's own writing style similarly employs not a linear narrative but rather story fragments that together convey something of his characters' encounters with the new world that they were beginning to inhabit. Similarly, this chapter uses an episodic, storytelling style to convey a sense of the moment when the play was written and the actors' later reencounter with that historical moment as they prepared to bring *Apples* to the United States.

DESIRE: FROM APPLES TO APPLES®

The Customer's wife, Khouira, is pregnant. Her body is crying out for a luscious red apple, but apples do not grow in Algeria. When they can be found at all, they are a luxury product that only the privileged can afford. Khouira insists, however, that she can smell fresh apples when she goes up to the roof to hang out her clothes. Now she cannot get the enticing scent out of her mind. Her husband sets out to follow the smell. It leads him to a local fruit and vegetable stand, its products displayed on the street for passersby to see. A crowd has gathered, staring silently at an unusual sight: a case of shiny red apples. But it turns out that they are not for sale. The grocer had rented them for two days, thinking that by displaying the apples, he could attract more customers. Yet the Customer is desperate. "How much?" he cries out. A neighbor standing behind him unceremoniously covers the Customer's mouth, whispering, "Behave yourself!" How has the Customer not understood, the neighbor says, that the apples are not for the likes of him, a simple factory worker? Isn't it enough just to see and smell the apples? But the Customer is not content to simply "breathe these heavenly perfumes." He struts to the middle of the crowd and makes a scene. The crowd, aghast, pushes him away, telling him to "shut up" and accusing him of "ruining our lives." The grocer goes so far as to close the store, zinging the Customer with a well-known proverb: "The donkey can't appreciate cinnamon." Suddenly afraid, the Customer retreats.

We next see him in an imaginary conversation with his wife. "Oh, Khouira . . . why did you choose apples? Don't you see the misery I'm living? Don't you see that nobody can afford fruit in our country? It's only for the rich, the businessmen and politicians, or people at death's door. People like us are only allowed to desire walnuts, carobs, and jujube fruits, dear Khouira." {**Video 01.01**}

—⟋⟍⟍—

When they were written into life, the Customer and the Attendant were already adults with established careers. The Customer had five children (with a sixth on the way) and a steady factory job. The Attendant had had a prior career in the labor union. They had no doubt come of age in the decade surrounding Algeria's revolution (1954–1962). They had experienced the heady postcolonial years of the 1960s. Perhaps they started working during the prosperous 1970s, when Algeria's economy was roaring with hydrocarbon wealth and the country was being characterized as the "Mediterranean dragon" (Martinez 2012). They most certainly experienced the acute recession of the mid-1980s, when the price of oil and gas plummeted on the world market and the Algerian economy started to fall apart.[9]

The Customer did not describe the changes he saw happening around him in terms of neoliberalism. This was not a term that a factory worker like the Customer would have used or likely even seen at the time. But he did have a word to characterize the changes he saw happening around him: democracy. For the briefest of periods in the late 1980s and early 1990s, the prospect of democracy in Algeria was potent and at times exhilarating. I spent a month in the country in 1990 as the national electoral field was taking shape, and I vividly recall how my interlocutors reveled in being able to say that their country now "had democracy." To Algerians at the time, the dethroning of the single-party FLN regime in 1989 was as significant as the nearly concurrent fall of the Berlin Wall in Europe in November of that year. "When we got democracy" became a temporal marker, a way that many Algerians referred to the country's post-1988 transformation.

As a form of governance, democracy in Algeria failed almost before it got started. But as an object of desire, the term initially percolated with possibilities. In the early 1990s, after nearly three decades of single-party rule, Algeria staged multiparty elections. People hotly debated the merits of the various candidates and platforms in cafés and around dinner tables. The newsstands now offered not only the handful of state-supported or tolerated newspapers but also a burgeoning and often critical (albeit still local) press. Algerian citizens could now form cultural and political associations at their own initiative, without going through an onerous process of government authorization.[10] The supermarket shelves no longer contained only shoddily made Algerian goods. Imports previously seen only in the suitcases of returning immigrants now started to become visible in the shops, though—like the apples—at prices that were out of reach for many. Algerians like the Customer would not have been able to articulate the political-economic history of this period as neoliberal transition, but everyone sensed that things were changing fast. Yet the hoped-for transformation always seemed just out of reach, like the apples the grocer rented to attract people to his shop. Desire for democracy soured as people like the Customer began to experience what it meant to live in a less regulated, free-market economy.

—⁊⁊⁊—

The Restroom Attendant is perplexed. Why is the Customer so desperate for apples that he needs to jump, stomp, and scream? The Attendant is clear: the Customer may not engage in these behaviors in the Restroom, but he is free to

do what he likes outside, where "democracy is on your side." "Democracy," the
Customer bemoans, the weighted word pressing down on him. "Democracy.
I don't even have a place where I can holler and release the pain. I can't even
afford a pound of apples."
The Attendant doesn't follow. "But what's the relationship between apples
and democracy?" he asks. {Video 01.02}

We talked about democracy and apples in rehearsal one hot August day.
"Apples," said Mustapha (who played the Attendant), "are about the pregnant
woman who has cravings—and also about democracy." But what, he asked,
was democracy? And in the context of democracy, what were apples? Maybe
apples represented temptation, he speculated. Mustapha was not referring to
the apple in the Garden of Eden that tempted Eve to stray from good to evil
(a symbol about which some US audience members wondered). Nor was he
evoking the apples found in a folktale in *One Thousand and One Nights*.[11] Instead, for Mustapha, the apple evoked desire for consumer goods that had once
been inaccessible and were now being marketed across the world. Were these
goods simply a way of placating populations, smoothing over political and
economic transitions that in fact made things worse for ordinary people? Was
democracy like that too?

Jamil thought so. "Today . . . the peoples who are in difficulty like in Syria,
Iraq, also Egypt and Tunisia, these peoples—they are sold democracy as if it
were a dream so that there will be a political change. . . . 'You want apples, go
ahead, fight to have apples [but] also to forget.'. . . Because in Algeria, as soon
as we started importing apples, we went into capitalism."

Jamil seemed to be suggesting that as people reached for democracy and
all that appeared to come with it, they did not realize they were still being
manipulated by those in power.

Moussa concurred: "The inventors of democracy, they aren't going to give
you just democracy. They're going to give you democracy and everything that
goes with it. When we take democracy, we are taking the economic system too.
In Europe, it took years and years of war and suffering before they really were
able to live in democracy." He continued: "In the Arab world, it's like, 'Here,
you can have democracy, one, two, three, democracy!' It's not normal."

"It's true," Jamil went on, "that Algeria, like many third world countries,
were victims of capitalism. . . . They were in a socialist system and suddenly,
one, two, three, they had to become capitalist. Right away." Jamil recalled a
line from the policeman in the play: "How do you want to catch up with the
Japanese, with the US, if we don't accelerate?" Didn't the Customer's wife start
craving apples at the very moment that his factory was overtaken by capitalist

Figure 1.2. Istijmam strikes a pose at an apple stand in Ashfield, Massachusetts, September 2016. *Left to right*: Jamil, Lila, Mustapha, Rihab, Djalel, Moussa. Author's collection.

entrepreneurs? Under capitalism, Jamil continued, "Your wife can maybe get apples, but you won't have a job."

Rihab agreed: "In the end, the important product is democracy. It isn't apples."

By 2016, Algerians' flirtation with democracy was long over, and a kind of cynicism had settled in. Democracy had moved from an out-of-reach entity, visible but inaccessible, to an imposed import that, like apples, was tantalizing from afar but that one couldn't actually get on the ground. "Why are you ruining our lives?" the neighbors asked of the Customer after he made a scene at the grocer's. Perhaps like apples, democracy looked better from a distance. When it actually came into one's country, democracy threw everything into disorder.

Apples and democracy emerge here as part of a linked affect of desire and distress. The people were like the donkey in the proverb that the grocer used to shame the Customer: "The donkey can't appreciate cinnamon." For the actors, democracy, like apples and cinnamon, was outside the orbit of the ordinary citizen in the Arab world. Like the fruits, spices, and nuts that were only for the wealthy and the well-placed, democracy could be desired, seen, and smelled but never inhabited. Were Mustapha, Jamil, Moussa, and Rihab giving voice to the conundrum that Lauren Berlant has called cruel optimism, wherein the very promise of democracy held out a false hope that worked to mask new conditions of disenfranchisement (Berlant 2010, 2011)?

"I remember when my father brought back two apples from Morocco that we shared among all our family members," Lila told me. "It was a 'wow' moment. Apples were like Coca Cola and chocolate. You offered them as a gift."[12] But by the 2000s, another kind of apple came to occupy the place of desire: the Apple computer (exorbitantly priced in Algeria when available at all) and, toward the end of that decade, the newly minted iPhone.[13] I was living in Algeria in 2008–2009 when iPhone sales started to take off in the United States following their June 2007 release. I saw my first iPhone in Algeria: an actor in another troupe I worked with had purchased it when she'd been in Sweden. It wasn't connected to any network, but all the icons were there. It looked sleek, sophisticated, and fun. But Apple had no market presence in Algeria. Some eight years later, in 2016, I started noticing shops that looked like they sold and serviced iPhones springing up across Oran. The brand's logo was clearly painted on their doors. Could this be true? I asked Djalel, who had an iPhone 5, where he'd gotten it. It turned out that he had procured it on the street from someone who had upgraded to a newer model abroad. The logo on the storefronts was fake, Djalel assured me. The fake Apple stores in Oran worked like the apples in the play that the grocer displayed to get people in the door so they would purchase other products. One couldn't actually buy or service an Apple in one of those storefronts, but the logo gave the store a certain cachet. (Just outside of Algiers, there is now an Apple distributor, though not a full-fledged Apple store.)

One day in rehearsal, Mustapha started to play with *apple*'s double meaning. In the script, a second client enters the Restroom and hears the Customer talking about apples. Never having seen an apple, he asks the Attendant to describe them. The Attendant, trying to hide the fact that he has not seen an apple either, responds in the most general of terms. "Their shape is between watermelons and grapes, and their color is . . . apples!" But one day, when they reached the point in the script where he was asked to describe apples, Mustapha (as the Attendant) broke with the script and pretended to pull an iPhone out of his pocket. We laughed. He repeated this improvised play for several more rehearsals. Although it was not ultimately brought into the mise-en-scène, the actors did sometimes evoke the newer meaning of Apple during audience talkbacks in the United States, and it always got a knowing laugh. Maybe Americans couldn't relate to a quest for an apple, but they knew all too well of Apple's allure. Didn't people camp outside Apple stores for days to be first in line for a new product? In the United States, Istijmam went on their own quest for Apple products, with trips to Best Buy outpacing visits to more conventional tourist sites (following the consumer pilgrimage traced by tourists from around the world seeking to benefit from the lower prices and taxes in the United States). More than half of the troupe members would leave the United States with new MacBook Airs.

In the end, the Customer's distress was due to far more than apples. The very fabric of his life was starting to come undone. The institutions that had anchored the Customer to his society were vanishing. His factory had disappeared, and his family had left him. He was bound up in an atmosphere that was increasingly coming to characterize life in neoliberal times, where many people were shut out, unable to buy an apple or an Apple, unable to find a job, unable to provide for a family, and unable to find a way out. The contours of the Customer's life had become almost unrecognizable. He was living in a world where what he once took for granted was in the process of disappearing.

DISAPPEARANCE: APPLES, FACTORIES, LIFEWAYS

The Customer returns home from his quest for apples chagrined. He managed to see an apple but was unable to procure it. The next day, he goes to work to find that his factory has vanished overnight: no machines, no administration, no roof, no workers ... just a big "emptiness" (*el-srahrah*) where his factory had long stood. Stunned, he wonders whether maybe he has taken a wrong turn. He retraces his steps. Still no factory—only some surveyors out measuring the land.

"There were walls here, and a textile factory," the Customer exclaims.
"We don't know *anything*," the Surveyor replies. "This is a *private* property."
"But I was working here yesterday," the Customer exclaims.
"This is a private property. ...." the Surveyor repeats. ...
"But what do they want to do with this land?" the Customer asks. ...
The surveyor can say only that "the owner will decide."
{Video 01.03}

Factories started to vanish in Algeria in the mid-1980s. The state-run textile factory where the Customer worked had no doubt been built as part of the "industrial revolution," one of the pillars of Algeria's centralized economy alongside the "agrarian" and "cultural" revolutions.[14] The Customer had probably heard the phrase "industrializing industries," a project Algeria launched in the 1960s that featured strong investment in upstream industries like hydrocarbons, chemicals, and iron and steel.[15] Such industries would presumably generate downstream manufacturers that would produce other goods, like the textile factory where the Customer worked. Perhaps the Customer had started working in the mid-1970s, when some fifty large-scale industrial contracts contributed to a flourishing economy. The Customer would probably not have known this figure, nor would he have known that it fell to ten in 1978–1979 and then to fewer than a half dozen in the 1980–1986 period.[16] The Customer would not have been able to explain exactly how Algeria was financing its industrial development, but he no doubt had a sense that it was dependent on the global market for hydrocarbons.[17] He knew that when oil prices plummeted in the mid-1980s, Algerian public enterprises started laying off workers. He probably wouldn't have known the figures—that hydrocarbon revenue, which constituted more than one-half of total budget revenue, fell by more than 50 percent in 1986 (Nashashibi et al. 1986, 17), or that job seekers began to outpace new job creation beginning in the mid-1980s, with the ranks of the unemployed growing by sixty thousand to one hundred thousand each year (Abdoun 1989, 140–41). But he knew when he became one of them.

The Restroom Attendant also knew firsthand that jobs were disappearing. He had been a well-placed labor union steward, advocating for the interests of workers.[18] His job was to help ensure decent working conditions for laborers like the Customer. The Attendant saw these workers lose their jobs, and then one day his job vanished too. It was now up to him to make his own way. He found the Restroom "empty, closed, and abandoned" and decided to make a go of it, cleaning it up and opening it to the public. He would now be a self-made entrepreneur whose livelihood came from keeping the Restroom clean, providing customers with water (not a given in 1990s Algeria, where water was heavily rationed and faucets were dry for days at a time) and a relaxing environment. By the play's end, he was even contemplating offering cultural experiences such as music and theater.

Seen from a distance, the Attendant, previously in a position integral to the socialist system, had become part of a service economy. Seen from a distance, Algeria had come to exhibit many of the recognizable hallmarks of neoliberalism, including deregulation, economic liberalization, and a move away from state-controlled monopolies (Ganti 2014; see Nashashibi et al. 1998). But the Attendant and the Customer were like most Algerians at the time in that they could not have framed their experience as "neoliberal transition." On the ground, the process unfolded so unevenly, and from so many different directions, that even the institutional actors inside or close to government circles did not necessarily see that a new political-economic order was coming into being.

Similarly, a factory worker like the Customer would probably not have been able to articulate why socialism, previously understood as central to Algeria's political identity, was disappearing. He would have known that the country's mission and mandate were framed in socialist terms. But he may not have known that whereas the 1976 constitution mentioned socialism in thirty-two of its articles, in the 1989 constitution, the term *socialism* had vanished altogether (Aït-Aoudia 2015, 83).[19]

It was not just the Customer's relatively lowly status as a factory worker that made him unaware of what was happening in the country. No one really knew at the time. Even from a later vantage point, what was certain about the 1989 transition was uncertainty and lack of overall direction. According to historian Myriam Aït-Aoudia, the significant constitutional changes of 1989 unfolded through a kind of improvised "bricolage" (2015, 67) with little input from either the population or many of the governing representatives themselves. The governing bodies and then-president Chadli Bendjedid sought to remain in power by placating demands for reform via a "controlled democratization" that would see the single-party FLN lose its central status as the sole governing party without any formal announcement of its demise. In another corner of the government, a small, informal group of political appointees and economists around then prime minister Mouloud Hamrouche had been working since the global oil crisis of 1986 to put in place reforms that would open the economy to private enterprise.[20] But these reforms were not explicitly accompanied by any corresponding plan to open the country politically. Uncertainty and chaos reportedly reigned at the sixth FLN Congress in November 1988. While the Congress adopted most of the proposed economic reforms, it explicitly repudiated political pluralism: "We, the delegates of the regional conference . . . adopt the project of reform . . . and reject multipartyism." Few believed that Algeria was on a path to a pluralist system. One representative even claimed that "there could be no political pluralism in a socialist country," unable to see that socialism was on the verge of vanishing (Aït-Aoudia 2015, 77).

Political and economic liberalization emerged in fits and starts, with no explicit goal to transform socialist Algeria into an economically neoliberal and politically pluralist polity. From the point of view of Algerians like the Customer and the Attendant, liberalization was experienced as a new series of desires and disappearances. There was new talk of rights. There were new products in the stores. There were new political parties. There was the promise of change held out by upcoming elections. But as some things appeared, others disappeared, such as factories, jobs, and state subsidies on basic goods like bread and coffee.

Talk of disappearance punctuated our discussion in rehearsal one day. Early on in the play, the Attendant makes an offhand remark to the Customer: "And I noticed that since we adopted democracy there is a lack of apples." {Video 01.04} The troupe puzzled over this line. Rihab wondered whether this meant that when democracy came in, one could no longer get one's basic needs met. But others reminded her that apples had never been a staple of the Algerian diet. For Jamil, the line called up another kind of disappearance. He shared with us his memory of the area surrounding the town of Mohammadia, outside of Algiers. It used to be full of orange groves, Jamil recalled. At the time, oranges were one of Algeria's leading agricultural exports. Then one day the orchards disappeared. "Everything has been transformed. . . . When I say everything, I mean everything!" Jamil exclaimed. Now, he continued, when one drives through this region, all one sees is big box home appliance stores on the land where the orange trees once grew. "Was it privatization that made the agricultural workers leave to work in . . . I don't know." Jamil trailed off, unsure of the economic details but sure that the region's livelihood had been upended. Jamil's example made sense to Mustapha. "It's like the Customer who talks about the factory: there were oranges and then everything was transformed."[21]

The actors' sense that everything was transformed became more important than the historic details. They were telling stories of a world disappearing with sometimes wrenching consequences. I asked if they knew of any disappearing factories. Djalel replied with a different kind of story, a nostalgic tale of Algeria's move away from what he called "socialism, or, rather, communism." "We all ate together, the same thing." I asked again whether he knew people who had worked in factories that had closed with no warning. He said he did but didn't share specifics. What he conveyed was the general sense of malaise as "from one day to the next factories went bankrupt, businesses were burned, enterprises closed because they were sold to the private sector . . . you start asking yourself, 'What is happening in Algeria?'"

Jamil also narrated the transformation as abrupt. "We were really socialist, communist, with the Russians and all that, and then we changed to be with the United States." Rihab, like Djalel, knew about factory demolitions but didn't have details. "I didn't live [this] personally," she said, "but the situation affects me, the difficulties of Algerians . . . that [the Algerian] has to fight every day . . . he is told that something good will happen and he believes it, only to be disappointed. . . . The Customer didn't find apples, his factory disappeared, he couldn't even get an answer for what had happened, he couldn't find the person who had demolished it; he just found people saying that 'it is the owner who will decide.'" Whereas under socialism people had work, under capitalism they no longer did.[22]

Like the Customer and the Attendant, what Djalel and Rihab articulated was not historical specifics, statistics, or policies, but a sense of cruel optimism—a sense that the country had gone off its track, that the lives people had counted on living were no longer available to them, that the promises that "something good will happen" were instead plunging people into despair. It was not only buildings that were being demolished but also lifeways. The play, in this sense, became a charter for the actors' sense of their own history. "*Apples*, I lived it," Djalel said. "I remember [Algeria's] 'Arab Spring' in 1988, I experienced . . . Algeria's change from socialism, communism to capitalism. . . . *Apples* has followed my life so far, even though I didn't know the text until 2007, but I feel like, wow! [When it was written,] I was only ten, but this play has followed me, it tells my whole story up to the present." Here, nostalgia for the country's socialist past becomes a way of giving voice to the kinds of losses experienced under neoliberalism.[23]

Disappearance of former lifeways is especially visible on the landscape. By 2016, the city of Oran was pockmarked by private enterprise. Multinationals competed with or replaced state-run businesses. The highway from the Oran Es Senia Airport into the city, once running through a virtually empty landscape, now sports foreign car dealerships from Chevrolet to Toyota—tangible signs of the Americans and the Japanese evoked by the Policeman in the play. A Sheraton hotel has gone up on the coast, gentrifying the area around it. Within the city, high-rises built by wealthy developers are producing a new urban skyline visible from the terrace of Istijmam's rehearsal space. When I rode through Oran with my taxi driver, Amo, he pointed out some new apartment towers sitting on a site that had formerly held two national factories: one had produced leather, he said, and the other had produced vinegar. The site had been purchased by a wealthy developer, who had torn down the factories to make luxury condominiums. In the neighboring city of Mostaganem, a local seaside theater known throughout the region was razed to the ground, replaced by a touristic boardwalk (Goodman 2017). Changes in the layout of the land become points around which stories pile up and start to bleed into each other, constituting an inventory of disappearance.[24]

In 2016, the disappearances evoked in *Apples* were also mobilized as a way for the actors to look back at the Dark Decade. Moussa recited for us a passage from a text he had been reading alongside *Apples*: "They destroyed all that is visible and all that is invisible in the country. They killed the children and erased the history of the ancestors." Moussa didn't tell us where this quote

Figure 1.3. High-rises have recently been erected near the Port of Oran, August 2016. Author's collection.

Figure 1.4. A plaque marks the spot where Abdelkader Alloula was shot on March 10, 1994, Oran, Algeria. Author's collection.

came from, and we didn't ask, but it triggered memories of the Dark Decade's horrifying surfeit of stories of vanishing. Many Algerians, like Rihab and Jamil, had experienced the searingly painful loss of a beloved family member. All of the actors had grown up knowing people who were killed. They had grown up seeing daily reports of the latest attacks on the evening news. They grew up accustomed to pulling out their national identity cards at police, national guard, and sometimes false (insurgent-controlled) checkpoints on every major road. They grew up as cultural life was vanishing. Theaters and cinemas were empty if not shuttered. Those who could secure visas left the country. The Istijmam actors grew up in a city whose inhabitants feared the night streets, coming home well before the government-imposed 11:30 p.m. curfew. They grew up watching urban norms disappear as rural populations poured into the cities to escape the escalating violence in the countryside. They grew up in a country that had become an international pariah, isolated from the world. Like the empty footprints of former factories, such memories of disappearance were also mapped onto the landscape. Plaques memorialize some sites of violence, like the one outside Alloula's home on the Rue de Mostaganem in Oran, or the one at the

National Theater of Algeria commemorating the assassination of its director, Azzedine Medjoubi, in 1995. Others live in memory and emerge in story.

—⚘—

On August 30, 2016, the six actors and I boarded the train from Oran to Algiers. We were embarking on our journey. The feeling was playful and anticipatory. I joined the women of the troupe in putting on lipstick, admiring ourselves in our pocket mirrors, and snapping pictures of each other on our cell phones. Then I looked out the window. An empty shell of what had once been a thriving factory loomed before me, falling into ruin. A scene from the play had opened up right before my eyes.

DISENFRANCHISEMENT

The Customer left the site of the vanished factory in distress. He had been told by the surveyors that his former coworkers were running from one administration to another seeking a solution. He searched the whole city but couldn't find them. "Then, I decided to go to the court," he declared.

At this, the Attendant broke role, moved the cube to the center of the stage, sat down, arranged his face in a big smile, and raised his hands to his shoulders, palms up and fingers pointing out. He formed with his body the symbol of the balanced scales associated with justice. "No, the court!" the Customer repeated. The Attendant's smile turned to a frown as he lowered one arm. Clearly the scales had been tipped from the beginning. No justice would be forthcoming. {**Video 01.05**}

The Customer had lost everything. He had no recourse, no way to learn what had become of his factory, no compensation, and no way out. He was utterly disenfranchised. Like desire and disappearance, a sense of disenfranchisement was starting to pervade the atmosphere in which many Algerians were living. Socialism's promise of full employment, backed up by sizable state subventions on basic goods, was yielding to an "everyone for himself" mentality.

In the court, the Customer recounts his story to a police officer. "I told him about the factory that disappeared. He told me that it was normal. Our country is developing rapidly. This is modernity." But the officer is not sympathetic: "How do you want to catch up with the Japanese and the US if we don't accelerate?" {**Video 01.06**}

As the actors talked about these scenes in 2016, it was not just factory workers whom they saw as disenfranchised. In their view, Algeria itself was disenfranchised, barred from the possibility of occupying an equal position in the world system. For them, the Customer running around the city and looking for his factory was like Algeria and its African neighbors. "We third-world countries, we have done nothing but run for the last twenty years," said Jamil. "We don't even know what we are running towards. But the gulf is only growing wider. That's capitalism: the gulf between the one with money and the one without it." The scales had been tipped against countries like Algeria from the beginning, and things had been that way for so long that there was simply no way to right the imbalance. Algeria could never accelerate fast enough. The gap between the United States or Japan and the rest of the world was widening. There was still a de facto colonial system in place. "For the rest of the world," Jamil said, "Algeria must never have its independence." Countries like Algeria would never be equals in the world system.

For Moussa, it was the larger "global economic laws" that had led to the demolition of the factory: "They started imposing global economic laws that made it so the factory was demolished and the Customer was out of work." Moreover, "nothing had changed" in this regard since the play had been written in 1991, added Rihab. "The United States and Japan are still the great world powers."[25]

> "But what about my rights, my efforts, my sweat, my blood, my job?" the Customer asks. In response, the police officer drags the Customer away from the crowd, telling him that "there is no way to pursue this case," that "someone who is able to buy and demolish a factory is also able to buy justice and corrupt it." {**Video 01.07**}

Bound up in disenfranchisement is a sense of no recourse. The Customer cannot find help anywhere. No one will listen to him. His sense of powerlessness is compounded when the policeman makes it seem normal. Moussa started to articulate what this might feel like: "The system puts people in the shit, and then tells them that everything is fine. You're in the shit (*dans la merde*) but they say no, you're fine. . . . In Algeria they didn't just change the political economy but especially the consciousness of the Algerian people." In other words, the sense of disenfranchisement does not generate opposition but further ensconces people "in the shit," like the family of twelve people living under the stairs in the courtroom because they were kicked out of their house and have no other place to go.

Jamil saw the lack of political opposition as a global problem: "There is no opposition in the world. In the world. Especially not in Arab countries." For Rihab, it was also local: she brought up an example of a wealthy Algerian whose large construction project had caused a nearby bridge to collapse, injuring people, but no one dared to say what had happened. Why? Because it was a rich man with enormous power. Even the wali (local governor) couldn't do anything, she said, "because power is money, money is power."[26]

I can add my own memory to the compendium of stories. In 2008–2009, I was renting an apartment in a relatively upscale building on Oran's Avenue Loubet, a street at the very center of the city that residents consider its Fifth Avenue. The building custodian lived in a small, cagelike room by the elevator shaft, under an imposing staircase. The colonial-era building had fallen into some disrepair, and one of the new, wealthier tenants sought to clean it up. She hired her own cleaning team, spruced up the lobby, and successfully evicted the custodian. Then one day, he left a plastic bag containing presumably his own shit in the doorway for her to discover.

—∿∿—

When the Customer asks the Attendant when he last ate pears, peaches, grapes, or almonds, the Attendant gets a wistful, faraway look in his eyes. "A very long time ago." Then the Attendant remembers bananas. "If apples are making you behave that way," he says to the Customer, "what would you do for *bananas*? Bananas will make you run away from the country." As he delivers the line, the Attendant playfully embodies it, pretending to drive across the border where bananas were presumably plentiful. {**Video 01.08**}

The border has become another site of global disenfranchisement. Getting across a national border requires a passport stamped with a visa. Algerian novelist Tahar Djaout (assassinated at the beginning of the Dark Decade in June 1993) had characterized a passport with a valid visa as a "coveted and slightly magical object that citizens love to feel in their pocket, like a promise of escape" (2002, 68). In the Dark Decade, getting a visa out of Algeria was all but impossible. An exit visa had become "the most sought-after of commodities" (McDougall 2017, 292). Getting a visa to the United States still requires a steady job, a stable family situation, and a bank account with at least two thousand euros.

Securing a visa to the United States from a country like Algeria is not straightforward even for artists in troupes like Istijmam, who have official invitations from the US State Department and have been preselected and vetted by Center Stage. The six Istijmam troupe members went together to the US Consulate in Algiers on July 31, 2016, the day before the rehearsal residency was to start, with all the requisite documents in hand. Five of them were granted visas, but one, Djalel, was not. The consular official who interviewed him apparently feared that Djalel had the profile of someone who might remain illegally in the United States. It was true that his employment situation was problematic: Djalel worked in a friend's shop in Oran, but he was not listed on the shop's official register of commerce, so he had to declare on his visa application that he was unemployed. His wife had a steady job, but her income was deemed insufficient by the consular officer. Djalel did meet one criterion—he had two young children, and family ties are considered a strong motivator for return to one's home country. But the consular officer balked. "Why wouldn't you stay in the United States?" he reportedly asked.

"Because I have a wife and two children," Djalel responded.

"Why would a woman marry you if you are unemployed?" the officer then queried.

"Um, because she loves me," Djalel replied. He pointed out that the stamps on his passport demonstrated that he had already traveled to several Schengen countries and had returned home each time.[27]

But the consular officer wasn't having it. "Leave the embassy," he said. "*Vous quittez l'ambassade.*"

Two days later, in rehearsal, the encounter was playfully evoked. Djalel, Istijmam's improvisation coach, asked the actors to experiment with an exercise called "*Je suis un . . .*" ("I am a . . .").[28] Someone was to call out an object, animal, or social character, and the actor had to find a way to enact it. Mustapha went first. "I am a . . ." he prompted.

"University professor of chemistry" Moussa said.

Mustapha pretended to speak like a chemist, talking about the chemical reaction of aspirin in water.

Next, Rihab proposed an unconventional topic: "Galeta [nickname for Djalel] when he exited the consulate."

Mustapha exaggerated the way Djalel acted. "But, I love her," he said, and then he made as if to enter a restaurant (the six actors had gone out to eat afterward) and order copious amounts of food to counter his stress. Everyone laughed, but this uncertainty would cast a cloud over rehearsal for the next couple of weeks. {Video 01.09}

Then it was Rihab's turn. "*Je suis un . . . .*"

"*Chomeur* [unemployed]," Moussa called out.

"I am unemployed," Rihab repeated. She first went over and leaned against the wall, a position Algeria's many unemployed had made notorious (leading them to be called *hittistes*, or people at the wall, *ḥiṭ*). She then laid down in the middle of the room and pretended to sleep. Here, Djalel stopped her, suggesting that she try something more active than sleeping. She began again. "*Je suis un . . .*"

"*Stylo* [pen]," called out Moussa.

"I am a pen." She glued her arms to her body and pressed her legs together, enacting the pen's sleek form as she launched into her improv. "I am fed up, guys! Do you know how long I've been in the pencil case? . . . I need to get out of here. I've got to find a makeshift boat.[29] Excuse me, I am going to call one of my pen friends in the United States." She motioned as if to call. "Come on, answer, Steven! Hello, how is it going? Can you hear me? [*To herself*] I think there is no cell coverage here. Hold on." She moved to the corner of the room by the terrace to get better coverage. "Look, I have to come. I am fed up. . . . What? [There is] a program? Center Stage? They help people come there? Really? Even people who don't have a job? How does it work? What do I have to do? . . . Let my hair grow and make myself look like an artist. No problem, I can do that. . . . I need to get married too? . . . When can I come? Is there a place for me? With who?" {**Video 01.10**}

The pen becomes the Algerian, stuck in place, immobile, but desperate to leave the country. Rihab herself was not among the many young Algerians who wistfully fantasize about leaving. She had a steady professional job and strong family ties in Algeria. She did not feel stuck in place, and she had been able to secure visas to perform and travel in Europe when she wanted. But like everyone else in Algeria, she was well aware of the pervasive feelings of boredom, frustration, and desire that led so many young people to want to leave.

The next week, on August 8, five visas were delivered to the troupe in Oran. Djalel's application was still in limbo. Although the troupe kept rehearsing, a pall had fallen over the rehearsals. The actors were prepared to cancel the trip altogether rather than leave without Djalel. It was hard to get enthusiastic when one of their members wasn't yet guaranteed a spot on the tour. Motivation started flagging. Mustapha told me that he had wanted to set a new running record for himself during their morning physical exercises but then got preoccupied with wondering whether they would actually go to the United States after all. They started telling visa horror stories—a familiar genre in countries like Algeria where visas are so hard to come by. They were especially haunted by the story of another performing group they knew who had been invited to the United States as part of a cultural exchange. One member didn't get the visa until the day after he was supposed to leave. Jamil was determined that this would not happen to Istijmam. They weren't going to be suspended in a state of uncertainty up until the moment of departure. On August 11, Jamil told Lila, the troupe's administrator and their liaison to the US Consulate, to convey to the consulate that they needed a definitive answer.

On August 15, Lila announced that Djalel's visa would be forthcoming. I could feel the heaviness dissipate. The granting of the visa also lifted the silence that had taken hold around the troupe's visit to the consulate. The actors started playfully incorporating aspects of the consular officer's exchange with Djalel in their improvisations. Djalel, the improvisation leader, at one point used the phrase "Leave the embassy!" to get the actors to leave the room. Everyone laughed. Then they started talking about their own experience at the consulate. They all had had to stand in line outside for two hours in full sun in hundred-degree heat. Because there were six of them, they could take turns, but others could not. Babies were crying in their parents' arms. Why weren't there more humane conditions? they asked. People would not be forced to stand for hours in unrelenting heat in Europe, said Jamil (who had spent several years in France).

As an American citizen and one of their US hosts, I was chagrined. I wanted the troupe to be excited about the prospect of touring in the United States. I didn't want their first encounter with my country to be like this. But there it was. The division of the world was awkward on an interpersonal level. Some people, like me, have passports that let them go almost anywhere. Others see their movement restricted to a tiny part of the globe, perhaps just their own country, and they encounter suspicion and mistrust when they seek to travel. They are like the pen who couldn't get out of the pencil case, immobilized for so long that it almost forgot how to move. The unevenness of global mobility was also conveyed in a story by Moussa, who by 2016 was living in France. He had been accepted into the University of Grenoble but was not granted a visa. He ended up marrying his French sweetheart and secured the visa that way. Before that, she had been going back and forth between her home in France and Moussa's home in Algeria. "The Algerian visa was accessible to her, but for me the French visa was not accessible," he lamented.[30]

Moussa compared the visa to the apple, but as he spoke, it became clear that the visa was more than a desired object—it was, for Moussa, a human right as well as a site of global discrimination against Arab and African worlds. "The right to travel is a human right, at UNICEF [he meant the United Nations] it is a human right. . . . I don't understand. If I work or don't work, that is not the problem. It is my right to travel. . . . [Denying that right], it's western, American politics and all of the western prejudices against the Arab world, against Africa." This is precisely what Abdelkader Alloula was getting at in his plays, Jamil contended. "It's the people who are always the victims of political decisions. No matter what we do, the people pay for the hypocrisy [of the leaders]. The leaders live very well, they can travel when they want, where they want, they don't need a visa."

Figure 1.5. At Reagan International Airport in Washington, DC, en route to Indiana, visas in hand, September 2016. *Left to right*: Lila, Jamil, Djalel, Mustapha, Moussa, Rihab. Author's collection.

For Lila too, the visa was like the apple: "Apples, it isn't just about the fruit, it's about the desire of an ordinary Algerian citizen to travel."[31] As I have been writing this book, the US government has made it increasingly difficult for visitors from certain parts of the world to enter the United States. The US Supreme Court allowed a partial travel ban to go into effect on June 29, 2017,[32] targeting refugees across the world as well as citizens from six Muslim-majority countries. On January 31, 2020, six more countries were added to the list.[33] Although Algeria was not one of the banned countries, I wonder what might have become of Djalel's visa application in the intensified exclusionary climate of 2017–2020. But in August 2016, "the impossible became possible," as Jamil put it. Djalel got his visa. Istijmam, whose members had never dreamed that they would be performing in the United States, would soon be leaving for the tour.

A visa to the United States is perhaps the ultimate symbol of cruel optimism. In much of the ex-colonized world, getting to the United States is held out as a promise of a better life. The United States has been seen as of a land of equality and opportunity, a place where anyone with enough drive can make it. But those who find their way across borders without documents face a life of clandestine poverty, working under the table (if they find work at all) and finding themselves at the bottom of a society that makes no room for them. Even those who win the annual visa lottery and come with proper paperwork start at the bottom. For Istijmam, of course, it was a different kind of trip: a cultural exchange in which they were valued as artists. It was never their intention to remain in the country. But as they walked through American cities, they were repeatedly shocked by the homeless living on the streets. They saw people like the family in the play who had been kicked out of their apartment and were living under the stairs at the court. They saw the signs of those who had not made it, those who were disenfranchised.

As the Istijmam actors brought their own stories together with those of the Customer and the Attendant, they began setting the stage for *Apples* to become a halqa—a storytelling forum that opens tales of the past to contemporary interpretations. The halqa as Istijmam reconstituted it became both a series of dialogic encounters among characters inside the play and an energetic exchange that brought the actors into an embodied connection with their audiences. The next chapter follows Istijmam as they sought new ways of creating an experience of halqa and bringing it to the United States.

NOTES

1. James McDougall cites an official death toll of 169 but notes that other estimates place it as high as 500 (2017, 384n126).

2. On this transition, see Aït-Aoudia 2015; McDougall 2017; Roberts 2003, among others.

3. Significant social upheavals are often evoked with a phrase or date that comes to stand in for the larger set of events. See Goodman 2005; Pahwa 2020.

4. As McDougall notes (2017, 290–95), the inability to determine an official death toll speaks to the uncertainty surrounding the events.

5. On the fatwa, see: https://www.nytimes.com/1993/11/05/world/leave-or-die-algeria-militants-tell-aliens.html, accessed June 26, 2018.

6. See Appadurai 1996, ch. 7, on implosive versus explosive violence.

7. The phrase "intimate, gritty" is from Center Stage's marketing materials. https://centerstageus.org/artists/istijmam, accessed June 26, 2018.

8. On neoliberal precarity, see Allison 2013; Appadurai 1996, 2013, among others.

9. On the move to liberalize the economy in Algeria, see (among others) Dillman 1992, 2000, 2001; Nashashibi et al. 1998. For a case study of Sonatrach, the major player in the state's hydrocarbon economy, see Entelis 2012.

10. Article 40 of the 1989 Constitution recognized the right of citizens to form political associations. See Aït-Aoudia 2015, 90–91.

11. This well-known work also goes by the title *The Arabian Nights*. See "The Tale of the Three Apples," found at https://middleeast.library.cornell.edu/content/tale-three-apples, accessed June 3, 2019.

12. Personal interview, October 1, 2016. With regard to the Apple computer, Lila told me it would have cost her 150,000 dinars (almost $9,800) to purchase one in Algeria in 2016.

13. The iPhone was released on June 27, 2007. Some 3.7 million were sold worldwide that year. This figure rose to 13.7 million in 2008 and to 25.1 million in 2009. See https://www.businessinsider.com/apple-iphone-sales-by-year-2016-4, accessed February 8, 2020.

14. For a brief overview of these "revolutions," see McDougall 2017, 256–270. See also Bennoune 1988; Stora 2001.

15. According to Benjamin Stora, the phrase comes from the work of French economists François Perroux and Gérard Destanne de Bernis (Stora 2001, 151). See Stora 2001, ch. 13, for an account of Algeria's development policies from 1965 to 1978.

16. Abdoun 1989, 137n6.

17. Nashashibi et al. (1998) provide a range of economic data on the importance of hydrocarbons to the Algerian economy.

18. That the labor unions (*syndicats*) were of utmost importance in newly socialist Algeria is apparent from their prominence in the 1964 *Charte d'Alger*, which charted the foundations of the new state: "The role of the unions is one of direct participation in economic life. It is in the union that worker initiative can grow with regards to establishing the norms, rhythms, and preparation necessary for their work . . . The union organizations have the essential task to remain vigilant with regards to open or veiled attacks on the socialist sector, to defend the interests of workers, and to do the work of advocacy (*propagande*) to expand the socialist sector" (Front de Libération Nationale 1964; see especially articles 18 and 20 on pages 108–109).

19. Aït-Aoudia 2015, ch. 2, analyzes this transition in greater detail. Information in this section concerning the transition comes from her work unless otherwise specified.

20. In 1986–87, Hamrouche coordinated three reforms that reduced the monopoly of the state on the economy: reorganizing of agricultural lands, previously inaccessible to private development; restructuring of public enterprise; and softening of regulation on foreign investment. See Aït-Aoudia 2015, 73–74.

21. Material in this paragraph comes from a group discussion on August 12, 2016.

22. The quotes from Djalel and Rihab come from personal interviews, August 28, 2016. The quote from Jamil comes from a group discussion in rehearsal on August 12, 2016.

23. Ganti (2014) identifies nostalgia for earlier political-economic formations as a common coping mechanism in the face of systemic change.

24. The image of piled-up stories comes from Lepselter 2016.

25. Discussion in rehearsal, August 12, 2016.

26. Discussion in rehearsal, August 12, 2016.

27. The Schengen countries are those European states that have waived border controls for people moving between them. At the time of this writing, it was twenty-six countries.

28. They drew this exercise from Tournier 2003, 114.

29. Rihab was referring to the often crude, makeshift boats that desperate *harraga* would use to attempt to cross the Mediterranean.

30. Personal interview, August 28, 2016.

31. Quotes from Moussa, personal interview, August 28, 2016. Quotes from Lila, personal interview, August 20, 2016.

32. http://cdn.ca9.uscourts.gov/datastore/general/2017/11/13/17-17168 %20order%2011-13.pdf, accessed June 25, 2018.

33. https://www.natlawreview.com/article/new-us-travel-bans-announced -friday-january-31-2020, accessed February 8, 2020.

TWO

—ᗑᗑ—

RESTAGING THE HALQA

From Algerian Market to Global Marketplace

"IT WAS A HALQA!" JAMIL exclaimed. The Istijmam troupe had just finished its first dress rehearsal of *Apples* in English for a friendly, invitation-only audience in Oran that included the two translators who had developed the English script along with a handful of the troupe's English-speaking Algerian friends. With only a week remaining before Istijmam was to leave for the United States, the actors wanted experience performing in English before an audience. Following the run-through, the dozen or so people in attendance gathered on the apartment's small terrace overlooking Oran's Mediterranean coastline. Over coffee and pastries, they talked animatedly about the play, the English translation, and Istijmam's upcoming journey. It was this postperformance discussion that Jamil called a halqa.*

"It's a halqa," troupe members proclaimed when they entered the performance space at the University of New Hampshire, where they would be surrounded by the audience on three sides.

"That was a halqa," they declared after a postperformance question-and-answer session at New York's La MaMa Theater.

They aim to "repopulate the halqa, Algeria's town square," the Center Stage promotional materials said about Istijmam's work.

"Halqa," Lila responded when an audience member at La MaMa Theater said that he didn't understand the play's ending.

In North Africa, a halqa refers to a circle of people who would gather around a goual,[1] or storyteller—a gifted crafter of words who wove together past and present tales with astute and often humorous commentary. The goual would

---

* Author's Note: An earlier version of this chapter was published as "Embodying Halqa: Algerian Storytelling on a Global Stage" in *Africa Today* 64 (4): 92–112.

take up a position on the market's edges, and as he began his tale, a circle would gradually form around him.[2] His tales spoke to ordinary people, to those who might stop to listen after stocking up on produce for the week. The halqa was reportedly an animated event, with the crowd becoming highly involved in the stories, interjecting comments and questions. Today, the marketplace halqa has essentially disappeared.[3] But the spirit of the halqa has been resurrected in contemporary North African theater. The terms *halqa* and *goual* recurred more than any others during Istijmam's tour. The actors evoked them almost every day throughout the rehearsal residency. They were prominently featured in Center Stage's publicity. They were brought up in virtually every interaction that Istijmam had with US audiences. In short, halqa and goual provided the cultural heritage that a cultural encounter scenario requires.

The halqa had been constituted as heritage decades before it was taken up by Center Stage. North African playwrights writing in the aftermath of French colonial rule mobilized the halqa in part to "decolonize" (Cheniki 2002, 41) their culture by restoring value to their own traditions. This was not a recovery of heritage for its own sake but was part of a broader postcolonial project that called for contemporary artists and intellectuals to "use the past with the intention of opening the future" (Fanon 1963, 232).[4] But the halqa was not the only vernacular theatrical tradition on the North African performance landscape. What made the halqa stand out from other North African performance forms? Why, by the time the Istijmam actors took up theater, did it seem so natural for them to engage with the halqa? Why, in short, did the halqa become such an effective scalar device—that is, a device used to propel local performance traditions to global heritage markets?

In the first part of this chapter, I situate the halqa in relation to related vernacular performance traditions in the Maghreb and provide a brief history of the emergence of proscenium-style theater in Algeria. I then consider how the move by North African playwrights to reconstitute the halqa as a forward-looking engagement with their own heritage was accelerated (Urban 2001) when they set it in relation to avant-garde theater coming from Europe and the Soviet Union—in particular, the work of Bertolt Brecht and his contemporaries. The Brechtian paradigm propelled the halqa into larger conversations about critical avant-garde theater, which in turn set the stage for Center Stage's ability to market the halqa. In the final part of the chapter, I take up the ways Istijmam built on Alloula's work by approaching the halqa as a style of embodied encounter among actors and audiences. Envisioning a halqa as an energetic field, Istijmam would draw as much on the physical method of actor training proposed by Jerzy Grotowski as Alloula and his contemporaries drew on Brecht.

NORTH AFRICAN POPULAR THEATER: A BRIEF HISTORY

The halqa was just one of a range of theatrical forms that constituted the vernacular performance landscape in North Africa.[5] Masquerade performances, often associated with religious or seasonal celebrations, featured both traditional and fantastical characters who enacted satire and parody in carnivalesque fashion.[6] Festivals saw farcical performances featuring a cast of recurring figures such as a wise man and his wife, a judge or authority figure, a donkey, and a Jew.[7] Al-Bsat performances in Morocco similarly highlighted archetypal figures who enacted social satire and farce for the Moroccan monarchy. Garragouz (qaragūz or garagūz),[8] a popular form of shadow puppet theater, featured comic dialogues, trickster figures, and sometimes sexual innuendo alongside social critique.[9]

Some of the figures associated with these performances did become incorporated into wider circulatory networks. In Morocco, the masked figure known as Boujloud (Būjlūd) anchors what has become an international pilgrimage to the village of the Master Musicians of Jakouka, where Boujloud appears in a goatskin costume alongside other stock characters in an annual festival following the Muslim holiday 'Aid Al-Kabir.[10] Boujloud and the Master Musicians inspired Rolling Stone musicians Brian Jones and Mick Jagger as well as such luminaries as Paul Bowles, Brion Gysin, and William Burroughs.[11] At a more local level, Paul Silverstein describes how Amazigh (Berber) activists used the annual masquerade associated with the Jewish Ashura to call attention to a land rights case (Silverstein 2010).

In Algeria, the character Djeha (Djeḥā)—long revered as a trickster in stories told throughout North Africa—was the first figure of popular culture to make the transition from local performance contexts to a formal proscenium stage.[12] Actor and director Selali Ali Allalou (1902–1992) staged his play *Djeha* at the French-built Kursaal Theater in Algiers on April 12, 1926.[13] The play was constructed around local tales drawn from marketplace storytellers as well as intrigues found in such classics as *One Thousand and One Nights* and the French playwright Molière's extensive corpus.[14] In putting *Djeha* on a proscenium stage, Allalou was making use of a theatrical infrastructure that the French had begun building in Algeria from the earliest years of colonization.[15] Most plays at these theaters were performed in French, drawing audiences from the large settler colonial population.[16] *Djeha* is widely recognized as the first play to be performed in Algerian Darija in a European-style theatrical setting. That said, an earlier play written in a mix of Darija and classical Arabic is attributed to the Jewish Algerian translator Abraham Daninos.[17] This play—with the lengthy title "The Pleasure Trip of the Enamoured and the Agony of Lovers in the City of Tiryaq in Iraq"—may have been staged in Algiers as early as the 1840s.[18] Yet Daninos's play did not launch an Arabic-language theatrical tradition in Algeria. *Djeha* was the first known staged play to feature a figure drawn from popular culture and to address Algerians in the language they spoke at home.[19] It was the first play that started to bring into being a new Algerian theatergoing public, able to see itself depicted with humor and satire by an Algerian troupe on a formal stage.[20]

Five years before *Djeha* was performed at the Kursaal came another turning point in Algerian theatrical history: the 1921 visit of the Egyptian company of George Abiad. Abiad's troupe put on two adaptations of historical dramas in classical Arabic, both adapted by Najib Al-Haddad: *Salah El-Din Al-Ayoubi*, inspired by Walter Scott's *The Talisman*, and *Taratu El Arab* (*The Vengeance of the Arabs*), adapted from Chateaubriand's *The Last of the Abencerrages*.[21] But Abiad's tour did not draw wide audiences, as most of the Algerian population had not been schooled in Arabic and had little experience attending formal theatrical productions.[22] The tour did inspire a new kind of vernacular production, prompting Algerian religious associations to stage morality plays for pedagogical purposes.[23] But like Abiad's troupe, they performed in classical Arabic that reached only a limited public.

If *Djeha* opened the way for Darija to become a primary language of Algerian theater, this was consolidated with the work of the renowned director Mahieddine Bachetarzi.[24] Bachetarzi had been classically trained, starting out as a singer in Edmond Yafil's famous El Moutribia music ensemble.[25] In the early 1930s, he turned to theater, and he would eventually tour throughout North Africa, France, and Belgium, creating some seventy plays over the course of his career. Anchored by lead comedian Rachid Ksentini (who had previously acted with Allalou), Bachetarzi's troupe performed both original scripts and loose adaptations of the works of prominent French playwrights, recast around figures and situations readily recognizable to Algerians. Bachetarzi's plays developed from another popular genre, the comedic sketches performed during local festivities. His scripts foregrounded the kinds of social and moral conundrums in which Algerians could recognize themselves.[26] In drawing on this beloved performance form, however, he was inspired more by the surrounding colonial situation than by a desire to explore traditional theatrical genres. For instance, he wrote humorous plays about the troubles that could arise in mixed (French-Algerian) marriages, spoofs on the dilemmas of emigration, or comedic portrayals of Algerians who assumed the mannerisms of French administrators.[27]

By the 1960s, then, two trends had been largely consolidated that would facilitate the redevelopment of the halqa into a form of contemporary theater: the practice of seeking inspiration for staged plays in popular figures and stories, and the use of Darija as a primary language of theater. What would truly propel halqa theater into new territory, however, were its affinities with the work of Bertolt Brecht.

HALQA MEETS BRECHT

As early as the 1930s, Bertolt Brecht (1898–1956) had begun developing a new form of theater: one that would promote critical reflection rather than what he saw as mindless spectatorship. From Brecht's Marxist perspective, classical drama constituted spectators as passive, bourgeois consumers of a story that was unfolding before them. They would be so drawn into the story, he thought, that they would lose the ability to stand back and think more critically about it. To counter this tendency, Brecht would eschew what he called Aristotelian theater, or theater built around a single dramatic story line or arc that generated and then resolved tension. Instead, he developed a form of non-Aristotelian theater that juxtaposed short episodes together, modeling his work on the narrative structure of the epic. Brecht also sought to develop staging and voicing techniques that would allow both actors and audiences to periodically stand outside their traditional roles. Sometimes his actors would move out of character and directly address the audience; other times, they broke into songs or chants to interrupt or punctuate the story. For Brecht, theater needed to incorporate these kinds of devices, or techniques of distantiation. Also referred to as the alienation effect, distantiation contrasts with identification, wherein the actor tries to associate so closely to her character that the spectator experiences them as one (as in Stanislavskian method acting). Brecht thought that identification tended to be mind-numbing: the spectator would get so carried away by the story that she lost critical perspective. Distantiation—where the actor visibly goes into and out of role and forces audiences to do the same—could allow for the possibility of a more nuanced and critical engagement.

Four features of the North African halqa made it amenable to being reconceived in Brechtian terms—a kind of "Brecht *avant la lettre*," as Brian Crow aptly put it (2009, 192): its organization of performance; the episodic form of the stories the goual told; the goual's style of storytelling, wherein a single figure took up multiple roles; and the participatory spectatorship the halqa encouraged. In its organizational structure, a traditional halqa was likened to a Brechtian play because it juxtaposed various kinds of performances. The storyteller or goual might be preceded or followed by a snake charmer, an acrobat, a flame swallower, or a group of musicians. Brechtian theater similarly incorporated elements such as songs or chants (though perhaps not flame swallowers) into the performance of a play, punctuating the play in ways that encouraged both actors and audiences to move outside the story itself. In terms of narrative form, the goual's stories typically took an episodic rather than a linear shape: that is, they were built as a series of intersecting tales or parables (somewhat in the style of One Thousand and One Nights). And the goual already utilized a practice that resembled the distantiation that Brecht called for: he moved between providing background and context (typically in the third person) and acting out each of the characters (typically in the first person), perhaps altering his pitch, accent, gestures, and related ways of indicating that he was entering into a new role. In terms of spectatorship, recall that a halqa took place in a town's outdoor market, where audiences would gather in a circle around the storyteller and interject comments into the flow of the story, sometimes reshaping it.[28] In short, North African theater makers pointed to these features of the halqa to underscore that this vernacular performance tradition already put into practice the kind of theater Brecht and his contemporaries were calling for: a theater that would enable audience members to stand apart from and critically engage with the stories being told. In effect, they reinterpreted the halqa through the genre conventions and Marxist perspective of Brechtian theater.[29]

It is unclear to what degree North African halqa spectators took up the kind of critical stance that Brecht was calling for in Europe. Brian Crow has argued that just because African audiences were more participatory did not mean that they were more critical. Instead of the "complex seeing" that Brecht promoted, Crow maintains, the Nigerian audiences he studied had a view of morality centered on "permanent truths" and "fixed essences" that was based in a "conservative moral framework" with decidedly undialectical ideas about what constituted "good" and "bad" (Crow 2009, 196, 197, 200). Karin Barber's work with Yorùbá popular theater similarly suggests that audiences coconstituted a play by "convert[ing] the narrative into a moral lesson which they can take away and apply to their own lives" (2000, 423). For North African playwrights, however, Brecht's notion of critique aligned well with their own postcolonial (and in some cases Marxist) politics. The halqa gave them a way of putting a vernacular practice in dialogue with avant-garde theater in order to speak to contemporary concerns.

In Algeria, Ould Abderrahmane Abdelkader (known as Kaki) was arguably the first to bring the story and performance forms found in the halqa into his own plays.[30] Kaki developed an episodic style that juxtaposed stories, songs, and dances within the architecture of a single production. Kaki was also the first to put a goual on stage. Like the marketplace storyteller, Kaki's goual would help to knit episodes together. Unlike in the marketplace, however, in Kaki's plays, the goual was a separate figure who provided context for and commentary on what the actors were doing. Kaki would also adopt the circular architecture of the halqa in an effort to "bring the atmosphere of the town square to the stage" (cited in Kali 2005, 48).[31] In Morocco, the playwright Tayeb Saddiki would similarly struggle with how to "transpose al-halqa . . . into a theatre building," retaining some aspects of the marketplace halqa while reconstituting others (Amine 2001, 61).[32] Kateb Yacine was among other Algerian playwrights who would find inspiration in the halqa form. He brought popular Algerian stories into a Marxist framework inspired by theater coming from Vietnam, China, and Bali. He was inspired less by Brecht's ideas about distantiation, however, than by a shared desire to create a revolutionary theater. Kaki and Yacine would join theater makers across much of the ex-colonized world in staging their own adaptations of Brecht's corpus of plays.[33]

In bringing halqa to a proscenium stage, all of these playwrights confronted the dilemma of how to retain the participatory and open-ended nature of the halqa. Whereas the marketplace halqa took place in a circular performance space that was constituted by the audience members themselves, the staged halqa was produced on a rectangular stage that was in front of and generally above the audiences. How could they work against the fourth wall that such a stage typically constitutes, retaining the feel of halqa as "process in motion rather than a final product presented to a passive consumer" (Amine 2001, 58)? In Morocco, playwright and director Abdelkrim Berrechid called for a "ceremonial" theater that would make use of Moroccan performance traditions in order to liberate "human potentialities" (Amine and Carlson 2012, 166).[34] Berrechid's actor, like the goual, would be free to improvise in relation to audience response, creating on stage not a "passive representation" but a "festive performance event with all of its multiplied participatory energies" (Amine and Carlson 2012, 167).[35] In Algeria, Abdelkader Alloula similarly saw the halqa not as a fixed or static event but as what Neil Doshi called an "attitude" as well as an "allegory" for "a form of democratic practice" (Doshi 2013, 114). One of the most significant ways Alloula would develop what he called a "modern halqa theater" was by envisioning the goual not as a separate storyteller (as he was in Kaki's theater) but as standing for a dialogic acting style in which each actor became a goual, simultaneously narrating and enacting the roles of several characters over the course of a play (Amine and Carlson 2012, 165).

ABDELKADER ALLOULA'S MODERN HALQA THEATER

Alloula's engagement with the halqa tends to be told and retold around a foundational event. In 1972, he went with his troupe to perform his play *El Meïda* (*The Low Table*) in the small town of Aurès Media, outside Oran. They set up for an outdoor performance, but they soon noticed that the audience gathered not in front of them but around them in a circle. Gradually, the troupe began eliminating the props and sets they had brought with them, and they started performing in the round. The performance took a shape that would lead Alloula toward the traditional Algerian halqa.[36] But in drawing inspiration from the halqa, Alloula wasn't out to unearth traditional theatrical forms for their own sake. He was not engaged in recovering artistic and cultural heritage in order to celebrate it as evidence of a precolonial history. Rather, he sought to reinvent this form for a contemporary Algerian population.[37] In Alloula's vision, theater would move from being primarily a pursuit of elites—the way it had been under the French—to become a popular artistic forum. He sought to make the theater a place where Algerians of all walks of life could recognize themselves, just as they did in the marketplace stories.

Alloula's plays were built out of the everyday situations that Algerians had to navigate. Constituted as a series of discrete episodes loosely connected around a theme, the plays used irony, irreverence, ruse, and humor to depict the small injustices of daily life, the foibles of petty bureaucrats, and the microencounters with the unwieldy state administrations with which Algerians had to contend. In repositioning the halqa as contemporary theater, Alloula was most interested in its potential for critically portraying the small daily dramas that ordinary Algerians confronted. When Alloula read Brecht's work, he found a new language to describe what the halqa had long been doing. "I consider Brecht, both his writing and his artistic work, a crucial 'yeast' in my work," Alloula would say. "I almost want to say that he is my spiritual father, or, better, my friend and my faithful fellow traveler" (cited in Djellid 1997, 23). Like Kaki, Alloula recognized that the halqa was similar in form to the Greek dramas and Asian epics that Brecht referred to as non-Aristotelian theater. Like the epic, the halqa unfolded in multiple temporalities. It did not tell a single linear story but instead presented a series of complementary tableaux around a common theme. Like the epic, the halqa had no stage set but instead invited spectators to imagine the show as it was being narrated. In the halqa, there was no distinction between onstage and offstage: no curtain would go up or down, and costume changes (if they took place at all) would happen right in front of the spectators.[38] Finally, whereas in classical European theater each actor played and identified with a particular character, in the halqa, the goual played all the parts but identified with none of them. Algerian theater expert Lakhdar Mansouri reiterated these points to me when we spoke in August 2016: "The goual in the traditional halqa was Brechtian: he broke the fourth wall, spoke directly to spectators, incited them to participation in the action [of the play]. It's the same thing that Brecht brought to his theater." Jamil would reinvoke this in 2016 with US audiences: "the spectator [metaphorically] leaves his seat and becomes a cocreator."

Yet for Alloula, the play-as-halqa was of interest not just because it contained Brechtian elements. It was a performance form that could speak to ordinary Algerians just like the traditional halqa did. It could resonate with those who might have stopped by on their way to the weekly market. It could portray people and experiences to which average folks could relate. For Alloula, the halqa offered a suggestive template for the critical and playful work that contemporary Algerian theater could accomplish. "My goal," he said in a 1985 interview with the reporter Abdelmadjid Kaouah, "is to make my contribution to the creation of an Algerian theatre which can display its own characteristics and in turn provide new elements for the universal theatre" (cited in Amine and Carlson 2012, 161).

In seeking to bring an experience of halqa to the stage, Alloula built his plays as a series of "tableaux," or scenes that loosely connected around a theme. *Homq Salim*, Alloula's 1972 adaptation of Nikolai Gogol's *Diary of a Madman*, was the first text that Alloula reworked in this style. As the protagonist descends into madness, he tries to make sense of a society paralyzed by bureaucracy and pervaded by corruption. As in all of Alloula's work, these social ills are portrayed not through ideological critique but via the petty humiliations that gradually led the protagonist to muteness and then to ferocious brutality.[39] In goual style, Alloula himself played all the parts. Alloula is best known for the trilogy *El-Agoual* (*The Sayings*, 1980), *El-Ajouad* (*The Generous Ones*, 1985), and *El-Lithem* (*The Veil*, 1989).[40] *El-Ajouad*, the most popular of the three plays, presents stories of quirky, marginalized characters who are connected only through the goual, or narrator. The stories are punctuated by songs and recurrent refrains—a coming together of Brechtian and halqa-inspired dramaturgical approaches. (Istijmam performed *El Ajouad* in Algeria in 2019—their first major work following the US tour.)

NARRATIVE EVENTS AND PLAYS OF VOICING

Performance theorists would say that both the halqa and Brecht's plays are built on a similar relationship between narrative and narrated events.[41] A narrative event constitutes the framework in which a story is told. It often starts with a particular kind of framing device (such as the familiar "once upon a time"). A narrated event enacts the story itself. In a traditional halqa, the goual moved between being the narrator and playing the characters. He would both frame the story (narrative event) and act it out (narrated event). In so doing, the goual created what Algerian theater scholar Ahmed Cheniki has called a "dual perspective," standing both "inside and outside" (Cheniki 2006, 179). The goual's move also articulates with Mikhail Bakhtin's distinction between the "inner" and "outer" orientations of a work (Bakhtin and Medvedev 1978). In moving between these perspectives or orientations, the goual could comment on the story itself—the very space that Brecht called distantiation.

Alloula's early plays gave the goual as storyteller his own role, as Kaki's plays had done. The goual would stand apart from the main action on the stage, supplying background, context, and framing for what the actors were doing. But by the time he started writing the trilogy, Alloula had reenvisioned the goual, merging the narrative and narrated event such that the actor-as-goual would simultaneously stand outside and within the characters he played.[42] Every actor in an Alloula play was a goual, sometimes speaking about the characters in the story in the third person while at other times enacting the characters, voicing their words in the first person.[43] Because they would constantly shift roles and perspectives, Alloula's actors could never be fully identified with any one character or voice.[44] They could never embody a single perspective the way a traditional actor playing a character would do. Instead, they would move into and out of different roles by changing their stance, voice, and body language. In the same play, then, Alloula's actor-as-goual could be narrator, protagonist, and supporting cast—much like the goual in the halqa itself.

Longtime Alloula collaborator Mourad Senouci explained it to me like this: in Alloula's theater, you don't need a separate goual because "the goual is present in the actors."[45] Through a creative play of voicing, each actor moves into and out of a number of different characters, roles, and stances.[46] The use of pronouns makes this possible. When an actor enters into a character, she momentarily inhabits that character's position, creating a temporary identification by using a first-person pronoun, only to move away as she enacts another character or provides narration in the third person. In shifting from third person narration to first person speech, the actor—as goual—is not in a one-on-one relationship between herself and the characters she plays. The actor does not just project herself into another self as she would in a traditional play, fully identifying with her role. In other words, in conventional theatrical productions, the audience understands that when the actor says "I," it is the "I" of the character, not the actor. This use of what Greg Urban calls the "theatrical 'I'" promotes identification between character and actor, allowing the audience to experience them as one (Urban 1989). By contrast, in Alloula's halqa, the "I" and the "he" "are constantly mutating," one changing into the other to cocreate the theatrical space (Cheniki 2005, 180). Jamil put it to me this way: "Distantiation allows an actor to do what a classical actor can't do. A classical actor can't directly look at or speak to the public. The goual can. . . . So there is distantiation [from his role] in that the goual can speak to the public, but there is also an identification with his role, which he creates. . . . It's not distantiation *or* identification, it's distantiation *and* identification."[47]

ISTIJMAM'S HALQA

Plays of Voicing

Istijmam's performance of *Apples* offers any number of examples of Alloula's goual-style play of voicing. For instance, Rihab both tells the story of the Customer and speaks as the Customer. She narrates the Customer's encounter with the Policeman and also enacts both the Customer and the Policeman. As Policeman, she changes her stance, speaking more deeply, putting her hands in her pockets, raising her collar, and thrusting her pelvis forward. She also speaks about and gives voice to the Neighbor, who chews out the Customer when he asks for the price of an apple; to the old man despondent at the surge in prices; to the attorney general's secretary; to the surveyors measuring the land; and even to the Customer's own daughter. By telling the story while simultaneously acting out the story from the perspective of each character, Rihab is performing on stage the way a goual would have acted in the marketplace halqa. Rihab, as goual, operates from a stance of distantiation, entering into every character, finding points of identification, and then moving back to take up another voice.

Consider the court scene. Rihab momentarily acts as the official who is showing Mustapha the family of twelve living under the stairs. Mustapha, too, moves out of his primary role of Restroom Attendant, momentarily becoming the Customer (in effect assuming Rihab's primary role) to whom the officer is talking. Rihab, as officer, describes how the family was evicted from their home by the courts and adds, almost as an aside, "the very same court that got them evicted." {**Video 02.01**}

Whose voice is this? Not the Customer's. Not the official's. The line resonates beyond the playwright, the actor, and the particular characters. It affords an opportunity for actors and audience to come together in a momentary

Figure 2.1. Rihab momentarily enacts another character through plays of voicing, September 2016. Photo credit: Istijmam Culturelle.

experience of complicity in which they collectively recognize the petty paradox that the scene describes. They know in their bones about the capricious and arbitrary encounters with power where the little guy just trying to get by is caught up in endless procedural webs from which he can't escape. As such, the line constitutes a third voice, a voice of social critique, which could perhaps be experienced as shared precisely because it stands apart, outside the story, unidentified with a single character's perspective. Here, then, the goual is not only a narrator and animator of stories but also a figure capable of opening up a space for critical reflection and commentary.

Another moment of collective recognition occurred in the United States in 2016, this time around the line the Attendant utters about the "red Russian demon." The Actor (played by Moussa) had been quoting Brutus's speech in *Julius Caesar*, but the Attendant (played by Mustapha) had no idea what the Actor was talking about. Shakespeare was entirely beyond the Attendant's experience. So he looked askance at the Actor and then diagnosed his problem: "Democracy drove you crazy!" This line itself generally provoked a laugh. Ever the entrepreneur, the Attendant had a solution for the Actor's over-the-top verbiage. The Actor should go find Si Mbarek, an African healer who could "cauterize your legs, exorcise you and release the demon who is making you talk this way." The Actor tried to explain that he was simply reciting a passage from a Shakespearean play. But the Attendant would have none of it: "Si Mbarek will exorcise it from you even if it is a *red Russian demon*." US audiences often laughed at this moment. The line may have worked to open a space for collective recognition of an issue that was just beginning to be discussed in the media: Russian attempts to influence the 2016 election, which was then two months away.

One of the clearest examples in *Apples* of how distantiation opens a critical space occurs at the beginning of the court scene. Seeking answers about why her factory (and her livelihood) had vanished, Rihab, as the Customer, describes to the Attendant what had happened, concluding with the statement, "Then, I decided to go to the court." Mustapha—suspending his role as the Attendant—places the cube in the center of the stage, sits down on it, and raises his arms to imitate the balanced scales of Lady Justice. "No, the *court*," Rihab reiterates. In the Algerian performances and in the early rehearsals of *Apples*, Rihab and Mustapha both broke here from the play, addressing each other with their real-life first names: "No, Mustapha, the court," said Rihab. "Okay, Rihab," replied Mustapha. The first time I heard them use their real names in rehearsal, I thought Mustapha had made a mistake that Rihab was correcting. As they repeated it, I realized it was intentional. But would this make sense to US audiences? Would they even recognize that Rihab and Mustapha were the actors' first names? It was a jarring moment, a moment that stood out from the rest of the play. Istijmam ended up leaving in the scene but taking out the names. Even without the names, it created a distantiating effect, allowing audiences to recognize that the courts were not always the sites of justice. Both in the United States in 2016 and in my subsequent video screenings of the play after the tour, this line often got a knowing laugh. {**Video 02.02**}

Performance Space

Another way Istijmam tried to create an experience of halqa was via performance spaces. They staged their first performance of *Et-Teffeh* in June 2009, on an outdoor terrace of a café near Oran. In so doing, they were following the example of Alloula, who had experimented with performing in various open-air spaces.[48] Istijmam's show was reviewed in the local press under the headline "Istijmam in the pure tradition of the halqa" (Morad 2009). The play was deemed a halqa because of the way it used space—the reporter described how a few rows of chairs were set up in a half circle, with a bare stage empty of all but a single prop (the cube). On the US tour, two of the stages the troupe performed on were thrust stages, or platforms surrounded on three sides by the audience (at Indiana University and the University of New Hampshire). Both times, as soon as troupe members saw the stage, they called out, "Halqa." But even on a regular proscenium stage, Jamil told me, they could reproduce the shape of

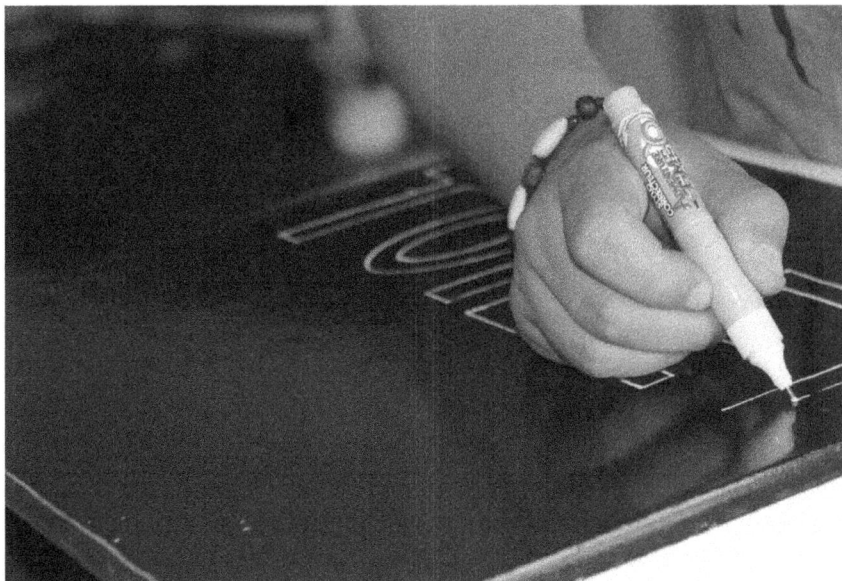

Figure 2.2. Jamil adds the English word *toilet* to the cube for the US tour, August 2016. Photo credit: Istijmam Culturelle.

the halqa: "The actors open a half circle and the audience completes it." What they were trying to accomplish, he said, was to put aside the usual theatrical conventions: "You go to a play, you sit down, you wait for it to start, the house lights go down, the stage is lit, there are actors playing, they finish, you applaud, they go off the stage, and you leave. Us, we didn't want it to be like that."

In creating *Et-Teffeh* for performance in both outdoor and indoor locations, Istijmam eschewed elaborate sets. Their only prop was a cube that could be readily dismantled and carried as a small piece of handheld luggage (a boon for the US tour). In North Africa, they would occasionally perform in the streets. Rihab described this experience for an audience at New York's La MaMa Theater: "Once we were playing in a distant town in the south of Algeria, trying the concept of the storyteller and the circle, el halqa, where the storyteller is always surrounded by people. And we started to play, and we were surrounded by people. A closed circle. And these people were talking at the same time, their telephones were ringing at the same time, drinking, buying, and selling—this was the street, and the street is, everything is hard. To perform in the street is hard: you must be engaged physically, vocally, you must adapt yourself at every moment. It is like you are ready, you must be ready, for everything, for every surprise, for every *imprévu* [unexpected thing]. It is very different and very ..."

Figure 2.3. Mustapha seated on the cube in performance, September 2016.
Photo credit: Istijmam Culturelle.

Here, she couldn't quite find the right word and so made scare quotes with her hands. {**Video 02.03**}

Mise-en-Scène

Istijmam further sought to generate the sense of audience engagement that a halqa would foster through staging, or the mise-en-scène. The troupe staged *Et-Teffeh* and *Apples* differently. Although they did not alter the script (aside from changes that took place in translation; see chap. 5), they significantly re-worked key aspects of the mise-en-scène. In both versions, they were trying to create a halqa. But they did so through distinct framing devices, such that the opening and closing scenes were utterly different and gave rise to competing interpretations of the play.

In the North African performances, Istijmam staged *Et-Teffeh* as if it were one of several performances, recreating the form of a marketplace halqa.[49] The play followed a short musical and poetic performance by Moussa and Rihab. As they were exiting the stage, Mustapha entered carrying the cube. The two groups of performers stopped on stage and greeted each other, and then Mustapha began *Et-Teffeh* as the others continued to exit. Mustapha, on stage alone, put down the cube and started to clean the floor, singing a popular Algerian rai song[50] about love and dancing as he cleaned. The audience clapped along. Then the Customer (Rihab) entered, and the story of the quest for apples began.

As Lila later explained to me, this opening was intended to suggest the form of a halqa by featuring multiple performances, one after the other, as would occur in a marketplace.[51] The troupe adopted this format to foster an experience of distantiation: the Istijmam actors were both actors in the play and marketplace actors. The greeting was intended to be interpreted as an offstage encounter, highlighting the space in between performances, the moment when one set of performers left the halqa and another entered it. Greeting each other between sets was a phatic performance that foregrounded their connection as actors who recognized each other outside their performance roles. In other words, the Istijmam actors performed the transition itself between two marketplace performances. The greeting generated an overarching framework of halqa, in which the poetry and play would take place. The actors created the context in which both events were situated. They did so in a conventional theater (in the video I saw), such that the performances become like nested Russian dolls, one performance containing another, which contains another. The halqa was made into the overarching narrative event that contained several different narrated events.

Toward the end of the script of *Et-Teffeh*, the Actor and the Customer encounter each other in the public restroom for the first time. Following the script, the Attendant introduces them to each other with these words: "That man is an actor, he will work with us in the business. This man will tell you his story of apples later." In the Arabic version, at this point the Attendant continued to recite the script but introduced a change in the mise-en-scène: he pretended to turn on a microphone and spoke the next lines in a different voice, taking on the tone and the speaking style of the Algerian president. "We have to structure this business and establish professional relationships, rights, and duties, and think about how to improve our services and profitability." Rihab at this point stepped out of her role as the Customer and momentarily entered the role of a video journalist who was filming the speech. The three then went back into their primary roles, coming together around their shared plan for a collective future. They sang the song the Attendant opened with, and they exited together—the Customer carrying the cube and the other two making as if to clean the floor.

The English language version, *Apples*, was framed differently. First of all, there was no prior performance. The Attendant entered alone carrying the cube. As in the Arabic version, he started cleaning the floor, but he then walked to the side of the stage and pressed an imaginary button on an imaginary wall. A sound of static came in from offstage, made by the voices of the other two actors. The Attendant turned his hand as if trying to find a radio station. From offstage, a voice (Rihab's) started singing in English the first strains of "Killing Me Softly," a song made popular in Algeria by the Fugees.[52] US audiences would almost always react at this point, surprised that an Algerian play was beginning with a song so familiar to them. The Attendant turned the dial again, landing on a station where a deep voice uttered, "Respect the law" (also delivered by Rihab, foreshadowing a line from the police officer whom she would enact later in the play). Startled, the Attendant turned the dial a third time and landed on a station playing a traditional Algerian rai song—the same one that began the Arabic version, except that this time it was sung not by the Attendant but by Rihab and Moussa, still offstage. Satisfied, the Attendant began to sing along as he went back to cleaning the floor. The play then unfolded more or less as did the Arabic version, until the end. In the Arabic version, the three characters—Restroom Attendant, Customer, and Actor—finished on stage together, seemingly united in their collective project to recreate the Restroom as a space where cultural entertainment would be added to the Restroom's offerings. In the English version, the Actor exited, then the Customer, leaving the Attendant alone on stage. He sat down on the cube/toilet to rest, happily dreaming of his future and almost nodding off. He was startled out of his reverie when the radio (again created vocally by Rihab and Moussa backstage) came back on, playing the same Algerian rai tune the Attendant had sung along with at the beginning. The Attendant jumped up in a daze, moved to turn off the radio, and then stumbled offstage, appearing stunned and confused.

In both the Arabic and English versions, the opening and closing scenes, or the play's frame, introduce another medium into the play via an act of remediation, or the representation of one medium within another.[53] In the Arabic version, the moment of remediation came at the end, via the microphone and the camera. The imaginary microphone and video camera momentarily transformed Mustapha from Attendant into the President. In this case, it introduced a fleeting instance of humorous critique, but it did not otherwise transform the interpretation of the play.

In the English version, a representation of the radio was added to the beginning and ending of the play. As a framing device, it changed the way the actors themselves understood the play, and it opened up a different set of interpretive possibilities for audiences. The transformation of the mise-en-scène was gradual. Jamil said that it came to him as an idea that he wanted to try out, so he introduced it one day in rehearsal. Initially, the Attendant's use of the radio was meant to suggest that the whole play was a dream sequence. At the beginning of the play, he turned on the radio, sat down on the cube, swayed his head to the music, and then appeared to nod off. At the play's end, he again sat down on the cube, appeared to be asleep, but then awakened with a start to the sound of the radio, which was playing the same song to which he had fallen asleep. He awoke in that state of postdream confusion, the state where we ask, Was that real? What just happened?

When I first saw this version in rehearsal, it raised new interpretive possibilities for me. Seeing the play as a dream, suddenly its nonlinear, fragmented construction made more sense: as in a dream, one scene morphs into the next without resolution. In a dream, one looks for a different kind of coherence: not a continuous narrative that builds from one scene to the next but rather a loose sense of how the various fragments connect (or sometimes fail to connect). The absurdist moments ("an elephant with jaundice trying to cross a border") also started making more sense to me. The play began to suggest elements of a social reality where desire, neoliberal transformation, and art continuously bleed into each other in unexpected and nonlinear ways.

But then Jamil altered the ending again. He no longer had the Attendant (Mustapha) nod off at the end. Instead, Mustapha would hear the music, appear startled and even a bit panicked, turn off the radio, and then stumble from the stage, spinning around, dizzy and disoriented. But there was no moment of awakening from sleep. For some audience members, the radio at the beginning and ending was still suggestive of a dream sequence, even without the scene of awakening. But for others, it was not. During the tour, the ending proved to be one of the most confounding elements of the play. In talk-backs after the shows, the question came up almost every time: What happened at the end? In the spirit of halqa, I offer some of these conversations, highlighting the ways the actors sought to foreground the halqa as a space of interpretation (see epilogue for more audience comments).[54]

At Indiana University

Audience member: I didn't get the last scene when the Attendant got distracted. I wonder why he got distracted, and what distracted him and distressed him.

Mustapha: *Maybe* we can say it's like I woke up from a dream. It's like the first time I listened, I sleep, so *maybe* it was a dream. The last time, another time this song, that's why I wake up . . . *maybe* I am a crazy man.

Audience member: So *maybe* it all happened and maybe it didn't. *Maybe* it was a dream.

Mustapha: *Maybe* dream, or people can understand his life, or his imagination.

At La MaMa Theater in New York

Audience member: What was the significance of the song at the end that pushed the Attendant out?

Rihab: The song is a popular song; the type is rai. Rai is very popular in Algeria. And he was just, in fact he was listening at the beginning to this song, and he loved this song, and it makes him traveling or dreaming or sleeping, *we don't know,* and at the end we find the same situation of dreaming, of relaxing.

Lila: *El halqa.*

Rihab: Yes, and when the Restroom Attendant woke up, it was just a little imagination, or *perhaps* it was real. It is *open, open to the imagination of everyone. . . . Even us.* [laughter]

Mustapha: Me too, *I don't know.* [laughter]

Rihab (joking): No, you must *know!* [laughter]

{**Video 02.04**}

At the University of New Hampshire

Audience member: What was the ending, where you like have a panic attack and run out?

Lila: What did you understand?

Audience member: Umm . . . [audience laughter] I don't know. Maybe he had like a realization about the world, or something. I asked the question because I was confused.

Jamil: Even us, we don't know. In this kind of theater, the imagination of the spectator is open, and each one's interpretation is different. For us, that is the objective.

{**Video 02.05**}

Istijmam's responses to these questions are replete with adverbs of indeterminacy like *maybe* and *perhaps,* and even by statements like "we don't know." As moderator of the talk-back sessions, I was initially frustrated by these responses. For instance, in the interaction at the University of New Hampshire, I could sense that the audience member (a young male student) wasn't satisfied by being told to use his imagination. He wanted more to work with. After Jamil's reply, I interjected, saying that a dream sequence was one way to interpret the ending. We discussed it later in the troupe. Istijmam wanted to leave it ambiguous. They wanted the audience to ask themselves the question "What just happened?" They did not want to orient the spectators toward a singular interpretation. They wanted to leave it up to the audiences to try to put together what they understood. In the troupe's view, the ambiguous ending opened up the space they called halqa. The mise-en-scène would be successful if it led the audience to ask questions.

In both the Arabic and the English versions, the actors sought to create a space of indeterminacy in part through the technique of remediation. That is, the theatrical medium created on stage a representation of another form of media that worked to momentarily lift spectators outside the play itself. In the Arabic version, a journalist with a video camera and a microphone suddenly entered the play, unexpectedly turning the scene into a different kind of encounter. In the English version, a radio opened and closed the play, suggesting alternative ways of interpreting the play's stories. In both cases, the introduction of another medium—camera, radio—worked to introduce a new narrative event or frame within which the rest of the play could be understood. This created a space of distantiation wherein an audience member might be pulled out of the main story and start asking themselves questions like the ones above. These fleeting but critical moments generated a space for reflection, when audiences could stand back from the story and see it *as a story* that was being presented through the lens of another medium. Remediation, in other words, helped to create the space of halqa by turning the play itself into a remediated story, which opened new interpretive possibilities for the audience. This space of remediation was a key part of how Istijmam envisioned a halqa.

Yet not all audiences were convinced that they had experienced a halqa. An audience member at the La MaMa performance in New York was getting at this when she asked, "When you play outside in Algeria, is the audience, participation of the audience a little different than what you encountered tonight? We didn't sing with you, we didn't cross into the stage in order to dance with you. Is the audience reaction in the Maghreb more physically participating than we did tonight?" This spectator's question was echoed in other talk-backs. Even when Istijmam performed on one of the thrust stages (as at UNH and IU), surrounded by the audiences on three sides, *Apples* was still a structured, formal performance. People would get a ticket, enter, take a seat, the lights would go down, and the play would begin. From this perspective, the audience was seeing the performance from within the kind of embodied decorum imposed by a long history of Western performance practice.[55] What might a halqa mean in that context?

Consider Jamil's reply: "We think that when there is an actor and a spectator, there is theater. We don't need [a certain kind of] space to do theater. In our experience in Istijmam, it's about going to meet the public (*d'aller à la rencontre du publique*). In North Africa, we played outside in the street and also in theaters. But what we are looking for, it's the participation of the spectator in the play; the space doesn't matter." A play, in other words, was an encounter. The audience member was right in that spectators were not reshaping the direction of *Apples*. They were not shouting out responses from their seats, the way people might in a halqa. *Apples* was not an improvisatory piece whose script changed each time. But Jamil seems to have been getting at something else: a play as a shared encounter with the audience that can perhaps best be characterized as an energy exchange.

HALQA MEETS GROTOWSKI

If Jamil were reading this chapter, he would be telling me that the halqa is not just a space for critical or intellectual engagement. He would be saying that creating a halqa is not a theoretical exercise. It is not only a result of voicing or mise-en-scène, although these can help to furnish the conditions for a performance to become a halqa. Above all, a halqa is a space of encounter that emerges through an affective connection between actors and audiences. Affect, following Brian Massumi (2002), refers here not to emotion but to the sensations generated by and on human bodies through vibration, resonance, volume, frequency, and related material forces. An affective encounter is also performative: it "does something . . . to the bodies and to the sensitive qualities we experience in a live performance" (Pais 2017, 244). It resonates with the way Portuguese choreographer Vera Mantero has described the way dancers generate a "string connecting us to them, a string that we keep on pulling and stretching" (cited in Pais 2017, 233). This is not a one-way process: the dancers (or actors) may initiate making the fabric of a performance, but the audience weaves and tightens it. Jamil could sense whether such an encounter was developing, he said, from backstage, which is where he usually listened to Istijmam's performances. In standing backstage, attuned to the energy of the room, Jamil was "listening with the whole body to the reverberations of the rhythms and intensities of performance" (Pais 2017, 236). A halqa, from this perspective, is precisely such an affective and embodied encounter.[56]

Whether it takes place in the market, the street, or a formal theater, the halqa is envisioned by Istijmam as a space of what Ana Pais calls commotion or "co-motion." Drawing on Teresa Brennan's work, Pais notes that humans, as material bodies, are "open beings who receive signals from and emit signals to others and to the environment, perceived by the senses and therefore materialized in our physiology" (Pais 2017, 240–41). Physical theater like that practiced by Istijmam puts into play rhythms and vibrations that viscerally impact the audience. As audiences are drawn in, they intensify the performance, turning it into an energetic exchange that the actor Tony Torn likens to the ocean: "The energy flows off the stage into the audience, it recycles and comes surging back. . . . You feel like there is this give and take, a suction and then a wave" (cited in Pais 2017, 247). This flow is experienced as surges of affect that are collectively generated between actors and audiences. Whereas audience members' interpretations may differ, affective intensities result from a shared sensory experience. Intensities are what prompt an audience to groan, gasp, or laugh together. The audience can feel the embodiment of the actor through "immersed sensuous participation" (Mazzarella 2017, 204). Experiencing a play as a sensory performance is why some of my friends and family members could tell me that they enjoyed seeing *Apples* even though they did not understand it.[57]

In this sense, halqa can be understood as a material architecture that works through tensegrity—a term coined by the American engineer Buckminster Fuller to describe the principle through which geodesic domes are held aloft. Through tensegrity, loads are borne not through compression but through tension. That is, the weight of one component is not held up by another but instead is distributed through a resilient network of cables that run between the load-bearing components while ensuring that they never touch.[58] The halqa as Istijmam talked about it was like such a dome, created and sustained through a continuous give and take of energy located not in the performers or in the audience but in the space generated between them. In order to generate a performance experience of tensegrity, the actors had to maximize their own bodies' capacity for biotensegrity. Biotensegrity is based in the insight that our bodies operate through the same principle that geodesic domes do: "forces primarily flow through our muscles and fascial structures and not in a continuous compression manner through our bones. In fact, our bones do not directly touch each other, and are actually 'floating' in the tension structure created by our fascial network."[59]

Istijmam's engagement with the physical acting called for by Jerzy Grotowski was the means through which Rihab, Mustapha, and Moussa sought to develop their own bodies as organizations of biotensegrity, though they did not use (or have access to) that language. The training was so critical to them that they could not imagine performing without it. I observed them when they began the training in 2009 (see chap. 4). They would spend hours trying to leap over large stacks of cushions, jump up on an unsecured chair landing on one foot, and move fluidly into backbends and headstands. The exercises led to many black-and-blues and some injuries, and almost split the troupe, but in the end, Grotowski's method became central to Istijmam's theatrical work. During the 2016 rehearsal residency, they devoted an hour each day to the training.

In the United States, the Grotowski exercises were a scheduled part of every engagement. The Grotowski method, though not based explicitly in principles of biotensegrity, works in the same "extreme" corporal range that training in biotensegrity calls for. It enabled the actors to maximally mobilize the capacities of their own bodies as instruments of performance.

Finally, Istijmam's focus on the embodied connection with the audience was also inspired by the "poor theater" approach pioneered by Grotowski. As Grotowski put it, whereas "theater can exist without make-up, without autonomic costume and scenography, without a separate performance area (stage), without lighting and sound effects . . . it cannot exist without the actor-spectator relationship of perceptual, direct, 'live' communion. . . . Text per se is not theater . . . it becomes theater only through the actors' use of it" (Grotowski 2002, 3). In all kinds of theater, of course, the actors use their bodies to translate a theatrical text into an experience for the audience.[60] But in poor theater, the actors also generate the stage and the story through their bodies. The body itself creates the mise-en-scène—another reason that embodied expression was so vital to Istijmam.

For Jamil, a halqa had a magic to it that was as sweet as a jasmine flower: "There is something that emerges between you and the public. We can call it magic." This "magic" is part of *el-furja* (al-furja), a term that Istijmam invoked throughout the rehearsal residency and the tour to characterize the quality of the experience that they aspired to produce for both themselves and their audiences. As Rihab explained it to me, el-furja encompasses the sense of embodied pleasure and well-being that builds up between actors and audiences over the course of a play.[61] The term extends beyond the theater, she said, also characterizing the energy generated through forms of community ritual or ceremonial gathering. In theater, an experience of el-furja can be facilitated by a range of stylistic and technical components, from the poetic quality of the dialogue and the dramatic shape of the play to the embodied, kinesthetic dimensions of the mise-en-scène.[62] But ultimately, el-furja transcends technique. It can perhaps be likened to the "utopian performativity" that Jill Dolan holds out as theater's promise and potential: "a processual, momentary feeling of affinity, in which spectators experience themselves as part of a congenial public constituted by the performance's address" (Dolan 2005, 14). Both Dolan's utopian performatives and Jamil's "magic" resonate with Victor Turner's view that performance, like ritual, can generate an experience that Turner called communitas (Turner 1974, 1982)—that fleeting feeling of belonging to something larger than oneself that transcends ordinary social and societal boundaries. Theater, Jamil told the actors the day after the first invited presentation of *Apples* in Oran, was 70 percent in the text and mise-en-scène, but the remaining 30 percent was in the play (*le jeu*), or the energy generated on stage among actors and between actors and audiences. "Why think that everything is on you," he remarked, "that you have to do this, do that, not do this, that if I don't do this everything will stop. No! You need to be conscious of these things—we have a text, we have a mise-en-scène, the rest, it's the night jasmine (*mesk el-layl*)."

—⁓—

The halqa and its lead character, the goual, are exceptionally fecund figures that can be scaled up or down in any number of ways. They were invoked on the US tour and in Center Stage publicity as figures of heritage, providing a language to talk about a specifically Algerian form of theatrical practice in ways that would appeal to contemporary audiences. They were also invoked to put Algerian theater in dialogue with other theatrical traditions, in particular the works of Bertolt Brecht. At the same time, these figures were invoked in ways that seemed to transcend culture altogether. For Istijmam, the halqa and the goual modeled a kind of theatrical encounter based in el-furja, one that could be experienced on an energetic, affective level. One audience member, at the talk-back following the Indiana University performance, was perhaps getting at this when she referred to the halqa as a figure of "humanity": "*Merci beaucoup,* you are marvelous, *magnifique, merci beaucoup,* you are fabulous. I am an American actor, you were able to transform this theater into not only a picture of humanity with each line, each thing you said, each movement of your body, but you also created for us just with your face, your eyes, your hands, so many other worlds and so much humanity that I say *merci beaucoup.*" Her words were greeted with applause, a fitting end to that night's halqa.

As it moves across scales, then, the halqa emerges alternately as a figure that represents North African tradition and an experience that transcends tradition. It was perhaps this very oscillation between representing culture and transcending culture that would give rise to some of the tensions of the tour.

NOTES

1. The word *goual* comes from the Arabic verb *qāla,* to speak. Related terms for storyteller include *meddah.* The storyteller, a popular figure across North Africa and the Middle East, has been incorporated into other forms of contemporary theater as well; see Slyomovics 1991. On storytellers and poets in the Arab world, see, among others, Caton 1990; Haddad 1982; Reynolds 1995; Slyomovics 1987.

2. On the Moroccan market as a space of performance, see Kapchan 1996. On the halqa in Morocco, see Amine and Carlson 2012; Kapchan 1995, 1996. For an account of a traditional Moroccan halqa, see Hannoum 2000.

3. Halqa-style performances continue to exist as tourist attractions at large markets such as Morocco's Djema'a El Fna. See Ladenburger 2010.

4. For a comparative case on the Palestinian theater troupe El-Hakawati, which named itself after the traditional storyteller, see Slyomovics 1991. The El-Hakawati company toured North America in 1989.

5. Salhi (2004, 53–59) discusses vernacular theatrical traditions in the Maghreb, including the Al-Bsat performances in Morocco (short humorous sketches performed during festivals); the Garagouz shadow puppet theater; carnival and masquerade burlesque performances featuring characters such as "Ba-Cheikh," the Aklan (slaves), the Aghul (donkey), and the Amghar (old man).

6. On masquerade in Morocco, see especially Hammoudi 1993. See also Amine and Carlson 2012, 39–43. On scalar dimensions of masquerade, see Silverstein 2010.

7. Described in Amine and Carlson 2012, 44. On carnival performances, Amine and Carlson 2012, ch. 4.

8. On the Garragouz, see Amine and Carlson 2012, ch. 4; Baffet 1985, 26–27; Bouzar-Kasbadji 1988; Kali 2014; Roth 1967, 14–17.

9. Theatrical productions on a proscenium stage began in Algeria around 1910 (Cheniki 2002). For histories of Algerian theater in the twentieth century, see Bachetarzi 1968; Bouzar-Kasbadji 1988; Cheniki 2002, 2006; Baffet 1985; Dahmane 2011; Roth 1967. For histories of theater in the Maghreb, see Amine and Carlson 2012; Salhi 2004. See also *The World Encyclopedia of Contemporary Theater, Volume 4—Arab World*, in particular the entries for Algeria (El Rukaibi 1999), Morocco (Berrechid 1999), and Tunisia (Al-Madani 1999).

10. On the Master Musicians of Jajouka, see Schuyler 2000.

11. On appropriations of Boujloud, see Amine and Carlson 2012, 43–44. Brian Jones chronicled his encounter with Boujloud and the Jajouka Master Musicians in Davis 1993.

12. On the figure of Djeha, see Baffet 1985; Cheniki 2006, 90; Dejeux 1978; Roth 1967, 25–26; Salhi 1998, 75; Salhi 2004, 42–45. Allalou's play *Djeha* was first performed April 12, 1926, in the Kursaal theater in Algiers (Roth 1967, 25). The character Djeha also appeared in one of Mahieddine Bachetarzi's first plays, *Djeha and the Usurer*, in 1934.

13. For a memoir-style account of Allalou's troupe, including the performance of *Djeha*, see Allalou n.d. On Allalou's theater, see Bencheneb 1977; Cheniki 2002. On Allalou's production of *Djeha*, see Bachetarzi 1968, 60–61; Cheniki 2006, 12–16; Dahmane 2011, 33–35. Roth (1967) situates Allalou's theater in the larger context of popular theater in Darija (which she calls "dialect") in Algeria.

14. Cheniki 2002, 21. The Molière plays from which Djeha drew included *The Doctor in Spite of Himself* and *The Imaginary Invalid*.

15. Moreh and Sadgrove (1996, 34–36) provide a history of the French theatrical infrastructure in Algeria. They draw on the work of Arnaudiès (1941). Work by Arnaudiès on the early history of French theater in Algeria is also documented here: http://alger-roi.fr/Alger/opera/arnaudies/textes/2_premiers _heures.htm; a history of the Kursaal theater is documented here: http://afn .collections.free.fr/pages/59_bulletin/kursaal.html, accessed March 29, 2019.

16. On French settler colonialism in Algeria, see Prochaska 1990.

17. According to Philip Sadgrove, Daninos was a guide and translator who served as assistant to Torpin, commander of one of the vessels that may have been part of the French invasion of Algiers in 1830. Daninos also "accompanied a commission of inquiry that came from Paris to Algiers in 1833," and his service to the French was rewarded when he was bestowed the title Chevalier of the Légion d'Honneur (Moreh and Sadgrove 1996, 46). This history does not appear in most accounts of Algerian theater. Daninos's close collaboration with the French makes it unlikely that he could provide an acceptable ideological starting point for a history of Arab Algerian theater.

18. For an extended account of Daninos's play in the context of early Arab theater, see Moreh and Sadgrove 1996. This volume also provides the Arabic script of the play.

19. On language in twentieth-century Algerian theater (French, Arabic, Darija), see especially Cheniki 2002, ch. 4; Roth 1967.

20. Djeghloul (1984, 123–39) provides brief histories of the troupes of Allalou and comedian Rachid Ksentini.

21. Documented in Amine and Carlson 2012, 75–77, 86; Roth 1967, 22.

22. Salhi 2004, 61; Roth 1965, 22

23. Goodman 2013a; Roth 1967, 22–23. See also Amine and Carlson 2012, ch. 10.

24. On the Bachetarzi troupe, see especially Bachetarzi 1968. See also Amine and Carlson 2012; Bouzar-Kasbadji 1988; Cheniki 2002; Roth 1967.

25. Dahmane 2011, 34n33. For more on Edmond Yafil and El Moutribia, see Glasser 2016; Merdaci 2008.

26. Bachetarzi (1968) describes in detail the development of his theater, and Algerian theater more broadly, in his memoirs.

27. Bachetarzi occupied an ambivalent position with regard to the colonial situation. Cheniki (2002, 29–30) details how he was recruited by the colonial administration to develop plays in support of the Vichy government during the Second World War. Overall, Bachetarzi's plays critiqued the institutions and mores of Algerian society more than the colonial administration. Yet a number of his plays were also censored by the French (Cheniki 2006, 16–21).

28. For an account of a traditional halqa performance in Morocco, see Schuyler 1984.

29. "Genre," notes Karin Barber, "is the principle by which texts converse with each other" (Barber 2007, 43). Genre, in other words, allows a text (or in this case a performance) to be linked to larger textual traditions.

30. Kaki began experimenting with the halqa as early the mid-1960s in his adaptations *El Guerrab Wa Essalhine* (el-Gerrab wi-l-Salhin, an adaptation of Brecht's *The Good Woman of Setzuan*) and *Kul Wahed u Hukmu* (Kul Wahid wa Hukmu, *To Each His Own Justice*) (Amine and Carlson 2011, 145; Cheniki 2006, ch. 3; Dahmane 2011, 113–16). He would go on to write original plays on French colonialism, including *132 Years* (*132 Sana*) and *Africa Before the Year One* (*Afrique Qabl al-Aam Waahid*, Afriqya qabl al-ʿAam wahid), which adopted a similar style (see Dahmane 2011, 113–16).

31. Mostefa and Benchehida (2006) discuss major influences on Kaki and provide French translations of excerpts of several of his plays and novels. Kali (2005, 47–49) also talks about influences on Kaki's theater. Cheurfi (2007, 653–54) provides a biography of Kaki. Cheniki discusses Kaki's career in the larger context of Algerian theater (Cheniki 2002) and provides a detailed textual analysis of three plays by Kaki that demonstrates the influence of Bertolt Brecht, Greek tragedy, and Algerian oral literature and poetry on his work (Cheniki 2006, 59–93).

32. Amine (2001) discusses Saddiki's appropriation of the halqa in Morocco. On the way halqa inspired contemporary Moroccan playwrights, see also Berrechid 1999.

33. On Kateb Yacine's work, see Amine and Carlson 2012, 152; Cheniki 2002; Doshi 2013. On the wider influence of Brecht in Asia and Africa, see Fuegi et al. 1989.

34. See especially Berrechid 1985, cited in Amine and Carlson 2012.

35. See also Jay 2016 for an account of how contemporary feminist theater-maker Fatima Chebchoub drew on halqa and trickster traditions to address feminist issues.

36. Alloula dates the end of the halqa as a regular practice to the decade of the 1950s (the decade of Algeria's war of independence from France). See Alloula 1997, 122–23. Alloula did have occasion to see a marketplace halqa, as did Kaki.

37. This project was similar to what Amazigh or Berber singers were doing at the time with New Kabyle Song, as developed in Goodman 2005.

38. Reportedly, the actor could even sit down for a time among the spectators and smoke a cigarette (Alloula 1997, 128).

39. For more on *Homq Salim*, see Djemai 1997.

40. The trilogy may be found in French translation in Alloula 1995. *The Veil* is found in English in Carlson 2008. Amine and Carlson (2012, 161–65) offer a critical summary of the plays in this trilogy. On Alloula's work, see also Alloula 1997; Bereksi Meddahi 2012; Cheniki 2000; Cheniki 2006, 91–93, 179–186.

41. On narrative and narrated events, see especially Bauman 1992, 2004; Bauman and Briggs 1990.

42. I am grateful to Rihab Alloula for this clarification. Personal communication by email, April 23, 2018.

43. In more formal terms, he would alternate between indirect and direct forms of reported speech.

44. Greg Urban put it this way: "The use of the theatrical 'I' involves a complicated sign process in which a speaker/narrator becomes in effect the substitutive ostensive referent of a third person form, and consequently capable of referring to that referent by means of the first person form" (Urban 1989, 41).

45. Mourad Senouci, personal interview, Oran, Algeria, August 15, 2016.

46. On shifts of voicing and stance, also known as footing, see especially Goffman 1981; Goodman, Tomlinson, and Richland 2014; Hastings and Manning 2004, among many others.

47. Personal interview, September 21, 2016.

48. Doshi (2013) provides an account of Alloula's open-air theater.

49. My reference for the North African staging is from a performance on May 5, 2010, in the Salle Mougar in Algiers, which Istijmam provided to me on a DVD. That performance was sponsored by the Algerian Office Nationale de la Culture et de l'Information. Istijmam's self-conscious attempt to recreate the scene of the halqa may be compared with the way Moroccan gnawa musicians set up a North African marketplace in the lobby of a French club where they were performing (Kapchan 2007, 153).

50. The song is "Lazrag se'ani" (Lazreg sʿānī) by Cheb Mami.

51. Istijmam was not the first troupe to adapt an organization of performance inspired by the marketplace halqa. Roselyne Baffet describes how Kateb Yacine's well-known play *Mohamed, Prends Ta Valise* (*Mohamed, Take Your Suitcase*) opens with a traditional berrah or town crier, in which the actors come on stage before the play begins to "warm up" the public with songs and popular sketches familiar to the public (Baffet 1985, 166–67).

52. The version of "Killing Me Softly" that inspired them was covered by the Fugees in 1996 and was very popular in Algeria.

53. On remediation, see Bolter and Grusin 1999; on intermediality, see Chapple and Kattenbelt 2006, among others.

54. The actors responded in a mix of French and English. I translated the French for the audiences. I report here only the English, but the French is audible on the video.

55. Cheniki (2006, 91) similarly notes that putting a halqa-style performance on a traditional stage worked against the popular marketplace storytelling atmosphere that Alloula sought to create.

56. Neil Doshi makes a related point in comparing accounts of Alloula's open-air plays with his own experience of the plays of the Indian troupe JANAM. Both, he argued, used the physical layout of the performance space to "intensif[y] the embodying effect of attention through the triangulation of performance, individual spectator, and collective audience." Viewed phenomenologically, attention was an "active process . . . shaped jointly by sound, visual stimuli, and the co-presence of spectators" (Doshi 2013, 121–22).

57. Patrick Eisenlohr's work on the performance and reception of nʻat devotional texts among Muslims in Mauritius offers an analytical and ethnographic approach to sound that usefully complements this chapter. Describing nʻat performance as a "sonic event whose effects rapidly spread like ripples on water," Eisenlohr approaches the sonic performance through the lens of transduction, wherein "sonic energy . . . is converted into different forms of energy in the body, creating new psychological and sensational phenomena in the process" (2018, 86, 84).

58. Geodesic domes were invented by American engineer Buckminster Fuller; see Pais 2017, 245. Pais used the spelling *tensigrity*; I am using the more familiar spelling *tensegrity*.

59. http://www.magicalrobot.org/BeingHuman/2010/04/introduction-to -biotensegrity, accessed February 9, 2020.

60. The issue of liveness in theatrical performance has been the subject of considerable debate; see Auslander 1999. On the body as a medium of and for artistic expression, see Royce 1984.

61. Rihab Alloula, personal communication by email, July 12, 2019.

62. On al-furja, see especially http://folkarts.ahlamontada.net/t185-topic, accessed February 9, 2020. I am grateful to Rihab Alloula for this reference.

THREE

—꘠—

ON THE ROAD

Cultural Encounters in Cosmopolitan Times

THE MEMBERS OF ISTIJMAM WERE standing with around twenty students from Sarah Lawrence College in a circle on the stage of the La MaMa Theater in New York. Everyone gave their first name and shared a sentence about their backgrounds and interests. Jamil launched into the first exercise, designed to free the body from the incessant watchfulness of the brain. He demonstrated five movements, calling out the numbers as he performed the gestures. {Video 03.01}

One: Raise hand above your head
Two: Put hand on your heart
Three: Slap thigh
Four: Clap hands
Five: Gently place fingers on your breastbone

The students imitated him, starting slowly and going faster and faster. Jamil then demonstrated six movements for the feet. {Video 03.02}

One: Step forward right
Two: Step forward left
Three: Open out right foot into wider stance
Four: Move right foot forward
Five: Move right foot back
Six: Move left foot back in line with right foot, in an ordinary standing stance

Jamil didn't say any of this. He demonstrated with his own body, simply calling out the numbers that matched the movements. The students caught on almost before he finished. When he added a finger snap to mark the rhythm, so did they. Then they started chanting the numbers with him. The whole circle moved in sync, calling out numbers as they moved their feet. As they sped up, a few fell out of the rhythm, laughed, and got back in.

"And now," Jamil said after a few minutes of moving together, his pitch rising in anticipation of what was to come. The students knew what was next. They were to put the hand and foot movements together, first slowly and then faster and faster. They again started chanting the numbers together as they moved. Some mastered it right away. Some struggled to coordinate. No one failed to understand. {Video 03.03}

Next, it was Mustapha's turn to lead. He put on music, and they all danced freely for several minutes, like they would at a party. {Video 03.04}

Then Mustapha stopped the music and addressed the students: "We must feel and listen and see another person. It's why we had to make a circle. . . . It's like a family, one body. It's like in theater, on stage, when we play, three or four actors. We must feel and see all things. And, second, we make a triangle. It's like Michael Jackson. . . ." He went on to explain the formation he envisioned: one in front, two behind, then three, and so on—just like in a Michael Jackson music video. "The first person is leader." Despite his somewhat cryptic English, the students immediately understood. Mustapha gestured with his body at the effect he wanted.

"With turning, or just front?" one student asked.

"It's 'follow-the-leader,'" another explained. The students fell into formation, assisted by Rihab and Jamil. The leader—a young man in front—nodded as Mustapha continued to explain. Clearly, the leader had done this before. Mustapha started the music, and the young man gracefully led the group in a slow, improvisational dance. The others followed as one body. There was a small hesitation, marked by nervous laughter, as the leader made a 180-degree turn. When the students followed, suddenly their backs were to him, and they could no longer see what he was doing. But they barely missed a beat. "You're the leader," the young man shouted out to the person at the other end. The group effortlessly shifted their attention to the student who was now in front. As they collectively turned again, they moved back to follow the first student. The music Mustapha put on was the only sign of Algerian culture. {Video 03.05}

The Center Stage tour was intended to foster cross-cultural exchange, and Istijmam was anticipating energizing engagements with their US counterparts. The workshop with students from Sarah Lawrence College in New York was one of a series of encounters that were key components of Istijmam's tour. The troupe led an afternoon workshop at an arts high school outside of Hartford, Connecticut. They spent a Saturday morning giving a workshop for University of New Hampshire theater students and an afternoon with a modern dance company in Portland, Maine. They also participated in panel discussions and classroom presentations at various stops along the tour. But rather than the stimulating exchanges Istijmam was hoping for, what emerged in virtually every case was a co-constituted performance of cross-cultural encounter with which all participants were already familiar.

Performance encompasses not only the marked display events that people come to watch (such as a staging of *Apples*) but also the range of communicative events in which people engage—from a simple greeting or a casual dinner conversation to a more structured event such as a presentation or workshop. The "communicative dynamics" (Bauman 2012, 95) that characterize a particular kind or genre of encounter include how the encounter typically unfolds (event structure); the anticipated roles and relationships of participants (participant structure); the context of the event; the content or topics associated with the event (referential dimensions); the expected postures and body language of participants; and the anticipated pitch, volume, tone and rhythm of speaking (prosody). All of these and more form the performance conventions that are associated with particular kinds of interpersonal encounters.

To talk about performance conventions is also to talk about genre.[1] In the now classic approach to genre developed by Richard Bauman and Charles Briggs, genre conventions entail "features and structures" that are "systemically related" and "co-occurrent"—that is, they occur together in virtually every performance in a similar way.[2] But a genre is not only a collection of co-occurrent features. A genre also provides a "conventionalized orienting framework for the production and reception of discourse" (Bauman 2004, 3). That is, genres contain histories that in turn set up expectations about how future performances will unfold. For instance, a phrase like "please welcome Istijmam" signals that a certain kind of event is about to start: one in which Istijmam will provide some sort of performance. The phrase would typically be uttered by an emcee or event organizer. The group's name would be verbally emphasized via changes in volume, pitch, and vocal emphasis. The phrase invites a visceral response, indicating to spectators that they should clap and then sit in anticipatory silence. It carries these expectations because it has been uttered in similar situations over and over again. In that sense, the phrase indexes or points to its own prior history.

Genres can also signal ideological orientations. For example, in Morocco, women were generally not involved in selling in the marketplace. When a female herbalist started marketing her herbs to a mostly male audience in the local halqa, she was upsetting the prevailing gender ideology, which viewed the market as a male domain (Kapchan 1995, 1996). Similarly, in the Algerian halqa, the goual has long been assumed to be male. A female goual would call attention to her gender in a way that a male goual would not. In breaking with the genre convention that the goual is necessarily male, she would also challenge the gender ideology that assigns men and women to particular socioeconomic and discursive roles. Whereas the male goual's performance was unmarked and thus unremarked, her performance would become marked by gender and subject to particular kinds of commentary and critique.

Genres, then, tell people what to expect based on past performances. Most genres are so ingrained that we do not think about them. However, genre conventions can be violated (as the female herbalist shows). In fact, challenging conventions can be a way to critique and even alter established orders. More often, however, people tend to reproduce genre conventions, because to violate the conventions of an event is to confront the wider structures of power, authority, and ideology that keep it in place. Ideology aside, violating a genre convention is simply uncomfortable because it will focus attention on both the violation and the person who has dared to challenge it. (Every year, in discussing the genre or performance conventions of the classroom, I ask my students why no one stands on their head in the middle of class; they laugh, but no one has ever taken me up on it.)

On tour, Istijmam was engaged in genres of encounter in which all participants were already highly practiced. They were globalized genres, in the sense of being associated with the economic and educational structures and institutions of capitalist modernity that have now spread virtually around the world.[3] Take workshops like the one with the Sarah Lawrence students. The Istijmam actors and the US participants could anticipate the kinds of activities they would be doing before the event began. They understood the structure of participation. The students fell into line almost before they were given instructions. The name the students had for what Mustapha was asking them to do— "follow-the-leader"—would be immediately recognizable by most children raised in the United States. The shared reference to Michael Jackson's music videos enabled everyone to visualize instantly what they were going to do.

Classroom presentations and panel discussions were even more familiar. Whether at the University of New Hampshire, Yale University, or Indiana University, the members of Istijmam would take their places in chairs set up for them at the front of the room. Those in attendance knew precisely what kinds of questions to ask (and not to ask). The actors knew just how to answer. By and large, similar questions and answers were repeated throughout the tour. In both workshops and presentations, everyone knew just how to sit, how to speak, and how to dress. They had rehearsed these kinds of performances for much of their lives. Common theatrical training, similar approaches to artistic creation, shared educational experiences, and generational cultures that were more global than national were typically foregrounded over difference.

The widely shared performance conventions associated with the workshop, the panel discussion, and the classroom presentation worked to shape the ways people participated in these events in highly predictable ways. The "performative potency" (Briggs and Bauman 1992, 159) of the encounters—or the potential effect that the encounters could generate—came less from the particular contents of the events than from the performance genres through which they were organized.[4] These genres of encounter were so ingrained in all participants that they may have worked to foreclose other kinds of exchange. Looking at workshops, classes, and panels as genres of encounter entails close attention to the concrete performances that make up the various events, including: phatic devices that open, close, or maintain connection; overall event structure; available participant roles; presentational styles; kinds of material presented; and anticipated forms of bodily and verbal engagement.

What makes these encounters challenging to take up is their inherent familiarity not only to the actors but also to most readers of this book. You have likely participated in these kinds of events yourselves. Yet close analysis of the encounters as performances can also help to defamiliarize them, showing how they too are learned cultural forms that work to promote certain kinds of interactions while discouraging others.

For much of the tour, then, Istijmam and their US collaborators shared a common performance culture in which everyone already understood the conventions of what constituted a cross-cultural encounter. But the cultural component of the cross-cultural encounter was vexed. In a program like Center Stage, culture is located in aesthetic traditions and practices that have been doubly scaled up: taken out of their local settings, they are first located in nation-states or ethnicities, from which they can then be propelled into dialogues with other parts of the world. For both ideological and logistical reasons, the nation state is necessarily the political unit around which Center Stage tours are organized. Artists are selected in part because they can share something unique about their national or ethnic heritage. Heritage is then situated in the context of a larger cosmopolitan conversation, with cosmopolitanism defined as a basic aspiration to bring into being "a borderless world of cultural plurality" (Werbner 2008, 2).[5] Artists selected for the 2018 Center Stage season, for instance, all offered a blend of the traditional and the contemporary. The Egyptian singer Dina Elwedidi was billed as "a sophisticated musical innovator" who could "channel the heritage and contemporary identity of Cairo"; the oud player Mohamed Abozekry was said to "convene . . . Egypt's popular and classical music traditions, Sufi calls, and secular poetry with a new instrumental project"; the Ukrainian group Kurbasy was described as "trac[ing] contemporary connections to an archaic past."[6]

In Istijmam's case, Center Stage highlighted the halqa and its master storyteller, the goual as part of an Algerian "populist tradition" and as cosmopolitan figures who could simultaneously point to an Algerian past, inspire Istijmam's contemporary theater, and suggest resonances with international aesthetic practices (such as Brechtian theater). As such, these figures both carved out an Algerian difference and made this difference speak to a common humanity—an inherently cosmopolitan initiative. But if differences in heritage were celebrated, other kinds of cultural differences were rendered virtually invisible, surfacing only as occasional flashes of friction (Tsing 2005) or phatic laughter. Istijmam, like other Center Stage artists, was supposed to come to the United States bearing difference, but not so much difference that they would not be able to recognize what kinds of performances they would be asked to produce. They were supposed to come bearing culture, as long as they shared the norms of the events where their culture was to be on display. They were invited guests and celebrated artists, fully commensurate on that level with their US counterparts. But Istijmam actors were also in the United States as privileged visitors from a country where much of the population would not be able to secure a US visa. These differences were never directly brought up. They were not considered to be cultural in the right ways. But at several moments, potentially uncomfortable disparities between troupe members and US participants could have become salient. Instead, however, both troupe members and those in attendance marshalled phatic devices—devices to maintain connection—to smooth over what might have become disquieting points of divergence. Indeed, the effort that went into maintaining connection sometimes became the most salient feature of an exchange.

Two tensions, then, lay just below the surface in at least some of Istijmam's encounters on the Center Stage tour. First, cosmopolitan expectations associated with a scenario of cultural exchange were put into play through familiar global performance genres of workshops, panels, and presentations that worked to erase all but the most banal of differences. Second, tensions within the cosmopolitan scenario itself meant that only some kinds of cultural differences were to be made visible while others were occluded or quickly smoothed over.[7] Scholars of cultural display have productively raised the question of difference, asking, "Just who counts as different or as different enough or as different in the ways that matter?" (Kirshenblatt-Gimblett 1998, 243–44, writing about the Los Angeles Festival of 1990). The flip side of this question is of equal importance: In what ways do performers have to be similar in order to participate successfully in cross-cultural exchange?

These questions are hardly unique to Istijmam's tour.[8] Since at least the early 1990s, scholars have been talking about the ways that a global stage homogenizes cultural expression. If performances of cosmopolitanism entail "an aesthetic openness towards divergent cultural experiences," they are also "a matter of competence" that demand "a state of readiness, a personal ability to make one's way into other cultures . . ., a built-up skill in maneuvering more or less expertly within a particular system of meanings" (Hannerz, cited in Werbner 2008, 48–49). It is not, said Richard Wilk (referring to the performance of international beauty pageants in Belize), that "we are . . . all becoming the same, but we are portraying, dramatizing and communicating our differences to each other in ways that are more widely intelligible." This occurs when we frame cultural differences through "universal categories and standards" (Wilk 1995, 118).

More than twenty years before Istijmam's tour, an Egyptian epic storyteller came to America without this "built-up skill." The poet Abu Zayd had been invited to perform selections of the well-known Bani Hillal epic for the large Arab-American immigrant populations who had settled in Dearborn, Michigan, just outside Detroit. Moving between accounts of the tour itself (Reynolds 1998; Shryock 1998) and a documentary film made about the tour (Mandell 1995) points to how some of the uncomfortable moments in performance were erased in the film. In effect, the film reconstituted the tour after the fact in ways that homogenized cultural difference and turned Abu Zayd's visit into a performance of cosmopolitanism. During the tour itself, the lack of shared genre conventions between Abu Zayd and audience members was especially apparent at a performance at the Lebanese Islamic Center of America, a primarily Shiite organization. The storyteller (from largely Sunni Egypt) was uncomfortable from the beginning by being asked to speak from the mosque's minbar, a podium used in this center for many performances but utilized in the poet's native Egypt only for readings from the Quran. Moreover, the poet had been asked to perform without his usual musical accompaniment in this sacred Shia space. This altered his recitation practice in ways that made him hard to follow. Further, Abu Zayd was accustomed to short audience responses punctuating his praise poems about the Prophet Muhammad, whereas this audience was used to giving longer responses. The poet, shaken by the differences in performance conventions, started speaking faster and faster. In turn, the audience stopped responding, "essentially going on strike," and the performance was brought to an early close. This event appears nowhere in the documentary. Instead, the film turned the poet into a "curio," part of the film's "colorful backdrop" but otherwise all but silenced (Reynolds 1998, 157–58). The poet, in other words, became a figure of celebratory otherness and a character around whom Arab Americans were shown coming together. Rather than bringing out differences, the film "accentuated shared human experiences" (Shryock 1998, 177).

This case is instructive because it shows how a cosmopolitan scenario came to reshape the tour after the fact, as the film turned the visiting Egyptians into figures of celebratory otherness, erased diversity in Arab American audiences, and created the very "colorful, cosmopolitan scene" that the presumed viewer "want[ed] to behold" (Shryock 1998, 168). By the time of Istijmam's tour, the conventions of cosmopolitan exchange no longer had to be retroactively imposed. By then, these conventions were so ingrained that they entered into and shaped the social relations of the tour itself as it unfolded. Both the actors and their interlocutors knew precisely how to create connections and smooth over any tensions almost before they arose. Going with the actors into the classrooms and workshops points in concrete specificity to how they did so.

GENRES OF ENCOUNTER

The tour was organized around three kinds of event: performances of the play *Apples* (sometimes followed by audience talk-backs),[9] panel discussions or classroom presentations, and workshops. In most cases, the US participants at presentations and workshops had not seen Istijmam perform *Apples*. This was partly intentional and partly circumstantial. As the tour organizers Lisa Booth and Deirdre Valente explained both to me and to the troupe, Center Stage books tours to include various modes of encounter in a range of settings so that the touring groups get a glimpse of some of the diverse ways of living in the United States. In Istijmam's case, this meant traveling from tiny Denmark, Maine (population 1,148 in the 2010 census), to the Midwest college town of Bloomington, Indiana, and from suburban Hartford, Connecticut, to the metropolises of New York City and Washington, DC. Two venues featured performances of the play: the Kennedy Center in Washington, where the tour began, and La MaMa Theater in New York. Two venues—Indiana University and the University of New Hampshire—sponsored both the play and one or several workshops and/or presentations. But because of scheduling constraints at both universities, the play took place after the workshop or panel, so participants had not yet seen the play itself when they encountered Istijmam. This meant that the play could not constitute a topic of shared experience and conversation.

Figure 3.1. Istijmam's show advertised on the roadside marquee at the Denmark Arts Center, September 2016. Author's collection.

At Yale University, the University of St. Joseph, and the Greater Hartford Academy of the Arts, the play was never on the program; the workshop and/or panel operated as stand-alone events.[10]

When performance genres and practices are similar, where is cultural difference located? In the panels and presentations, the Algerians were physically set off from the others, sitting together at the front of the room. At two of the venues (Indiana University and Yale University's Pierson College), the actors dressed the part of cultural others, wearing the attractive, African-inspired outfits or fabrics that they also used to perform Living Communication.[11] By and large, they entered classrooms expecting to be asked about Algerian culture and Algerian theater. Students came prepared to ask about cultural differences. The halqa, the goual, and Istijmam's impressions of the United States were topics of almost every conversation. These events— structured primarily as Q&A-type verbal exchanges—highlighted the referential dimension of the encounter, directing attention to the substance of what was being said. The importance of transmitting cultural content in these events was apparent in that every presentation included a translator (except in one advanced French class, where the students were expected to practice their French with the actors). Genre conventions of classroom presentations also oriented the questions in a single direction, framing the actors as the sources of cultural material about which other participants would learn. Difference, then, was constituted in the presentations through physical separation, through the cultural contents of speech, through a participant organization in which students asked questions and actors answered them, and sometimes through dress.

Conversely, in the workshops, similarities were foregrounded. The actors and the participants dressed alike in jeans and T-shirts—the unmarked global youth costume par excellence. Unlike in the presentations, no one translated (aside from the occasional assist by me, Theresa, or a French-speaking host). And if the presentations highlighted verbal exchange, the workshops relied more on a shared language of the body. Although specific exercises may have been new to some students, everyone understood that they were expected to imitate what the actors were showing them. The participant structure and the organization of performance in the workshops were akin to what students had been doing in dance, acting, yoga, or physical education classes their whole lives. Their shared set of embodied experiences worked to override or make invisible other kinds of differences.

The tour also included two exchanges with theater troupes—the HartBeat Ensemble and the Double Edge Theatre Company. The HartBeat encounter,

though brief, was by far the most satisfying for Istijmam. It included a cofacili-
tated workshop that culminated in the joint creation of several scenes as well
as a panel discussion open to the public in which members of both troupes
participated—the only time on tour when Istijmam was joined on stage by another troupe. With Double Edge, Istijmam's visit unfortunately coincided with
the final days of rehearsal for one of the company's major performances, so most
of the troupe was unavailable.[12] Istijmam did manage to hold an impromptu
rehearsal of *Apples* that led to one of the richest spontaneous exchanges on the
tour, but they did so only by working against the expectation that they would
give a workshop. In both encounters, the possibility of exchange was raised—
held out like the apple—only to be frustrated. Still, there were moments that
hinted at what exchange might look and feel like.

Central to all of these events was their phatic orientation—that is, their
focus on establishing and maintaining a channel of communication. Typically,
phatic communication is concerned with opening and closing channels, as
when a moderator opens a panel discussion with introductory remarks or when
an actor calls together workshop participants into a circle. A channel is generally experienced as unmarked, part of the background to a performance event
that takes place through it. In other words, a channel is generally established
to allow other communicative acts to take place. Here, however, the channel
itself became a central part of the performance.

The "phaticity" (Lemon 2018)—or the emphasis on connection—that sat-
urated the cultural encounters worked on two levels. On the one hand, the
panels and classroom discussions became sites for the representation of cross-
cultural encounter itself. The very fact of phatic connection between Istijmam
and their US counterparts was itself put on display: it was turned into a series
of Facebook-able moments in which the two groups were seen to be in connection. Photos and videos of each encounter were taken and duly circulated on
social media by both Istijmam and Center Stage. These posts displayed images
of exchange itself, without reference to the substance of the encounter. Indeed,
display and dissemination of images of the encounters over social media was
an explicit focus of the Center Stage program. Istijmam's administrator Lila
and the Center Stage tour manager Theresa were charged with posting such
images throughout the tour. On Facebook, the encounters looked for all the
world like cultural exchange. The social media audiences of both Istijmam
and Center Stage would see the troupe interacting with young Americans. But
in effect, the posts worked more as simulacra of exchange, wherein the image
purports to represent something that was never really there. The performance
of encounter came to stand in for encounter itself. That is, the channel served

less as a means for exchange (of some other content) than as a performance and a display of exchange. {**Video 03.06**}

Phatic connection also emerged as central in the workshops that Istijmam led, but here, it worked differently. The workshops highlighted ways of connecting through the body via what Lemon (2018) has called a phatic "technology for intuition." Embodied exercises were used to build a collective field of energy. The exercises appeared to be enjoyable for participants, but it was unclear what made these encounters cultural. Indeed, the exercises may have worked to erase cultural difference. As Mustapha put it: "When you share with people, [whether] verbally or through the body, it's beautiful because you forget your nation, who you are." For him, in an embodied encounter, one's sense of being a separate cultural self vanishes. As in the classroom presentations, the workshops were also predictable, featuring an organization of participation with which everyone was already familiar.

Close ethnographic examination of the staging and the substance of the various encounters points to the moments in which connections were alternately generated, hinted at, frustrated, or even put at risk. If the workshops engendered an embodied sense of connection, they did so via widely shared norms of improvisation practice that made cultural difference almost vanish. They were less performances of cosmopolitanism's "borderless world of cultural plurality" (Werbner 2008, 2) than performances in which that plurality largely dropped out. By and large, the encounters felt thin, leaving the actors (if not the participants) unsatisfied. Layered into many of the encounters, sensed but not made explicit, was a "wounded cosmopolitanism" (Rose 2015, 41) in which the promise of cultural exchange was always just out of reach. The encounters made the possibility of cultural exchange simultaneously tantalizing and inaccessible—like the apple.

CULTURAL CONNECTION ON DISPLAY:

PANELS AND CLASSES

The explicit focus of panels and classes was on the material or the content being exchanged. The implicit focus of these sessions, however, was on the performance of the cultural encounter itself. What was being performed in these events was a highly circumscribed kind of cross-cultural connection. Thematically, or in terms of their substantive content, the events were oriented as question-and-answer sessions in which certain kinds of questions tended to be repeated almost verbatim from one audience to the next. As performances, these events feature organizations of participation so thoroughly ingrained

Figure 3.2. In a class at the University of New Hampshire, September 2016.
Left to right: Lila, Rihab, Mustapha, Moussa. Author's collection.

that they pass virtually unnoticed. Any student raised in a modern educational system knows how they unfold. The event starts with a spatial arrangement that creates a clear separation between artists and audiences and puts the artists on display. At the four universities—St. Joseph's, Yale, Indiana, and one UNH class—the Istijmam members sat in a row of chairs facing the audience. At a second UNH class, the chairs were arranged in a layered circle, with the troupe members occupying the chairs at the front of the room. At each event, an organizer or moderator would introduce the troupe and open the floor for questions. Audience members would raise their hands in turn. One or several actors would reply. In most cases, both questions and answers were translated (from French except at Yale Pierson College, where Egyptian Arabic was used due to the moderator's fluency in that language). Participants knew precisely what could violate the performance conventions of panels and presentations: picture the audience member who goes on for too long, or who tries to redirect the conversation to his own ends, or who asks overly personal questions. Participants also knew what kind of bodily comportment these events entail.

They remained seated, perhaps with a notebook or laptop at their disposal. They knew to raise their hands to ask questions. They knew that they would not be asked to get up and improvise with the actors.

"So what?" you may ask. The genre conventions of panels and presentations are so ingrained as to be boring to read about. But that is precisely what is at issue. What kind of cultural encounter can emerge when participants all know from the beginning what to expect? Wherein lies the culture? What exactly is being performed? Culture in these events becomes contained to the content of what is being said. The performance conventions themselves not only leave little space for divergence but also make such divergence potentially uncomfortable.

That the events would begin with an introduction of the troupe seems so self-evident that it is easy to miss. But in considering how the troupe was introduced, the phatic emphasis on cross-cultural connection was repeatedly foregrounded. For instance, at Yale's Pierson College, host Stephen Davis opened like this: "I just want to say that it's very meaningful to me . . ., we do a lot of work here in teas and other ways to try to connect with the arts. Pierson is in the arts corner of campus, and so we really like to think locally as well as globally in the way that we do that." Professor Davis was clearly describing the event as a performance of connecting the local and the global through the arts. He continued: "Our ultimate goal is to get you all in conversation with these performers." Again, the establishment of conversation, the setting up a frame to allow conversation, is what is being performed. "Getting in conversation" was the goal; the contents of the conversation were a means to this phatic end. From the beginning, the audience was told that they were to create connections, generate mutual understanding, and perhaps experience a common humanity. Audiences knew what to ask to generate just the right amount of cultural exchange: different enough to be tasty and intriguing, but not so much as to be unpalatable or challenging. And Istijmam members knew just how to answer to provide cultural nuggets while avoiding areas that could have been disquieting.

Audience questions tended to cluster around three or four subjects: the halqa as an indigenous theatrical form, and the goual as a model for a halqa-type form of acting; the troupe's impressions of or experiences in the United States; their theatrical practices and history; and (less frequently) the relationship between theater and politics in Algeria. Istijmam members would pull out similar responses at every event.

Halqa and goual: tell us about your difference. Halqa and goual could hold cultural otherness in palatable and enticing ways. Any number of questions could lead Istijmam members to invoke halqa or goual: questions about theatrical practices, about Algerian audiences, about Alloula as playwright, or about Is-tijmam's performance techniques. Halqa and goual became, in these sessions, scalar figures who were capable of simultaneously containing cultural differ-ence while also transcending cultural boundaries. At UNH, for instance, one student said that she thought every culture's theater had something specific. What, she asked, did Algerians have? Mustapha offered the goual as an answer, making the goual sound rather like a contemporary cosmopolitan: "He is a traveler, a nomad who travels everywhere, to meet [people], to gather stories, for education, for information." Rihab situated the goual in relation to a cul-ture of oral tradition that was shared across Africa; he was a figure who told religious stories or recounted historical events. But she also brought him into contemporary focus as someone from "the streets": "He was a very good actor, but he came from the streets, not Hollywood."

Halqa and goual were also evoked as bridges between vernacular Algerian culture and western avant-garde theater, in particular the theater of Bertolt Brecht. At a panel with HartBeat Theater Company, Jamil linked Brecht, Al-loula, and the goual as approaching storytelling from a stance of distantiation. Alternatively, halqa and goual were marshalled as indigenous figures that of-fered a contrast with the culture of French colonial theater. Or they became figures who held the key to differences in Algerian theater by locating it in an interactive space: the halqa was situated as a marketplace encounter where the goual would incorporate the actions and responses of those around him into his story.

US audiences also tried to draw the goual into relation with similar figures in Western traditions. At the HartBeat panel, a US panelist brought up the Italian playwright Dario Fo, who had been inspired by a medieval Italian storyteller called the guivari. The guivari sounded, to this panelist, a lot like the goual: "It sounds like there's some kind of artistic connection definitely because the guivari would perform in the streets the things that couldn't be said in official places." In short, the figures of halqa and goual made Algerian theater simul-taneously vernacular and universal—the very definition of cosmopolitanism.

Tell us about ourselves. Another prominent line of questioning is typical of contemporary cross-cultural encounters throughout the world. Again, most of us already know what these questions are. We have asked or answered them ourselves. Any nation can be substituted for the United States or Algeria. *What did you think of the US before you came? Is it like what you imagined? What has most surprised or shocked you since you've been here? What do you think of US cul-ture? How is it different from Algeria?* These are all versions of the question: "Tell me what you see in my culture and how it is different from yours." Someone perceived as a cultural other is asked to refract their view of US culture back to those within, so that those inside can see for a moment through another's eyes. Even foreign students in the classes would pose these kinds of questions. For instance, a UNH student from Senegal said, "I know you've only been here for two weeks, but what do you think?"

Istijmam's responses would range from jokes to generalities. "Coffee," Moussa replied in response to a question about the difference between Algeria and the United States. Throughout the tour, the actors were constantly on the lookout for a strong cup of coffee. Everyone laughed. Lila said that she simply wanted people to know where Algeria was. She was not entirely joking—Algeria had already been confused at least once on the tour with Nigeria. She also brought up Algeria's socialist past, saying that capitalism was much more deeply rooted in the United States. Moussa raised the familiar and fairly stereotypical contrast of Algeria as a place of Arab hospitality, whereas the United States was a place of economic, political, and cultural development: in Algeria, "you find people capable of giving everything to someone they don't even know." Mustapha talked about America's "yes we can" mentality and how "if you have an idea," you can make it. As for Rihab, she was still looking, she said, for a "wow" moment. Both the actors and several foreign students talked about how their previous image of America as a more violent place than what they encountered on the ground had been fostered by film. These were all one-off responses to one-off questions. The next question, whatever it was, would redirect the conversation. Nothing went very deep—as per the genre conventions of this type of event.

Several actors did talk about how they had come to the United States wanting to engage with US audiences around the play more than to discover America. Lila, for example, said during the UNH presentation that she had wanted to "show the American people our culture, our way of doing theater, and to have a lot of exchange around it. . . . I wasn't [coming] in a dynamic of getting to know America. America, it's the glitter (*la paillette*)." But as noted above, the students in the classes had not seen the play. For logistical reasons, it had been programmed after the class discussions at both Indiana University and the University of New Hampshire, whereas at other venues, the play was never on the agenda. This meant that there was no shared point of reference around which discussion could center. The play, in these discussions, became an empty signifier that pointed to its own absent presence. The actors could invoke it, but it did not call up a shared experience around which discussion could unfold. In these venues, the play itself came to stand for the potentiality of exchange that was never quite realized.

It is not surprising that these kinds of events, as well as the surface nature of this kind of tour itself, would give rise to a kind of "thin description." Tour organizer Deirdre Valente described the tour to me as like a "Survey 101."[13] The actors, too, were well aware of the limits of what could be accomplished in a month. At the University of New Hampshire, when asked about the "difference between Algeria and the United States," Moussa acknowledged that they "would need fifteen years to answer this." Rihab added that in the short time they were in the United States, they couldn't really get a sense of the country, though she did note the openness and receptivity of the Americans she had met and the country's cultural and racial diversity. They also acknowledged that the structure of the tour itself fostered a certain kind of openness while insulating the troupe from some of the harder aspects of life in the United States. "In two weeks," Rihab said, "will we really be able to see the depths of America? Because it's [only then] where we can really push up against people and sense their differences." Istijmam's hosts and audiences, as well as the troupe members themselves, were predisposed to be welcoming, to be tolerant, "to be completely open to the difference of the other" as Rihab put it. But "we can't penetrate deeply into America," Rihab said again to me at the end of the tour. "We're not directly encountering its reality."[14]

Moussa may have offered the most telling response: "I don't really want to penetrate deeply." He didn't want to see what he called the "underground," the "hidden things." He knew that the tour was showing him only the surface of things, and that was enough for him. The tour itself operated in a kind of bubble that worked against deeper engagement. By traveling in a van and staying primarily in hotels or inns, we were relatively insulated from the daily goings-on in the country, which at the time was in the heated final weeks of the 2016 presidential campaign. Then-candidate Donald Trump was making pronouncements about the "Muslim ban" that he would put into effect and spewing anti-immigrant rhetoric. By and large, however, the actors did not encounter this side of US society (aside from in yard signs across New England). To the contrary: they were surrounded by Americans who could not have been more welcoming.

The structure of the tour and the performance conventions of the various encounters, then, fostered a thin engagement between the troupe and their various interlocutors. The six troupe members and the US participants had an opportunity to sit in a room together for an hour, perhaps two, communicating through translators and disfluencies. What could have been exchanged? The encounters were captured and disseminated via group photos, which were taken at every event and posted regularly on Facebook by both Center Stage

Figure 3.3. At Yale University's Pierson College, September 2016. *Left to right,*
back row: Rihab, Lila, Mustapha, Moderator Stephen Davis, Moussa, HartBeat
director Steven Raider-Ginsburg, Jane; *front row*: Djalel, Jamil. Photo Credit:
Istijmam Culturelle.

and Istijmam. The images gave the impression that exchange was taking place.
Everyone tried their best. Everyone was well meaning. But experiences of exchange were repeatedly foreclosed.

Like the Customer in search of an apple or the Actor in search of rehearsal
space, Istijmam had come seeking cultural encounters. Before the tour, Jamil
voiced it to me this way: "We are trying to bring out the spirit, the something
other that goes beyond the human being, that is there, that happens between
us, that lives between us." "I really felt this need to exchange with them," Rihab
told me at the end of the tour. Yet the stuff of cultural encounter, the moment
itself, the "something other," always seemed elusive. The spark that they sought,
the creative energy that they hoped to unleash, was not quite there in most of
the panel and classroom discussions, and they could all sense it. The transfor-
mative potential of theater—its capacity for "utopian performativity"—was
largely unrealized in the encounters themselves (Dolan 2005).

I feel the flatness of these encounters as I write about them. They do not lend
themselves to ethnographically thick discussion. They are based largely on a
one-way transmission of information about the halqa, the goual, the playwright,

and so on. I could do no follow-up with workshop or classroom participants. Even if I had taken names and done post-tour interviews in some virtual format, not only would I have encountered the same problems, but I also would have been working to circumvent the very genre conventions of the events I was writing about. I could have gone looking for that tidbit or "rich point" (Agar 1993) that would illustrate a vivid and moving moment of exchange. But this would have obscured the way these events worked as performances whose very structure discouraged a more mutual encounter. These were performances of phatic connection, images of something they were supposed to represent, but lacking the "something" that would have given them greater substance. Perhaps, Rihab said to me at the end of the tour, it was not possible to both tour with the play and try to have richer encounters. Perhaps that was too much to expect in just a month's time.

PHATIC FRICTIONS

Part of what frustrated Istijmam in the various encounters (except for the workshop and panel with HartBeat) is that they were by and large one-sided. Participants could ask Istijmam about their reflections or experiences, but there was no structured opportunity for the troupe members to ask questions of the audience. To redirect the event from a panel or presentation to a dialogue would have violated performance conventions. Istijmam was there primarily to answer questions, not to ask them. Moussa, while lauding Americans' "curiosity" and "desire to know the other," was a bit taken aback by this: "I didn't come with the idea that I have things to show you or present to you. . . . I was in the dynamic of 'I want to share something with you.'" Sharing implied for Moussa a give and take, something more mutual.

If most presentations unfolded along predictable lines, there were occasional moments of what I have been calling phatic friction—moments when the interaction veered into territory that was uncomfortable enough to threaten the connection for either the actors or, as in the following example, the US instructor. This exchange took place in an introductory French class at the University of New Hampshire. The instructor was translating. One student asked what had influenced the troupe members to want to become actors. As the instructor translated, the actors looked at each other, and then Lila took the floor. I provide both French and English, as translation here is part of the issue.

Lila: Alors, moi, c'est vraiment un peu particulier pour moi.
Instructor: It's particular.
Lila: Quand j'étais petite, j'étais toujours une fillette grosse, une grosse fille.

Instructor: Okay, so when she was little, she was a little bit, how to put that?
[she gestures with her hands]
Lila: Fat. [Everyone laughs.]
Instructor: No, not fat. No, no, no. We don't use that word. Alors . . .
Rihab: It's forbidden in America?
Instructor: She was very well . . .
Lila: [inaudible]
Instructor: Well built.
Rihab: Well built!

Lila went on to explain that as a young girl, she had been self-conscious about her size, and theater gave her a way to enter into other realities: she could become a princess, for instance. But what interests me here is Rihab's response to the teacher's refusal to use Lila's own word, *fat*: "It's forbidden in America?" This could have opened out into a discussion about political correctness, about the way certain words come to hold indexical charge that make them difficult to utter, about what words might take on this kind of charge in Algeria versus in America, about what aspects of women's bodies can (and cannot) be openly discussed. Instead, everyone chose to move on. {**Video 03.07**}

This being said, as a university professor myself, I cast no judgment on the instructor's response. It can be hard to know where to direct conversation that threatens to unfold in unexpected ways. It may also have been considered off-topic by the instructor—the troupe was there, after all, to talk about theater, not about political correctness or women's bodies. Moreover, Rihab uttered the remark in an off-the-cuff, almost back-channel way, more as a side comment than as a question she was putting on the floor for discussion. It is unclear how many students in the large lecture hall even heard her. Still, this offers a telling example of how moments of potential discomfort were smoothed over. No one pursued the momentary rupture in the interaction in a way that could have opened up a richer conversation.

WORKSHOPS

If the classroom discussions were largely organized in a Q&A format that foregrounded discursive content located in the actors as cultural others, the workshops were designed as embodied activities in which everyone would participate. Again, however, with the exception of the workshop with HartBeat, cultural expertise and practice flowed in only one direction. Istijmam led and participants followed. This is not unusual, of course: guest artists nearly always facilitate workshops at the institutions that host them. "That tends to be the model of cultural exchange," noted one participant in a discussion I organized at Indiana University after the tour. "We don't do it the other way."

Whereas classroom presentations foregrounded differences, workshops were designed around similarities. Even more than the panels, the workshops were structured to produce connection. They did so through theatrical techniques designed to generate "phatic energy" (Lemon 2018, 33) among the participants, evoking in them an intuitive, embodied sense of when and how to move together. This was the case for the "prison break" exercise that Rihab led with the Sarah Lawrence students. Everyone was to line up on one side of the room. The task was to sense the moment to escape by running at the same time to the other side of the room.[15] They had to generate a collective energy, intuiting its presence among them until their bodies all moved at once.[16] {Video 03.08} In a related exercise in Portland, Maine, participants were seated in a circle and had to stand up one at a time, their movement not overlapping with anyone else's. {Video 03.09}

Another exercise that Istijmam used repeatedly both in the United States and in their own training was "Allo Mami." At the Sarah Lawrence workshop, Djalel placed people in parallel lines facing each other. "There is no time to reflect," he said. He called out a number and then demonstrated the vocal call and/or the embodied gesture that went with that number:

One: *Allo Mami*—raise hand to your ears like a phone
Two: *Hi Ami*—pretend to shake hands
Three: *Oui oui oui oui oui*—crouch down with hands by temples
Four: *Get up stand up*—raise fist
Five: Jump up and down (no verbal component)

He would then call the numbers out in random order, quickly, so students wouldn't have time to reflect. Next, he would shout out a sequence—*one two three five five two*—and they would have to recall the sequence along with the vocalization and action quickly and, ideally, in unison, sensing the collective energy and moving together.

The workshops occasionally incorporated a more elaborated linguistic component. With the Sarah Lawrence students, Djalel introduced an activity that involved making an advertisement for an imaginary product. Participants were to begin in pairs: one person would verbally introduce the product, and the other would try to depict it with her body. They had thirty seconds to devise their ad. The first half dozen pairs to come forward were all Sarah Lawrence students and fluent speakers of American English. The "sellers" spoke quickly and colloquially in ways that may have been hard for the Algerians to fully follow, but the students knew just what to do. Then Djalel modified the exercise, asking for more people. Four came forward: three from Sarah Lawrence plus Mustapha. The seller, one of the more experienced Sarah Lawrence students, chose to market magical glasses. {**Video 03.10**}

The student says, "Do you have bad vision? Do you wish that something could help you because you just can't see a goddamned thing? Well, try these new Amaz-o-vision glasses. They can help you see what's in front of you, what's behind you, what's above you, and what is in between the states of matter. They can help you see into the future, into the past, into other dimensions. They can help you see who people were when they were babies. They can help you see what people will be like when they're old. They can help you see into your past ancestors as well as your progeny for thousands and thousands of generations. You will see into all sorts of new colors, colors beyond the colors you even can imagine."

"Freeze!" says Djalel. He asks one of the three to continue the story. The new seller elaborates on the glasses for several seconds, and then Djalel adds a fourth actor, a customer.

The student playing the seller doesn't miss a beat. "Would you like to buy these fantastic wonderful glasses that can make you see everything?" The customer takes off Mustapha's glasses, puts them on his own head, and looks out at the audience as if seeing them for the first time, exaggerating his movements. Everyone laughs and claps except Mustapha, who plays along, closing his eyes as if he can no longer see a thing.

The customer puts them back on Mustapha and exits, but the seller exhorts him to "Come back! They're only four dollars! For these mind-bending, world changing, perspective-deepening spectacles."

"Cheaper?" the customer asks, trying to bargain.

The seller responds: "I don't know, you know, the manufacturing. . . . Sure, sure, you know what, just for you, sir. Just today, right here, right now, with the code word 'swordfish,' you can get them for $3.99."

"Take it," someone yells from the audience.

"Such a good deal," the saleswoman continues. "You can't get a better deal anywhere. Walmart is selling them for seven dollars."

The customer asks for a new pair in a box and makes as if to take them when Djalel calls out, "Freeze! Another customer."

A young woman assumes the role of customer and takes Mustapha's glasses. "How much is this?"

"For you, ma'am, $3.50." They continue enacting this scene until Djalel again says, "Freeze! Change the situation. Go!" They continue to banter and bargain.

"Freeze!" Djalel cries out, this time giving them a new situation: "The police-man comes." No sooner does one customer hear the word *police* than she goes running away, to general mirth.

Another woman, playing the policeman, comes out onto the stage. "Okay, ladies and gentlemen, break it up, break it up, break it up! I know what's up with this black market shit. Give me the glasses," she orders, hand outstretched. "Give me the glasses." The owner makes as if to look around for the glasses, but the policewoman interrupts. "Cheryl, I saw you the other day. I'm not doing this game again." Mustapha, still silent, then makes as if to pull money from his pocket as a bribe (meanwhile, his own glasses are nowhere to be seen). The policewoman takes it, sends him away, and starts to count the money.

The owner again comes forward, begging: "Officer. You don't understand. If there were any glasses here, and clearly there aren't, they're my livelihood. . . . Please, I have a family who needs me, and I need to be there for them, I need to support them, and, and, it just so happens that, potentially . . ."

"Freeze! Children of this guy," Djalel calls out, and a number of others rush forward to join the scenario. Bedlam descends as the "children" roll around on the floor.

The officer loses it. "Will you tell them to get up?" she beseeches the seller. "I have no money to pay for child care." The officer lets out a wail.

"Okay, good!" Djalel then says with finality. The scene ends to applause, the seller still sporting Mustapha's glasses. Djalel wraps up the exercise by moving to the front and providing pedagogical framing. "This is the way that each one of us can take a piece of rock [he points to the walls, made of brick] and put it on the stage, and the others come and put another rock, and we make [a] story. Don't ask questions. . . . Don't say no. Okay? Don't reflect. Take your concentra-tion in the center and play. Thank you, everybody."

I chose to write about this exercise not only because it was one of the more well-developed ones, featuring both embodied and discursive components, but also because it raises questions about what counts as cultural exchange. Was it an exchange because it included coparticipation of Sarah Lawrence students and at least one Istijmam member? Did it become more cultural when people from both countries took part? What about those Sarah Lawrence students who may not have been from the United States? Did they count as cultural? Or was culture specifically located in the Algerians as the featured workshop leaders?

Istijmam members did not experience these events as cultural exchange. In fact, it was quite the opposite. Moussa told me that in the US workshops, he felt more of a shared dynamic, a shared way of of way of seeing things, than he did during improvisation workshops that Istijmam had offered in Algeria: "People [in the United States] understand what we're doing because they're doing this also, it's a country that allows us to be doing advanced research in the theatrical domain, and that's what we're seeking. . . . This opening already exists here, people are ready to receive it. . . . By contrast, in Algeria no . . . in Algeria, people share, even if they don't understand, [but] they are not in a dynamic that says, 'I have to understand what he wants to tell me in order to share [the work] with him.' But here in America, you feel that not only do people share with you, but they understand exactly what you are doing because they're in the same dynamic, you're on the same wavelength."[17] For Moussa, then, the workshops were designed to foster a shared "wavelength" in which culture itself vanished. A phatic connection, or a sensed and intuited feeling between participants, was invoked to override cultural difference, putting everyone on the same playing field.

Workshops, like class presentations, worked to obscure the places where participants were not in a shared wavelength. Recall the student from Sarah Lawrence who asked about the possibility of working with Istijmam in Algeria (see the introduction). If the troupe could come back the following summer, "it would be amazing," she had said. "Maybe we can give you our mails so you can let us know when you are here so we can do a workshop with you." The troupe members and I knew that this was impossible. Who would pay for it? Who would organize it? Jamil articulated this to me later: "It's interesting that . . . the person wanted to come work with us, but we're in *Africa*." In Jamil's inflected *Africa* was a history of cultural, geographic, and political-economic distance and disparity. There was simply no mechanism that was going to bring US groups to Algeria to work with Istijmam. Nor could Istijmam return to the United States. Similar conversations took place at the HartBeat workshop: the two troupes talked about getting together again to do a joint project. "But we know it will be financially difficult," Jamil said to me later. "It's frustrating."[18] The questions pointed to structural barriers rooted in a global order that made future travel between the two countries all but impossible for the artists. These conversations were haunted by a difference in horizons of expectation, a knowing-without-saying that future connection would likely be impossible. Material infrastructures did not easily support travel and exchange between Algeria and America. Indeed, this lack of access was part of why Algeria was selected by Center Stage. {**Video 03.11**}

Rihab too knew that a return visit would be all but impossible. She did flip the student's question a bit, saying that the troupe was frustrated by the lack of opportunity to deepen the exchanges on the tour and making it clear that Istijmam was interested in a two-way conversation in which each could learn from the other. At the same time, she pointed to a possible future: "Perhaps we'll have the opportunity," she said, and offered to stay in touch via Facebook and email. Why did she evoke a potential future, even if qualified with *perhaps*, and offer to stay in touch? Consider what might have happened had she said what she knew—something like, "Unfortunately, this is next to impossible. It will be hard for us to get visas, almost impossible to find money, and then where would we perform?" Such a statement would likely have closed down the conversation altogether. Pursuing its implications would have forced people to confront the awkward and uncomfortable reality of differences in resources and mobility, of the difficulties African artists face when they want to visit America, and of the uneven ways that global flows of artistic travel are structured. It would have made apparent the naive sense of privilege in the Sarah Lawrence student's question, her assumption that Istijmam had the resources and the setup to of-fer training workshops that Americans could attend. Rihab knew otherwise: There was simply no institutional structure in place whereby students from the United States could come to Algeria to work with Istijmam. There was no way for Istijmam to receive financing that would support such an initiative. Istijmam couldn't even support their own activities. Again, participants in the encounter were situated within different horizons of possibility.

The Center Stage program operates within a cosmopolitan logic "rooted in the idea that the meaning and value of human life rests less on circumstances of where a person is born . . . than the existential fact of their belonging to the human race and their capacity to act with and alongside others" (Irving 2015, 66). Such a logic gives rise simultaneously to a capacity to imagine such a world and to an awareness that political, legal, and institutional borders limit who can fully realize this aspiration. The Sarah Lawrence student's question harbored an almost utopian imagining of a world in which Americans and Al-gerians could easily work together. Sensing this possibility while also knowing that future work together would be virtually impossible gave rise to a certain psychic pain or "wounded cosmopolitanism" (Rose 2015, 41). The pain comes not because such encounters cannot be conceived of but because of the gap between utopian imaginings and material possibilities. Like the apple, future encounters were enticing but virtually inaccessible.[19]

Differences in horizons of possibility may have been mitigated by more co-eval forms of encounter on the tour. Rihab had gestured toward this in her reply to the Sarah Lawrence student. When I talked individually with the Istijmam actors, they all highlighted some of the ways that exchange had been foreclosed. It felt too uneven. As Jamil put it, "You meet people from another culture; you don't know what they do, but they want to see what you do." Moussa stated,

"It's been eight years that Istijmam has been giving [workshops] without receiving anything [in return]." Lila, who was not responsible for leading workshop exercises, by the end chose to stop participating in them altogether: "I didn't participate in the last two workshops because for me, we're [supposed to be] in cultural exchange. Exchange goes two ways: I give and I receive. Other than with HartBeat, where I really felt the exchange with two groups, the other workshops were always led by Istijmam. We showed them what we do, but we didn't get anything back."[20] After the tour, in an email, Rihab reiterated these points: "For me personally, and I had the opportunity to discuss this with the troupe, I felt a certain frustration at the end of some of the workshops. The others did too, even if we did everything to lessen this feeling. . . . With HartBeat, we would have loved the opportunity to discover each other more. It was the worst with Double Edge; the tour didn't allow us to meet around our artistic practices. We were spectators, and they were [spectators] in turn, and it's really too bad because our aspirations are the same, or almost the same."[21] The "uneven intersections" (Feld 2012, 7) that these statements point to found no place in the cultural encounter scenario.

EXCHANGES: HARTBEAT AND DOUBLE EDGE

If the workshops and panels were understandably structured with Istijmam as the leaders and featured guests, the encounters with the HartBeat Ensemble and Double Edge Theatre were envisioned as artist-to-artist exchanges. With HartBeat, the genres of encounter were similar, combining aspects of presentations and workshops. But the encounters were more collaborative in that both troupes alternated in leading the various exercises. At Double Edge, the encounters were more observational than collaborative. As Rihab had noted, Istijmam primarily observed Double Edge's performance preparations. Istijmam did offer two impromptu performances of their own that were not on the Center Stage itinerary: a rehearsal of *Apples* for a handful of Double Edge interns that led to one of the richest exchanges on the tour, and an evening performance of their Living Communication repertoire in a local café. The encounters with Double Edge, in particular, included several moments of friction where potential discomforts or disparities were partially sensed but quickly smoothed over.

HartBeat Ensemble

"I loved the exchange with HartBeat," Lila told me. "It gave me something. They work with real stories, they speak directly with people, they tell their

Figure 3.4. Lunch after a morning workshop with the HartBeat Ensemble, Hartford, Connecticut, September 2016. *Left to right around the table*: Theresa Teague (tour manager), Mustapha, Hannah Simms, Julia Rosenblatt, Jamil, Brian Jennings, Steven Raider-Ginsburg, Rihab, Jane, Moussa, Lila. Photo credit: Istijmam Culturelle.

stories on stage . . . that touched me, made me think, Maybe we could do this in Algeria, or do an exchange with them [HartBeat] in the future. I was in seventh heaven with them."[22] Though perhaps not as emphatically as Lila, all the Istijmam members agreed that a glimmer of something different had started to emerge with the HartBeat Ensemble in Hartford, Connecticut.

Founded in 2001, HartBeat describes itself as "tell[ing] extraordinary stories of ordinary people."[23] For Istijmam's visit, HartBeat cofounder Steven Raider-Ginsburg had organized a morning workshop with the two troupes as well as an evening panel titled "Theater in Times of Crisis" in which both troupes participated. The events took place at the University of St. Joseph, where Raider-Ginsburg directs the Carol Autorino Center for the Arts and Humanities.

On the morning of September 12, 2016, Istijmam and HartBeat gathered on the stage of the Autorino Center for what had been billed as a workshop. The six Istijmam actors were joined by five HartBeat members, including cofounders Steven Raider-Ginsburg and Julia Rosenblatt, along with actors Debra Walsh, Hannah Simms, and Brian Jennings. HartBeat led the first hour, beginning with a series of physical and vocal warm-up activities.

Debra opened with an introductory exercise based on the familiar lyrics of "Twist and Shout." "Come on, come on, come on, baby now," she cried out, twisting her body. "Shake it all out!" Everyone followed, jumping and shaking their bodies while repeating the lyrics. The song was clearly part of a shared musical culture. "Topeka bodega bodega topeka," they recited over and over, warming up their mouths and tongues. Then Brian led an extended exercise in movement and visualization based on what he described as the three movement principles of tai chi, chi gong, and the work of Jerzy Grotowski: all motion begins in the center and moves out, all motion always moves in all directions simultaneously, and every actor's motion should take her to the edge of balance. {Video 03.12} This was not dissimilar to warm-ups that Moussa had led in his Living Communication sessions back in Oran. It generated among the actors a space of phatic connection, allowing them to sense and flow with the energy of the group. HartBeat members then introduced their various projects and showed a brief video of their work, which the troupes watched together, sitting on the stage before the large screen.[24]

Next came the only exercise in cocreation that Istijmam would undertake on the tour. Julia introduced it, with Hannah translating between English and French: "We're going to take a few minutes and decide on a topic, a problem. Then we're going to create a tableau of the climax." They threw out a few themes: Immigration? US policy on immigration? Lila raised her hand. "*La vue des américains par rapport au printemps arabe*," she said. "What Americans think about the Arab Spring," Hannah translated. They set to work in two groups. Each was to create three scenes or tableaus: the first would depict the height of the action, the second would precede it, and the third would follow it.

I stayed with the first group: Debra and Brian of HartBeat and Jamil, Djalel, and Lila of Istijmam. Debra began, asking, "Can I take a risk?" She moved to Djalel, looking at him aggressively and holding her fist up to his throat, but then she backed away, muttering, "I don't know." Lila then walked over behind Debra and made as if to slit her throat. This throat-slitting moment became the centerpiece of the image they would use. Once they had this image, the before and after scenes came together quickly. Again, the Istijmam members led the way. Brian, representing American media, was directed to focus only on the problems. "You see the killing, but when they are getting along, you look elsewhere," Jamil put it.

In the group's first scene, two men (Jamil and Djalel) stand together on the street. One has his hand out, apparently begging. The other is smoking, giving nothing to the beggar except the ashes from his cigarette. By contrast, the two women are hugging. The photographer (Brian) takes a picture of the beggar, not seeing the women's display of friendship. In the second scene, Brian, still acting as "the media," focuses on the throat slitting as Lila slays Debra with an imaginary knife. In the third scene, Lila looks with sadness at Debra, now lying dead on the ground. Djalel and Jamil put their hands in each other's pockets in a display of trust. For "the media," represented by Brian, the killing is over and the scene is no longer of interest. Brian turns his back and makes as if to leave. {**Video 03.13**}

This series of tableaux was intended to depict how Americans saw the Arab Spring. The Algerians clearly had ideas about this, as they were the ones who had proposed the idea and the series of images. Both Debra and Lila had viscerally proposed an image of physical violence, with one person slaying another. But Debra backed away from it, saying, "I don't know." Lila picked up on her idea and intensified it. Perhaps Debra did not want to presume she knew what had happened. Perhaps she was reluctant to show aggression toward a guest, even in improvisation. Would it have been uncomfortable to allow an American to conduct the slaying, even if in play? For an American to depict Arab violence? Moreover, whereas Debra had gone to Djalel, Lila went to Debra—the only other woman. Did Lila move to "slay" Debra because it was more comfortable to work with one of the HartBeat women, or because Debra had proposed the idea, or for some other reason (including no clear reason at all)? These kinds of questions could have led to an enriching exchange. But the genre conventions of the event did not foster metalevel discussion about the process that was unfolding between the troupes. As in the class presentations, the performance conventions of group improvisation worked to orient participants to the event in specific ways and to foreclose others. With more time and a more focused collective project, such discussion may have taken place. But in barely fifteen minutes, not much could happen.

Group two focused less on media representations than on what had happened during the Arab Spring in Algeria. They depicted people simply going about their business, as if nothing out of the ordinary was occurring. This was, in fact, how the Arab Spring unfolded in Algeria: outside a few demonstrations, not much took place. Algeria had had demonstrations back in 1988 that in some ways anticipated the Arab Spring (see chap. 1). The aftermath of these demonstrations had led to the Dark Decade. In 2011, Algerians were not about to go back to anything resembling those years. Group two, then, modified the assignment a bit, perhaps to show the Americans that not all Arab countries had participated equally in the Arab Spring. {**Video 03.14**}

After a break, it was Istijmam's turn to lead HartBeat. They took up the two performance genres that they had been using throughout the tour, presentations and workshops. Again, the goual provided cultural ballast. This time it was the tour manager, Theresa, who used the goual to launch the conversation: "So, you guys wanted to learn about the goual?"

"Yes," some of the HartBeat members replied eagerly.

"Anything," added Julia. "Anything they want to teach us."

Jamil launched into opening remarks about how the goual moves between styles of narration, going into a character, coming back out, and continuing to tell the story. "This requires being present... not in the past with thinking," he said. He used the goual's imagined mastery of embodied presence to move into the first improvisation exercise, which, he said, was intended to help "evacuate thinking." He demonstrated five movements, the same ones that open this chapter.

One: Raise hand above your head
Two: Put hand on your heart
Three: Slap thigh
Four: Clap hands
Five: Gently place fingers on your breastbone

Then he added the feet, here with seven steps.

One: Step forward right
Two: Step forward left
Three: Jump
Four: Right foot to side
Five: Right foot to front
Six: Right foot behind
Seven: Move left foot back to join right foot

They started chanting the numbers together as they executed the hand movements, speeding up at Jamil's command. "Do you feel when your thoughts get in the way?" he queried. Then they put hands and feet together. Because there were five hand movements and seven foot movements, they did not coincide, making the exercise challenging.

"It keeps you in the moment," Debra affirmed.

"*Oui*, in the present," Jamil reiterated.

Rihab was up next, similarly emphasizing the need to stay in the present. She brought out a sword prop she had found backstage and asked people to take turns acting out what it could be. It became, in turn, a magnifying glass, a baby, a cane, an oar, a horse, a dog bone, an ear of corn, and a lollipop. She closed with a leader and follower exercise that Istijmam had often used in their own improvisations: one person comes into the center and carries out a simple action, then another person joins in, adding to the scene in ways that support the leader. Up to five or six may eventually join in, as long as they are all enhancing the first person's action. Collectively, they build a scene.

Whereas when HartBeat led, they had started their improvisation from an agreed-upon idea, here the scene was devised in the moment as each person took a turn. Debra began, starting to push as if on someone's heart. Djalel lay down and made as if to be dead while she administered CPR. Mustapha held Djalel's hand, raising his face to the sky as if in supplication. Steven and Hannah enacted medical professionals in the room, with Hannah recording vitals and Steven perhaps reaching for an instrument. Jamil made the sound of electric paddles used to shock the heart into beating again. Then Rihab squatted down and emitted a continuous, high-pitched sound like a cardiac monitor when a heart flat-lines. *"Il est mort?"* someone asks. "He is dead?" She laughed. "Yes!" **{Video 03.15}**

Then they reconfigured the exercise in pairs and trios: one would start an action, and others reinforced it. "No thinking," Rihab repeated. She wrapped up: "Spontaneously, you gave us the beginning and the end of the scene. It is interesting to see it in the action before speaking about it."

Jamil took the floor to conclude, again taking up the performance conventions of presentations. Before wrapping up, he and Rihab consulted off to the side. The HartBeat director wanted them to say something about Algerian theater, she told him. So Jamil closed as he had opened, with the goual: "The goual goes to the public markets. He tells stories. He's a nomad. He brings stories from the past and he recounts them in the present. . . . Around the story-teller there is the circle (halqa). People come to hear the story and to watch the story and to intervene in the story. The story isn't fixed. Anybody can add something. . . . The play is living." He went on to situate the goual in relation to oral history in Africa and to the specifically Algerian theater that Alloula had created around the goual, which Istijmam had taken up. Clapping ended the session. "I want more time," one HartBeat member said, voicing what many were feeling—that two hours just wasn't enough to truly engage in collaborative exchange.

Throughout the workshop, the goual served as a labile figure, capable of being evoked, reshaped, and marshalled to a range of ends. He represented an imagined Algerian difference, grounding Istijmam's work in performance practices drawn from their own heritage and linking their contemporary theater to a long Algerian marketplace tradition. The goual was alternately evoked as a figure of history and tradition, a figure who was socially engaged with the issues of the moment, a figure firmly rooted in the storytelling event and maximally attuned to the energies around him, a figure whose stories were built on what is today called improvisation, and perhaps above all, a figure of difference who in practice perhaps wasn't so different.

The session closed with the requisite group photo, testimony to the fact that a cultural encounter had taken place, followed by a congenial lunch, also duly documented and shared.

Double Edge Theatre

"Istijmam will love Double Edge," Lisa Booth said when she and Deirdre Valente were watching Istijmam's intensive physical warm-up at the Kennedy Center in Washington, DC. Known for its acrobatic, visceral, very physical theater, Double Edge seemed an appropriate match for Istijmam. But Double Edge had a full schedule, and the only time Center Stage could set up an encounter was just before one of Double Edge's major community performances.

We pulled into the Double Edge compound in the tiny town of Ashfield, Massachusetts, late on the afternoon of September 19, 2016. Most of the company was off-site, well over an hour away. They were preparing for their "Springfield Spectacle," a large-scale installation and performance in that city's expansive Forest Park. Associate director Jeremy Eaton had stayed behind to welcome Istijmam. We walked with Jeremy around the company's impressive one-hundred-acre complex, located on the site of a former dairy farm, complete with a beautifully restored eighteenth-century barn and other outbuildings that the company had creatively repurposed. She showed us their two performance and rehearsal spaces, their large studio pavilion, their scenography and costume shop, their offices, and their community kitchen, where we would share soup, salad, and bread with Jeremy and some of the interns that evening. We walked with Jeremy by the pond, a set where they had staged one of their outdoor shows still mounted in the water. We passed former stables that had been made into an outdoor suite of open rooms, each painted and decorated, the last one housing working goats and chickens. We saw the big organic vegetable garden. Everywhere we looked, it seemed that there were mini installations of found objects aesthetically repurposed. In one spot, a handcrafted mosaic was laid into the earth around what seemed to be a rustic sundial, framed by native flowers. Cottage gardens surrounded intimate patios and benches where a few people could share a morning cup of coffee. Trees and flowers of all kinds flourished in the late summer humidity. Cows were pasturing in the

fields beyond. It was a community where artists lived and worked, an intentional community fashioned as "a world in which artistic, political, and ethical
sensibilities align with daily life."[25] It was simply idyllic. And for an Algerian
theater troupe, it was simply unimaginable.

After a shared dinner, we gathered in a small music room for a brief slide
presentation about the company's work. In the ensuing conversation, Istijmam
members asked about Double Edge's training, how they envisioned the body in
their work, and their vision for theater. Not until nearly the end of the evening
did Jamil pose a question that stood out from the others: "How can you afford
this?" At the time, Double Edge was supporting a troupe of some fourteen
actors who lived and worked at the theater complex. There were directors of
development, food operations, food systems, and costume design; there was a
cook, a carpenter, a bookkeeper, an artist, a graphic designer, a buildings and
grounds supervisor, and more.[26] Jeremy described some of the sacrifices the
thirty-four-year-old company had made and the hours of labor they had all
put in to transform the old farm into a communal theater space. Their personal
investment was clear, but it was also clear that Double Edge had access to an
impressive roster of funders that included private foundations, federal and state
agencies, local businesses, and individual memberships, as well as volunteers
and in-kind donations of goods and services.[27] They had access to an economic
infrastructure in the arts that was nowhere to be found in Algeria.

More signs of this infrastructure became apparent the next afternoon, when
we piled into our Mercedes Sprinter van and headed down Interstate 91 to observe Double Edge putting the final touches on the installation for their upcoming show. Unfolding in the green expanse of Springfield's 195-acre Forest Park,
the performance featured a traveler (played by Double Edge codirector Carlos
Uriona) returning to his home in Latin America. As he journeyed through the
park, he evoked memories of his past, which were enacted by actors positioned
along the path, in the stream, and in the treetops.[28] The audience itself would be
traveling, walking from one end of the installation to the other and encountering different performances along the way, including Double Edge's trademark
aerial theater, which featured actors swinging from the branches of trees. Jeremy walked with us through the grounds. "We made the story ourselves . . . the
main event is a huge flood that destroyed a village," she explained. She pointed
to small houses that the company had erected along the stream. "From the very
first moment," she said, the audience "will be surrounded by us, and there will
be live music, people up high on stilts, all around." The audience focus would
shift depending on what scene they were passing, she went on, responding to a

question from Rihab. {**Video 03.16**} Accompanied by distant sounds of drums and music, we walked until we reached a dance rehearsal, led by Double Edge's dance director, Milena Dabova, with students from the Springfield Conservatory of the Arts, who had been recruited as local participants. Just beyond, we saw actors rolling down the path atop large wooden spools. Bird calls and the hum of late-summer cicadas enlivened the soundscape. {**Video 03.17**}

Continuing our trajectory, we ran into Matthew Glassman, artistic director of the performance. We sat on the grass around him as he spoke about the company's history. Ashfield used to be a farming community, he explained, but the economic policies of the federal government had changed in the early 1970s under then president Richard Nixon, upending the way food was grown. Most of Ashfield's local farms had closed. Double Edge had been helping to reinvent the town's identity as an artistic mecca in rural western Massachusetts that would draw in both professional artists and local community members. Picking up on Jamil's question of the previous evening, I asked about how they managed to do this kind of large-scale community performance with no admission fee. This led into a more extended conversation about how Double Edge financed their work. Matthew talked about raising grant money, partnering with other organizations, and finding creative ways to reduce the usual costs associated with a performance. For instance, instead of providing a per diem to each actor, they have a chef who cooks for the group. On the farm, they eat the food they grow themselves. On the road, they might be housed with community members instead of in hotels. This allows them to maintain what Matthew called their "laboratory approach"—the same phrase that Istijmam has long used to describe their work. Jamil asked Matthew about the status and compensation of actors in the United States. There was the Actors Equity Association, Matthew replied, but he added that all but the most famous actors have to subsidize their income by working other jobs. "So if [actors] don't perform, they're not paid?" Jamil asked. That was true, Matthew said, reiterating that Double Edge was sustained not only by performance fees but also from the activities of the farm. {**Video 03.18**}

As I revisit this conversation, I realize that it doesn't quite align with what Jeremy had told us the night before—due more to the lack of a shared language and context than to any attempt to dissimulate. In fact, the actors who are a permanent part of the Double Edge troupe are compensated with a regular salary, however modest it may be. As Jamil well knew, in Algeria there are few opportunities, short of working for a state theater, that can give an actor a regular salary. And even in the state theater, actors could become frustrated, like the Actor in the play, who had to go into a Restroom to develop his art. Acting as a profession, like apples, was tantalizingly out of reach. This is not to deny, of course, the considerable sweat equity and economic sacrifice that Double Edge actors have invested, but they also have had access to a well-established network of support from federal, state, and local governments; private foundations; community groups; and individuals.

In Algeria, the Ministry of Culture does provide state funding for projects it decides to support.[29] In 2007–2008, the El Moudja troupe I worked with received a sizable subsidy to mount and stage more than forty performances across the country of Amin Maalouf's play Love from Afar (al-Hub ʿan Baʿd). Budgets for such productions, which include professional stage sets, costuming, lighting, actor and director fees, and coaching fees, can reach upward of one hundred thousand euros. But the El Moudja company, despite its forty-year history of award-winning productions, has received no awards since that time; in fact, some of their applications have had no response at all—not even an official rejection. Moreover, state subsidies to cultural organizations like El Moudja have considerably decreased over the years. Increasingly, state funding supports large-scale events associated with annual themes such as the Year of Algeria in France, the fiftieth anniversary of Algerian independence, Tlemcen—Capital of Islamic Culture, or Constantine—Capital of Arab Culture. Small companies like Istijmam are not competitive for these awards.

In talking with Matthew, no one brought up these comparisons. We got up and continued to walk with him through the installation, passing painted backdrops ready to be suspended from the trees and crossing paths with a wandering accordion player. Actors, hidden in the surrounding trees, started to sing and make forest sounds. A drummer pounded out a steady beat from under a bridge by the stream. A woman sang while arranging flowers on the stream's far bank. Bird songs pierced the air. We passed another rehearsal scene with singers and dancers enacting a village carnival behind the lead character, played by Carlos. Then we headed back up to the main lodge, passing actors singing as they walked by us on stilts. {Video 03.19; Video 03.20; Video 03.21}

Who wouldn't be taken in by such an aesthetically stunning performance? Moussa later called it magical. It mobilized the body along virtually every dimension—singing, dancing, drumming, stilt-walking, flying through the air. It made exquisite use of all spatial planes, drawing attention now to the treetops, now to the stream, now to the dancers circling in a field. It pulled the eye into playful sets in unexpected spots like streams and tree branches.

But the encounter with Double Edge was not an exchange. It was a display of Double Edge's work for Istijmam to observe from outside. "Follow me, like an audience would," Matthew had said as he started showing us around. {See Video

03.19} Under the circumstances, it was all that was possible. As a performance genre in its own right, the visit was like a guided tour in which Double Edge displayed and explained their activities while Istijmam observed. As in a tour, there was time for questions. As in a tour, these questions were directed by the observers to the featured exhibit and performers. "We were spectators, and they were spectators [of Istijmam's rehearsal of *Apples*], and it's really too bad because our aspirations are the same, or almost the same," Rihab later wrote to me in an email.[30]

A hint of mutual connection did emerge after the dinner that Istijmam shared with the dozens of actors, interns, and local community members participating in the show. Members of Double Edge grabbed their instruments and sang a couple of rousing songs from the performance. Then they invited Istijmam to share some of their music. The troupe hadn't brought their percussion to Springfield, so they took up the instruments that Double Edge had used and launched into their song, "Goumari." Rihab, sporting a crimson Indiana Basketball T-shirt, was singing lead. Derived from trance music, the piece started slowly and gradually built to a frenzy. The audience loved it. At the end, Matthew rose and said, "We're very lucky—we have a show Friday and Saturday nights. You guys can join us." In saying this, he was recognizing Istijmam's considerable abilities. But he was also evoking a tantalizing possibility that was, of course, impossible. Istijmam would not be performing that weekend with Double Edge. They clearly had the talent, but they didn't have the material conditions—the time, the shared rehearsal process—to bring about such an encounter. Matthew's comments were greeted with friendly laughter—a phatic laughter that seemed to recognize both the desirability and the impossibility of such a collaboration. Here again, laughter averted a potential moment of friction, a moment where the unevenness of material horizons could have become salient. It also smoothed over what everyone knew: that there would be no follow-up. Istijmam could observe Double Edge engaged in its own artistic practices, but they could not come together in a shared encounter. Again, there was the apple: simultaneously visible and out of reach.

Even before the visit to Double Edge's rehearsal in Springfield, Jamil had sensed that something was off. The first night, after we toured the complex with Jeremy, we gathered with Double Edge's interns for soup and bread in the beautifully restored barn. Jeremy and Jamil talked about what the next few days could look like. Istijmam could use any of the rehearsal spaces, she told us; they could visit the troupe in Springfield; they could lead a workshop for the interns. For the only time on the tour, Jamil pushed back, perhaps feeling able to do so because a workshop was not on the official schedule. "We want to rehearse the play," Jamil told Jeremy. A workshop, he said pointedly, is not an exchange. Then he backed off a bit, telling her that Istijmam was happy to do a workshop for the interns, but that the troupe also wanted time to rehearse. This rehearsal of *Apples*, which took place the following morning with Jeremy and the Double Edge interns in attendance, became a highlight of the visit, leading to the only extended conversation about the play on the tour (see epilogue).

At the end of the tour, I followed up with Jamil. "I chose to perform the play and not do a workshop with the students," he told me. "I wanted to put on the play because we had to say something. It just wasn't possible!" Jamil experienced the visit to Double Edge as an unfortunate "cacophony," as he put it, in the program: "Throughout the world, we're fighting for the artistic cause because the artist doesn't have his place. So, let's start with ourselves: we can't arrive, a troupe from Algeria, and find Double Edge in rehearsal [off-site]. It's just not normal. It's clear they have an extraordinary space, the tree from which you can jump into the pond [as part of a performance], this space, that space. . . . Wow. There's nothing to say. Us, we don't have that, so what are we supposed to do? Cry? Feel excluded?" He continued: "You have to be very careful in doing exchanges. There can't be a question of superiority or inferiority. It has to be about sharing. . . . If Double Edge had understood that, they wouldn't have planned the visit the way they did."

I countered: It wasn't Double Edge who had set up the visit. They had wanted Istijmam to come later in the fall, but that was not possible. As I understood it, this was the only time that worked in Center Stage's program. But it mattered little to Jamil. "Us, we were following something. Someone put it in place. Whether it was them [Double Edge] or someone else, I'm not blaming them. I don't need to know who did it. There was someone organizing, and then there was us, and sometimes that didn't work together. We could have removed this frustration by meeting them in [mutual] work."

Not everyone in Istijmam shared Jamil's perspective. Moussa found a lot of similarities in each troupe's efforts to create an artistic community. He was also taken by the way Double Edge played anywhere: in the water, in the sky, on wheels. "That means they are trying to leave the space of the stage to go exploring other spaces," he said. In that way, it was similar to Istijmam's efforts to break the fourth wall, even though it took a different form. "I've never felt such an energy or dynamic," he said, as when they sang with Double Edge. "They gave us good energy, because we saw that they were like us, that we're not alone, that there are people on the other side of the planet that are in the same dynamic we are. Meeting people like that, it did me some good." Similarly, for Lila, the encounter was by and large positive. She was able to make a personal connection with Carlos, the Argentinian lead actor, because of her fluency in Spanish. "Frankly, I was touched by their art. . . . It was very strong and we're in the same dynamic. I felt that we have a lot in common." But she also had regrets: "Unfortunately, we weren't able to do an exchange."[31]

HORIZONS OF POSSIBILITY

On September 22, 2016, we had driven all afternoon and evening from Double Edge Theatre in western Massachusetts to Denmark, Maine, making several long stops along the way. So it wasn't until after nightfall that we turned down a tree-hugged dirt road in the woods that would lead to the cabin where we would be staying. Despite being enveloped by the pitch-black of the dense New England forest (and being led slightly astray by GPS), we managed to find the place. Theresa heroically backed the Sprinter down a steep muddy driveway, unsure whether she would be able to get it out in the morning. Spent from the trip, we soon retired for the night. The next morning, we would discover a tiny, sparkling pond down the hill, where some would venture out in kayaks and canoes. The presenters of Istijmam's show in Denmark had graciously vacated their summer cabin so we could all stay there. It was the only time on the tour when we were lodged in a shared living space.

Two nights later, after a rousing rendition of Living Communication in Beth's Kitchen Café in nearby Bridgton and a successful performance of *Apples* in Denmark's rustic theater, we gathered on the large screened-in porch, surrounded on three sides by the woods. The actors began to fantasize. What would a cabin like that cost? they asked me. A lot, I replied. They were undeterred. By the evening's end, they had envisioned buying land in the United States and building a place for their own theatrical laboratory—a place where they could train and rehearse, where they could collaborate with others, where they could foster and develop their creativity. Such a place would be almost impossible to create in Algeria, they told me. But in the United States, they sensed its potential. A new horizon of possibility had momentarily opened up. Of course, it was a utopian fantasy, but for just a moment it became palpable.

Istijmam's US tour was premised on a paradox: a scenario based in a cosmopolitan desire for exchange around cultural difference could be realized only through globalized performance genres that were shared by all participants. This paradox is clearly not of the actors' or Center Stage's making but results from worldwide markets for particular kinds of culture, from shared theatrical traditions, from historically shaped conventions around how to enact cultural encounters, and from the "survey 101" nature of this kind of tour as it has emerged over the last century. The genre conventions of presentations and workshops swallowed up or smoothed over moments of friction rather than using such frictions as deeper opportunities for exchange. This is not to say that cultural differences have no bearing on theatrical practices. But familiar, onstage events like presentations and workshops may not be the place where such differences emerge.

Moving behind the scenes with Istijmam into their own space of rehearsal (their Restroom of sorts) affords a different perspective on how their engagement with theater may be inflected by culturally specific pedagogies, systems of discipline, and textual ideologies.

NOTES

1. In this book, I use "genre conventions" and "performance conventions" interchangeably. Whereas all performances belong to genres and thus follow genre conventions, not all genres are necessarily performances (literary genres, for instance). My discussion of genre is inspired by the work of Bauman 2004; Briggs and Bauman 1992; Hanks 1987; Kapchan 1996, among others, as developed in Goodman 2005.

2. Bauman (2004, 3) consolidates this definition of genre as follows: "a constellation of systemically related, co-occurrent formal features and structures that serves as a conventionalized orienting framework for the production and reception of discourse."

3. On this use of the term global, see Turino 2000.

4. Inspired by Briggs and Bauman 1992, I have previously show how generic (genre-based) frames shape the interpretation of the material they hold (Goodman 2005).

5. Discussions of cosmopolitanism that I found useful in drafting this chapter include Glick Schiller and Irving 2015; Hannerz 2006; Turino 2000; Werbner 2008.

6. https://centerstageus.org/artists, accessed May 5, 2018.

7. An instructive comparison may be drawn with the performance of Maasai dance on the Mayer's ranch in Kenya. Certain kinds of performance markers were suppressed to make the event seem authentic, and some forms of dress and behavior were entirely disallowed: the performers, for instance, had to remove watches and other signs of their adoption of nonindigenous customs. See Bruner and Kirshenblatt-Gimblett 1994.

8. Along with more recent programs like Center Stage, the Smithsonian Institution has been one of the primary federally funded sites for cultural presentation and encounter. For an account of the Smithsonian Institution as a cultural broker, see Kurin 1997; for an account of the Smithsonian Folklife Festival, see Kurin 1998.

9. Postperformance talk-backs are discussed in the epilogue.

10. The Greater Hartford Academy of the Arts is a high school, so participants were under the age of eighteen and thus not eligible for my study.

11. At Indiana University, they may have dressed in this way because they were doing Living Communication immediately after the classroom events. At Yale, Living Communication had not been on the agenda, but the actors did perform several pieces for the audience.

12. Both Double Edge and Center Stage organizers acknowledged that this was an unfortunate conflict. Double Edge had no time available to work directly with Istijmam while the troupe was in the United States.

13. Personal interview, October 17, 2017, via Skype.

14. Personal interview, September 30, 2016, New York.

15. Paul Silverstein has noted the popularity of the American TV show *Prison Break* in North Africa (Silverstein 2013, 117).

16. Alaina Lemon described a similar exercise among theater students in Russia, without the prison image (Lemon 2018, 33).

17. Personal interview, October 1, 2016, New York.

18. Personal interview, September 20, 2016, New York.

19. The difficulty of moving between the United States and Algeria is also rooted in Algeria's specific history. In this regard, a comparison with Morocco is instructive. Morocco imposes no visa requirements on US citizens for tourism or short-term study (such as summer language programs), whereas Algeria's visa requirements are fairly onerous. Morocco offers easier access to US universities and private scholarly institutions, many of which have well-established language programs in Morocco. Morocco also did not suffer the kind of instability and violence that Algeria did during the Dark Decade and its aftermath and was marked only minimally by the Arab Spring. In Algeria, the United States Information Service (USIS), which offered classes and cultural opportunities to Algerians, closed in 1994, at the beginning of the Dark Decade, and embassy staff was reduced from twenty-two to six. Cultural services were not restored until 2001. I am grateful to Adam Sigelman, Cultural Attaché in Algiers at the time of this writing in 2020, for these figures.

20. Personal interviews, September 30, 2016 (Jamil); October 1, 2016 (Moussa); October 1, 2016 (Lila), New York.

21. Personal communication by email, October 25, 2017.

22. Personal interview, October 1, 2016, New York.

23. For more on HartBeat Ensemble, see https://www.hartbeatensemble.org, accessed February 14, 2020.

24. https://www.hartbeatensemble.org, accessed February 14, 2020.

25. https://doubleedgetheatre.org/supporters, accessed February 14, 2020.

26. https://doubleedgetheatre.org/who-we-are, accessed February 14, 2020.

27. A list of Double Edge supporters can be found here: https://double edgetheatre.org/supporters.

28. See http://www.masslive.com/news/index.ssf/2016/09/forest_park_in _springfield_was.html; http://www.masslive.com/entertainment/index.ssf /2016/09/its_going_to_be_a_spectacle_do.html; http://www.masslive.com /entertainment/index.ssf/2016/07/double_edge_theatres_annual_sp.html, accessed February 14, 2020.

29. An overview of legislation and budget pertaining to the arts in Algeria can be found here: http://www.medculture.eu/country/algeria/structure/302.html, accessed June 7, 2019.

30. Personal communication by email, October 25, 2017.

31. Personal interviews, October 10, 2016, New York.

FOUR

—⚉—

BEHIND THE SCENES
The Disciplines of Rehearsal

THE ACTOR IN *APPLES* HAD been relegated to the sidelines in the state theater where he worked. He had wanted to act in Shakespeare's *Julius Caesar* but instead had been given the role of a wardrobe—a large piece of wooden furniture used to store clothes in houses lacking closets.[1] He was literally made into dead wood on stage, his part reduced to animating the sounds of a creaky old door as he opened and closed his arms: "zeet, zeet." When he came into the Restroom, the Actor told the Attendant about his frustrations with his job, much as the Customer had done. Whereas the Customer vomited up his frustration, the Actor sought to transform it into art. He was brimming with ideas for an original play he wanted to stage. But he needed a place where he could improve his skills, where he could do exercises, where he could work out ideas for his play. He had been looking all over for rehearsal space. He had tried the public baths and the beach, to no avail. The Restroom, with its resonant acoustics, would be ideal.

Recall that the Actor had entered the Restroom after a long exchange between the Customer and the Attendant. The Customer was desperate for a place to release his anguish. He had lost his job, his wife, and his family, but he hadn't managed to procure a simple apple. He begged the Customer to let him scream, stomp, and holler. When the Actor entered the Restroom, he was seduced by its potential as a theatrical space: it was clean and acoustically compelling. The Restroom became, for the Actor, a space where he could realize one of his dreams: to create and stage his own play. The Attendant initially opposed his clients' requests. He was concerned about propriety. Having lost his previous job as a labor union representative, he wasn't about to risk his current position. But gradually, as he heard his clients' stories, he was won over.

The Actor's quest for rehearsal space and resources articulates with Istijmam's own search for theatrical training. Their performance of *Apples* in the United States is inextricable from the backstage endeavors that enabled Istijmam to create themselves as a theater troupe that one day would be selected by Center Stage. Following them into their "Restroom" of sorts—that is, into Istijmam's rehearsal space in Algeria—helps to illuminate their own efforts to develop as actors in a country that provides little support for independent theater.

The difficulty of finding training and resources for acting in Algeria was so palpable for Istijmam members that they brought it up more than once during a panel discussion with the HartBeat Ensemble titled "Theater in Times of Crisis." The event was open to the public, and audience members wanted to talk about theater as a way to respond to social and political issues. HartBeat actors talked about how they gathered stories from local neighborhoods and devised plays out of those stories.[2] They talked about how they wove into their theater issues surrounding drugs, gun violence, and poverty. Istijmam members talked in turn about how playwright Abdelkader Alloula had sought to use theater to speak to Algerian society by portraying ordinary people in their daily run-ins with bureaucracy and other tragicomic absurdities of social life. They talked about terrorism and the Dark Decade, and about how Alloula had been assassinated outside his home as he was leaving for an event at the Regional Theater of Oran. They evoked other directors, playwrights, and artists who had been assassinated in the city streets. They talked about how the very real threat of violence in public spaces had gotten Algerians out of the habit of going to the theater. But Istijmam also told a different story of theater in crisis than what their US interlocutors were perhaps anticipating. They told a story about the sheer difficulty of doing theater in Algeria to begin with. The crisis in Algerian theater, as they saw it, concerned not only societal issues that could be taken up in plays. The crisis was also one of training and resources for aspiring actors. The Actor's plight in *Apples*—his quest for rehearsal space—was a real problem, not a symbolic one: "Even now, we suffer from that," Rihab said. Lila elaborated: "Algerian artists have no place to rehearse. There are no spaces specifically for actors, dancers, musicians. . . . Even with money, you can't find rehearsal space." In short, theater did not just respond to societal crises—it was itself in crisis.

The Actor in *Apples*, then, opens up stories that point in two directions. One story (taken up in chap. 5) goes toward the stage and the incisive theater the Actor hopes to produce. The backstory goes behind the scenes. It points to the conditions that would allow him to develop as an actor, including the most basic one of all—a space to rehearse, a space where he could hone his skills and create the plays he was envisioning.

If going backstage with Istijmam into their rehearsals points to some of the challenges of doing theater in Algeria, it also illuminates culturally specific ways of engaging with theatrical practice that were not visible to audiences in the United States. The workshops and presentations Istijmam provided for US audiences tended to foreground similarities. In contrast, Istijmam's ways of rehearsing, executed behind the scenes, open up issues around discipline and pedagogy that were not evident during the tour—at least not to their interlocutors. Examining Istijmam's "pedagogical interactions in rehearsal" (Lemon 2004, 315) raises questions about cultural approaches to discipline, self-formation, and authority—some of the very points that might have constituted vectors of difference with their US interlocutors.

I spent four months sitting in on Istijmam's rehearsals during the second year of their training, in 2008–2009. While I was there, they began to work with the method of actor training developed by Polish theater theorist and practitioner Jerzy Grotowski, which they found in his book *Towards a Poor Theater* (1968). From their earliest years, they also worked regularly with improvisational theater, drawing largely on Christophe Tournier's *Manuel d'Improvisation Théâtrale* (*Manual of Theatrical Improvisation*).[3] The exercises in both of these texts have been practiced by theater groups around the world. Yet the ways Istijmam framed and taught these exercises—that is, their metapragmatic or "how to" engagement with them—suggests a pedagogy that fosters creativity through particular kinds of discipline. The troupe's reliance on these texts also points to how they worked to overcome disparities in access to theatrical training. In what follows, I take up the ways they engaged with these texts to develop themselves as actors. Before they could begin in earnest, however, Istijmam had to develop an administrative existence in a bureaucratically structured field of theatrical practice in Algeria.

PRACTICING THEATER IN ALGERIA

On June 18, 2009, I embarked on the ten-minute uphill walk from my apartment in the center of Oran to Istijmam's rehearsal space on the Rue de Mostaganem. By 2016, this road would be bisected by a new tramway that turned it from a major east-west artery anchoring the city's electrical and lighting district to a quieter residential street.[4] But in 2009, the neighborhood was still bustling with traffic and pedestrians. I entered at number 19, a once stately building constructed decades earlier by the French, and climbed four winding flights of stairs (the elevator having long since fallen into disrepair) to the Alloula household, where Rihab and Jamil had grown up. Half of the apartment was still occupied by a branch of the Alloula family. Rihab and Jamil had inherited the rest, giving Istijmam access to a rare commodity in Algeria—rehearsal and meeting space.

Upon entering the living room, I joined twenty-two others gathered around a big oval table. Five were current actors with Istijmam, several were former actors, and the rest were friends who joined the association in support of Istijmam's mission. We had come together for the troupe's second annual general assembly. As a cultural association registered with the state, Istijmam was required to hold a general assembly each year at which their members would elect officers, pay their annual dues, and outline projects for the coming year. I signed the membership card, paid my five-hundred-dinar fee, and listened with interest to their discussion of a proposed new project to sponsor artistic workshops for underprivileged children. At this point, the troupe had had its *agrément* in hand for some seven months—the formal, stamped document from the Ministry of Culture that gave Istijmam the right to practice theater as a cultural association.

Forming a cultural association is one of the two primary ways that Algerian citizens may practice theater outside the state-supported network of professional theater institutions.[5] Creating a cooperative is the second. Both cases require administrative approval, but the path Istijmam chose—becoming a cultural association—is more laborious. A cultural association must have a minimum of fifteen dues-paying members, a physical locale in which to meet, clearly spelled out objectives and plans, and a slate of officers elected at an annual meeting called a general assembly (*assemblée générale*).[6] A prospective association submits an application package to the wilaya (administrative offices at the regional level) for initial review; the wilaya then forwards it to the national Ministry of Culture for final approval. A cooperative is somewhat easier to create, requiring only three members with a common project, who submit a notarized application reviewed at the wilaya level only. Cooperatives are more nimble than cultural associations, but they must pay taxes on their earnings whereas cultural associations are nonprofits. And although cooperatives have a singular focus, cultural associations may operate as umbrella organizations for a range of activities. For instance, Numidya, the Amazigh (Berber) association that I worked with in Oran, offers Tamazight language classes, lectures, Amazigh holiday celebrations, music, sports, and children's activities as well as sponsoring an amateur theater troupe.[7] When they are approved, both cultural associations and cooperatives receive a formal, stamped, and numbered agrément that gives them the right to carry out their projects and practice their craft. Without an agrément, they cannot apply for state funding (*subventions*) or participate in state-sponsored regional and national festivals.[8]

The formal theatrical infrastructure in Algeria centers around the Algerian National Theater (Théâtre National Algérien, TNA) in Algiers and a sprawling network of state-funded regional theaters.[9] This network began under the French, who built theaters in the cities of Algiers, Oran, Constantine, Annaba, and Sidi Bel-Abbes.[10] The 1962 Tripoli Program, which would establish the constitutional and policy orientations of the Algerian state following independence (McDougall 2017, 240), called for a cultural program that would constitute "the link between the ideological effort of the popular democratic revolution and the concrete, daily tasks that building the country would require" (Front de Libération Nationale 1962, 696).[11] The following year, the theaters were nationalized, envisioned as cultural and ideological arms of the state. Considered a "national public service," theater was initially funded by the state and administered under the auspices of the Ministry of Cultural Affairs, itself located in the Ministry of Education.[12] A national theater troupe was established at the TNA in Algiers along with a center for national theater charged with defining the theater's mission in the new Algerian state, selecting theatrical works, and organizing festivals.[13]

In 1972, this infrastructure was formally decentralized.[14] The locus of theatrical production, including programming and artistic direction, moved from Algiers to the regional theaters, which were granted a measure of autonomy. In November 1972, what had been called the Opera of Oran (l'Opéra d'Oran) was rechristened the Regional Theater of Oran (Théâtre Régional d'Oran, TRO), with Abdelkader Alloula at its head (Kali 2005, 75). A report from the early 1980s shows that between 1972 and 1981, "theatrical activities" in Algeria—presumably including the regional theaters—regularly received state funding. But whereas theater received fifteen times more funding than other cultural initiatives in 1972, by 1981, this figure had dropped to only 1.8 times more.[15] By 2018, some seventeen regional theaters were operating; the larger regional theaters, like that in Oran, are anchored by professional companies.[16]

From an actor's perspective, the only way to receive a guaranteed annual salary is to be on the staff of the national or one of the regional theaters—as was presumably the case of the Actor character in *Apples*. Yet this was not unproblematic. Over the years, more money went to administrators than actors, creating a top-heavy bureaucracy.[17] In 1994, for instance, of the 440 salaried employees in the seven regional theaters at the time, there were 149 administrators, 126 technicians, and 163 actors. For the TRO, nearly half (41) of the

Figure 4.1. Posing in front of an outdoor toilet in New York City, September 2016. *Left to right*: Djalel, Jamil, Rihab, Mustapha, Moussa. Photo credit: Istijmam Culturelle.

87 salaried employees in 1994 were actors. A decade later, in 2003, less than a third were actors (22 of 68 salaried employees). Funds were sometimes directed to those with inside connections, leading to the production of plays not for their artistic merits but to reward friends. Actors could wait years to get any roles at all, and would work on the side as taxi drivers or television repairmen. At times, it was more lucrative for actors to refuse to tour. Mohamed Kali describes one particularly egregious example wherein an administrator in the city of Annaba imposed an economic text on the regional troupe, which they had to perform or risk being let go.[18] Further, the theaters were poorly maintained. In 2000, Azri Ghaouti, then director of the TRO, talked about the lack of comfort and even—as would *Apples*—the "state of the toilets" (cited in Kali 2005, 80).

Troupes that form as cooperatives or cultural associations lack operating support from the state, though they may apply for state subventions to fund particular projects. They also develop their abilities and reputations by participating in regional and state theater festivals. An amateur troupe may apply to perform at one of the four annual regional competitions, with winners advancing to the state level. The most visible platform has long been the annual Festival of Amateur Theater in the city of Mostaganem. Beginning in 1967 as a small regional festival organized by the Muslim Scout Association, by 1970 it had become a national festival drawing dozens of troupes from around the country for a week of theatrical activities culminating in juried awards.[19] A similar festival structure exists for professional troupes housed under the auspices of cultural associations or cooperatives: they may rise through regional competitions to perform in the juried annual National Festival of Professional Theater in Algiers. Cooperatives generally perform as professionals who expect to be paid for their work, whereas cultural associations typically house amateur theater troupes. But the line between amateur and professional is fluid.[20] A troupe housed in a cultural association may start out as amateur and eventually find themselves participating in professional theater competitions, as was the case with the El Moudja troupe I worked with (Goodman 2013b, 2017). Or an association may house several troupes—a children's troupe, an amateur troupe, and a professional troupe, like the El Ichara and El Moudja associations in Mostaganem. It's not always clear whether a troupe is amateur or professional: Mourad Senouci, director of the Regional Theater of Oran since 2017, recounted to me that when he was part of a university troupe in the late 1980s, they were forced to perform noncompetitively ("en off," or hors compétition) at both the Mostaganem Festival of Amateur Theater and the National Festival of Professional Theater. They were told that they were too professional for one but too amateur for the other.[21] Actors in the professional troupes attached to cultural associations or cooperatives receive a fee for performance but are not guaranteed salary the way the actors are in state-supported companies.

Istijmam initially formed as a cultural association. But when the law on associations changed in 2012 (law 12-06), they did not renew their application.[22] Part of the reason was that the troupe did not have a lot of activities planned at the time. But the law also became both more onerous and more restrictive. It required governmental preauthorization for the first time since 1987.[23] It also forced associations to submit a burdensome amount of documentation for both the organization and its individual members. Istijmam supported the demonstrations against the law that a number of associations undertook at the time.[24] In practical terms, not being registered with the state meant that Istijmam did not have access to government funding. But even when they had been registered, they took an unconventional route. They never competed in the regional festivals. Instead, they chose to organize their own national tour, during which they performed in venues across Algeria as well as in neighboring Morocco and Tunisia. They funded the tour from sponsor fees and, to a degree, out of pocket. That being said, for Istijmam, touring and performance were not initially their primary objectives. They used performance in the service of their larger aspiration to be a theatrical research laboratory (*laboratoire de recherche*). Their goal was to be continuously engaged in *la formation*—a training program encompassing both formal study and hands-on learning.

Too many troupes in Algeria, Jamil told me, would simply put an actor on stage without much training at all. Rihab concurred, telling me back in 2009 that her experience with Istijmam was significantly different than with other troupes she had worked with. In other troupes, she said, "we rehearsed a lot, but we didn't base ourselves on any school or technique; we had the desire to get on stage and pull out all the stops, without looking at what was being done elsewhere, without any research, without knowledge of what the leaders in the field had developed.... With Istijmam, we put everything we thought we knew aside, and we said, Let's see what others have done, let's gather documentation.... There's theory; let's try to see what it offers."[25]

Jamil and Rihab's assessments echo those of other Algerian practitioners. As theater scholar Hadj Miliani put it, "Each troupe repeats what others have done ten or twenty years earlier ... they don't build on each other ... because there is no research."[26] Omar Fetmouche, former head of the International Festival of Theater in Bejaia, Algeria (as well as an actor, director, and writer in his own right), similarly lamented the lack of training and transmission: "We are still living on practices inherited from the 1960s" (cited in Kali 2005, 57).[27] So when Jamil started working with the group that would become Istijmam in 2007, he made sure that *la formation* was their primary activity.[28]

LABORATORY THEATER

Istijmam devoted their first year together (2007–2008) to study and practice. They read theater theorists and tried to translate what they found into their own work. As Rihab described it to me, they had boarded a kind of "theory train," stopping at the Stanislavski, Brecht, and Peter Brook stations. They would get off at each station, sample the theoretical wares, and experiment with how to bring that theory to life. Rehearsals were spent discussing and experimenting with the various approaches and techniques about which they were reading. Different members of the troupe would also bring in texts to share. Sometimes they would take turns leading exercises that they found in their readings. For instance, in December 2008, they each took several sections of Grotowski's "Technique of the Voice."[29] In each rehearsal, a different actor would prepare and present exercises from their assigned section: carrying power, respiration, opening of the larynx, resonators, vocal imagination, and so on. {**Video 04.01**}

Training was not only about learning theory as a kind of intellectual exercise. Istijmam sought to embody theory, to experience for themselves what it meant. In training to become actors, Istijmam members were training above all to transcend their limitations, to open themselves maximally to the possibilities of creative stagecraft. As one actor wrote in Istijmam's 2008 blog *Theatrical Adventure*, "Between theory and practice there is a veritable journey of introspection. Above all, we are learning to discover ourselves, to always go further, to surpass ourselves."[30]

In calling themselves a theatrical laboratory, Istijmam can be broadly situated in a lineage that includes (among others) Grotowski's Theatre Laboratory, Julian Beck and Judith Malina's Living Theater, Joseph Chaikin's Open Theater, and Richard Schechner's Environmental Theater.[31] Of these groups, the only one I did not hear my Algerian interlocutors refer to was Schechner's. Living Theater had performed at the Avignon Festival in France in 1968 and would likely have been known in the Algerian theater community at the time. Open Theater made a mark in Algeria itself in 1971 as part of the Mostaganem theater festival, where Chaikin's troupe performed *Mutation* and *Terminal*.[32] Schechner was a pioneer in intercultural and experimental theater and worked with companies around the world.[33] Istijmam would no doubt have found much in common with Schechner's trajectory, but his work was not available to them, and their pathways did not overlap: his long-term collaborations were oriented more to China and India than to Africa (and, within Africa, to South Africa rather than the Maghreb).

In styling themselves as a theatrical laboratory, Istijmam was following in the footsteps of their ancestor, Abdelkader Alloula. In 1985, Alloula formed the first theatrical cooperative in Algeria, the *Coopérative du 1er Mai* (May 1st Cooperative), which focused on what he saw as a "burning need" for actor training as well as research into vernacular Algerian traditions (Belhadad 1997, 105). Alloula would have certainly known about Open Theater and most likely would have seen their 1971 performances in Algeria. What Alloula added to the mix—which Istijmam would later take up—was the Algerian halqa. In the halqa, Alloula saw many of the theatrical characteristics that the laboratory groups—inspired by the approaches of Brecht, Meyerhold, and Piscator—were claiming to have invented (Cheniki 2000).

The hallmarks of Istijmam's theater resemble those of other laboratory groups. As Open Theater's director Joseph Chaikin put it, in a laboratory approach, the concern was with "open questions," not answers (Chaikin 1972, 12). Rather than focusing exclusively on the story being told on stage, laboratory groups sought to cultivate a new form of actor-audience relationship that broke down the fourth wall. A corollary focus was on the actor's body as a "body in motion" or a charged "electric field" (Chaikin 1972, 21). This focus on the body was apparent in Open Theater's performances in Algeria, which were described in the Algerian weekly *Algérie Actualité* as offering "a remarkable panoply of expressions in which mastery of the body is sovereign" (Bendimered 1971, 18). Djilelli Boudjemaa, director of the El Moudja troupe, vividly recalled nearly forty years after the fact how the physicality of Open Theater's performance had impacted him.[34] Above all, laboratory theater was concerned with "find[ing] the conditions that make it possible to grow" (Chaikin 1972, 80). In short, acting in laboratory theater was understood not only as what takes place on stage but also as an unfolding journey of self-discovery in and through theater. When I asked Mustapha what laboratory theater meant to him, he replied, "It's as if you took a motor and disassembled it into all its pieces . . . as if you had a blackboard and were told to try putting red with yellow . . . it's life, how you're going to develop by using all the elements of life, all the elements of being human."[35]

By the time Istijmam came together in 2007, theater in Algeria was becoming increasingly eclectic. This had not always been the case. Theater expert Ahmed Cheniki (2002) characterized postindependence Algerian theater in terms of three periods. A first period (1962–1970) featured relatively conventional topics that took up aspects of Algerian social life in comic or burlesque fashion—although some groups and playwrights, like Ould Abderrahmane Kaki, were starting to experiment with the goual or marketplace storyteller as a model for a new kind of contemporary theater. Cheniki's second phase (1970–1980), which he locates in the wake of the May 1968 uprisings in Paris, saw a wave of new, experimental productions by Algerian playwrights and directors. He situates Abdelkader Alloula among this experimental group. But as the decade wore on, troupes increasingly became mouthpieces for state propaganda, mounting plays that illustrated social realist themes inspired by the socialist state's agrarian and economic policies.[36] With the death of President Boumediene in 1978 and the increasing societal and economic tensions of the 1980s, a number of troupes folded, while others turned even further toward an agitprop-style theater of ideology and propaganda. Of course, theatrical history cannot be confined to a singular trajectory, as Cheniki himself acknowledges. Other ways of approaching Algerian theater focus on theatrical adaptation (Cheniki 2006), independent theater (Kali 2005, 85–104), activist theater (Dahmane 2011), foundational figures (Cheniki 2006; Kali 2005, 41–54), theater and language (Dahmane 2011; Roth 1967), and theater and society (Ben Achour 2002, 2005). The development of halqa-style theater was particularly prominent because it could be brought to bear on many, if not all, of these approaches.

Istijmam was emphatically against the idea that a play should transmit a particular message. They repeatedly emphasized both to me and to US audiences that their plays did not contain a message or a meaning that they wanted audiences to grasp. When they attended a French class at the University of New Hampshire, the instructor wanted them to tell the class in what ways the play was political. Rihab responded that it was not political, that it was instead "a play that speaks about Algerian society." In a panel at Yale University's Pierson College, they made a similar point in response to a question from an audience member about whether their theater was a way of educating Americans about Algeria. Whereas most of this event was in Egyptian Arabic, which moderator Stephen Davis translated into English, for this question, the troupe wanted to respond in French (which they had better mastery of) and asked me to translate. "We start from a dynamic of learning (*apprendre*)," Jamil said. "Not of educating (*faire apprendre*). We first want to learn ourselves, and then to learn from the people who surround us. For us, learning and listening are essential." {**See Video Epilogue 02**}

For Istijmam, a play was an experiential and dialogical engagement in which audiences are not recipients but cocreators of a play's meaning. Istijmam liked nothing better than for spectators to come up with different ways of understanding their work. To them, a successful play would raise questions, not provide answers. It would offer pleasure and entertainment (*el-furja*), not instill dogma. It would draw in audience members as coparticipants in the play much like the goual had drawn in spectators in the halqa. Learning to create a halqa by becoming gouals themselves emerged as a key focus of their training. They made this point at almost every stop on the tour. At Yale's Pierson College, for instance, Jamil said that "the audience was considered to be a collective actor in the performance, participating through acts of their own imagination." Similar to the halqa, a play "becomes like a conversation that engages with the viewer's imagination."[37]

In taking up goual and halqa as the central figures of their theater, Istijmam deviated from previous practitioners in one key respect. The goual had long been understood as a master of the word. Alloula never tired of describing a pivotal outdoor performance by his troupe in the rural village of El Meïda in 1972.[38] Surrounding the actors in a halqa-style circle, some audience members turned their backs on the actors to absorb what they were saying, and they could reportedly repeat lines from the play after hearing it just once. One spectator even told Alloula he saw better with his ears than his eyes, a line that Jamil would repeatedly reference. Whereas Alloula's troupe had started out with a large stage set, they gradually eliminated it, approaching the play instead as a form of storytelling. The performance at El Meïda came to constitute an *aha* moment for Alloula. Through the word alone, he realized, theater could invite audiences to imagine the scene. He likened the goual's performance to that of Aeschylus or Sophocles, where people came more to hear texts than to see the action materialized, where "it was up to the actor to master all the categories of the word, from psalms to song, from the cry to the murmur." "It's up to the spectator to materialize the action in his imagination," Alloula would say (Ouazani and Hadj Slimane 1995, 97, 99).

For Istijmam, however, the body was central to what would become their brand of physical theater. As gouals, the Istijmam actors sought to generate the scene not only with their words but also through their bodies. Two areas emerged as foundations for their work: the Grotowski method of actor training, and theatrical improvisation.

GROTOWSKI IN ALGERIA: TRAINING FOR TRANSCENDENCE

September 3, 2016, Washington, DC. It was Istijmam's first stop in the United States. Their debut performance at the Kennedy Center would take place the next day. Tour organizers Lisa Booth and Deirdre Valente were excited to meet the actors, but they were understandably a bit anxious. They had taken a risk with Istijmam. Lisa and Deirdre had seen excerpts of the troupe's performance of *Apples* in Arabic, so they knew that Istijmam had strong acting skills. Language was another matter. The troupe had assured Lisa and Deirdre that they were up to the challenge of putting on the play in English. But that first morning, during Istijmam's orientation with Center Stage staff, it was apparent that only one of the actors, Rihab, had reasonably good mastery of spoken English. Could they really pull this off? Would US audiences be able to understand?

On that first afternoon at the Kennedy Center, Jamil and Djalel worked on stage with the lighting technicians, and I joined the three actors and Lila in a rehearsal room. Lisa and Deirdre came with us. They thought they would be seeing a run-through of the play. Instead, the actors put some Algerian rai music on their boom box and used the full hour for a rigorous physical warm-up. I wondered whether Lisa and Deirdre were nervous because they still weren't hearing any English from the troupe. As they would discover, instead of running through the play, the actors were doing the Grotowski warm-up sequence. By 2016, this training had become integral to Istijmam's practice. They devoted a full hour to the Grotowski work during every rehearsal and before each performance. They could not imagine performing without it. {**Video 04.02**}

Figure 4.2. Mustapha and Moussa do backbends as part of the Grotowski sequence. University of St. Joseph, Hartford, Connecticut, September 2016. Author's collection.

But in 2008, that was far from the case. Throughout the fall of 2008, Jamil and Mustapha would leave a long evening rehearsal with Istijmam only to continue working late into the night with a dog-eared copy of *Actor Training*, the manual of physical exercises for actors that Grotowski had developed nearly fifty years earlier (Grotowski 2002).[39] Mustapha, his muscles taut and his twentysomething body fluid from years of martial arts and capoeira practice, would try out each exercise in Jamil's kitchen on a punishing tile floor (several times injuring himself in the process, he later told me). He had come on board with Istijmam a few months earlier, in the role of the troupe's physical trainer. In this capacity, he led their exercise sessions twice a week at a local gym or at the beach, where he would have the whole troupe run laps for an hour, then spend another hour or two jumping rope and doing pushups and abdominal exercises in a rigorous workout that was not for the faint of heart (or the over-fifty, as I found out when I attempted to join them). After several months of this pretraining, as Mustapha would call it, they started the Grotowski series. This proved to be a turning point for the troupe. In the fall of 2007, Istijmam included around a dozen people. When I started working with them in early November 2008, they were

Figure 4.3. Running laps for an hour before an all-day rehearsal, Oran, Algeria, August 2016. *Left to right*: Moussa, Mustapha, Rihab, Djalel. Photo credit: Istijmam Culturelle.

nine. In January 2009, they began the Grotowski work. By mid-February, they were down to the five who, along with their administrator Lila, would come to form the nucleus of Istijmam. Initially, the whole troupe (except the director, Jamil) was expected to participate in the Grotowski workout. It is not clear whether those who left did so because of the Grotowski work. When I talked with the troupe about this during a brief visit in June 2010, they said that there was simply a difference in the kind of project they wanted to work on.[40] But the Grotowski work did accompany a transformation in the troupe.

Grotowski's training is based around the premise that an actor must anni-hilate the ordinary habits and limits of the body, freeing it to serve as a vehicle for and conduit of her craft. To this end, from 1959 to 1962, Grotowski devel-oped a sequence of rigorous physical actions called "Actor Training," following Stanislavski's "Method of Physical Actions."[41] The "key to the actor's craft" was being able to develop, embody, and reproduce what Grotowski called a "line of physical actions" (Richards 1995, 31). This "small truth" of physical ac-tions was designed to "stir the 'great truth' of thoughts, emotions, experiences" (Richards 1995, 66). Istijmam worked with a photocopy of "Actor Training" in French translation. The work outlines a three-part program beginning with what Grotowski called "Physical Exercises," designed to promote flexibility and dexterity, which Istijmam began in 2008. The second stage, "Plastic Exercises," is intended to help actors develop the ability to make rapid transitions between opposed conditions—a skill thought to be necessary for Brechtian acting (Mitter 1992, 92). Istijmam was working on this stage when I saw them in 2010. The third stage focuses on the muscles of the face. More advanced work emphasizes transcending what we imagine as the capacities of the body: for example, actors are enjoined to "use your voice to make a hole in the wall" (cited in Mitter 1992, 92).

Istijmam zealously took up the Grotowski method. To my untrained eyes, they seemed to be exaggerating its already challenging practices (though I later learned, in talking with theater students in the United States, that this was generally par for the course with Grotowski training). I was with the troupe on January 3, 2009, the night they began. Mustapha introduced Grotowski's eight-part "Warming Up" series: "running on tiptoe," "walking with knees bent, hands on hips," "walking with knees bent, gripping the ankles," and so on (Grotowski 2002, 134–135). Each of the eight exercises they did that night went on for at least twenty minutes. They were visibly exhausted, but no one uttered a word. They apparently took to heart Grotowski's injunction that "All the exercises described in this chapter must be performed without interruption, without pause for rest or private reactions" (Grotowski 2002, 146). One woman, I wrote in my notes, looked like she was about to die; at one point she leaned over for a few seconds but then said "C'est bon" (It's good) and kept going. Another, after over an hour of this strenuous work, apologetically requested some water, which she drank while continuing to perform the exercise. A third woman pulled a ligament in her foot during one of the very first exercises but said nothing; she would wind up under a physician's care for her foot, and after getting a concussion from a subsequent exercise, she would leave the troupe.[42] As the weeks wore on and the training became more grueling, all actors experienced some level of physical pain. Before or after the sessions, they would display their black and blues and grumble to each other about where they hurt. But they continued stoically, trying to do what Mustapha asked of them.

"Why are you doing this to your bodies?" I would ask (my own background becoming painfully clear—I was the American trained in hatha-style yoga with its model of listening to the limits of one's own body).

"It's good for us," they kept telling me. "We need it. We need to be ready for anything on stage." Rihab later told me that when they first started engaging Grotowski's work, it was "jaw dropping." Grotowski, she said, "was discovery in the largest sense. . . . We found ourselves waging a battle within ourselves . . .

because he pushes you to go beyond your limits. . . . I started doing things that I never imagined being able to do."[43]

Following Grotowski's program to the letter, Istijmam made no adjustments for differences in training, ability, or body type of the actors. Exercise II-7, for example—"Keeping the legs together, jump up onto a chair"—was relatively straightforward for actors of a certain height. But one shorter actor repeatedly bumped her lower legs on the seat of the chair to the point of having bruises up and down her shins. Yet she kept trying. Moreover, the chair was unsecured—it could tip over under actors' weight if they didn't land the jump just right. Why not use chairs of different heights? I later asked Rihab. In her view, that would weaken the practice's impact: Grotowski did not present options, so neither would they. And why not secure the chair? This would eliminate the element of risk, she replied, adding that risk is an integral part of doing theater. You're leaping into the unknown, she said, every time you go on stage. {Video 04.03}

Watching the troupe's initial attempts to learn the Grotowski sequence was challenging for me. I viscerally experienced the way bodies transmit affect—an energetic force—to those watching such that spectators feel the actor's body inside their own. But my interpretations differed from Rihab's. Where she saw risk as an opportunity, I saw danger. I saw a punishing tile floor with only a thin rug for actors to land on. I saw them being asked to do exercises that to me seemed impossible for all but the most highly trained bodies. I saw Mustapha, the trainer, forcing them into positions—like a one-sided shoulder stand—that caused them to grimace and sometimes cry out in pain (Mustapha later told me that he hated doing this). My heart would leap and my pulse would race when I saw them try to execute Grotowski's Tiger Spring (exercise V-7): "with or without a preparatory run, arms outstretched, spring over an obstacle into a somersault, landing on one shoulder. Get up in the same movement" (Grotowski 2002, 138). In Istijmam's case, this meant leaping over a tall stack of cushions, flipping in the air so they could land lightly on a shoulder, rolling into a somersault and springing up—all in one motion. To my eye, these were ordinary people with ordinary (and in some cases, not well-trained) bodies being asked to do extraordinary feats.

Even before the Grotowski training, the troupe had already begun developing a discipline that—as they described it—would govern their whole lives, not just their time in rehearsal. When I joined them in November 2008, they were working with an adaptation by Rihab of Mourad Senouci's script *The Seven-Headed Monster* (*Al-Ghul bi Usbu'a Risan*) (Senouci n.d.). Rihab titled her adaptation *The Rumor* (*Al-Da'aiya*), and the actors worked with what that meant.

Figure 4.4. Moussa leaps over a stack of cushions, Oran, Algeria, January 2009. Author's collection.

They might get into a taxi and ask their driver and other passengers about what rumors they had recently heard or spread. They would bring to rehearsals texts they had downloaded and offer them up for discussion. They were expected to work on their breath and vocal technique and to continually revitalize their own performance. And they were expected at rehearsal five evenings each week after they got out of work or finished their classes. During the fall of 2008, on three of those days, they would work with Jamil on interpretation and vocal performance of the script. They experimented with different ways of animating the text through breath, intonation, and vocal shading. They would do a table reading of the text and then spend up to another hour or more on debriefing or self-critique before doing another table reading. Rehearsals lasted until Jamil dismissed them, and it was not unusual for us to spend three, four, or even five hours around the table. Moreover, script rehearsals officially began at 5:30 p.m., but after the actors were chastised for failing to adequately prepare, they began arriving an hour earlier to work together on new ways of voicing particular scenes. The other two days, the troupe met up (without me) in a gym or on the beach for physical training.

Deviations from this exacting rehearsal schedule were not tolerated. When some of the actors were fifteen minutes late to one workout session for reasons that they (and I) felt were beyond their control, they were roundly chastised. The troupe's dedication to its project was apparent: from the time I began working with Istijmam in mid-November 2008 until they began the Grotowski exercises in January 2009, not one actor missed a rehearsal. They would show up even when they were sick, exhausted, or had an exam the next day. This display of dedication seemed to act as an index of their commitment to their own desire for self-discovery and self-transcendence.

The Grotowski exercises raised the bar by several orders of magnitude. According to Grotowski, the actor's body needs to be broken down muscle by muscle, fiber by fiber, at both physical and mental levels in order to liberate her for performance. Before an actor could enact characters on stage, she had to build up her own character by developing her mental, moral, and muscular capacities. Once she liberated her body and mind from all constraint, she would be able to reach the "total act"—a gripping and seemingly effortless performance at the very limits of human capacity. As Grotowski (2002) put it, to act was to "cross our frontiers, exceed our limitations, fill our emptiness, fulfill ourselves" (21). In the "total act," the actor would attain a kind of "holiness" by "eliminat[ing] . . . the resistances and obstacles caused by one's own organism, both physical and psychical" (128). The aim was "not a muscular development or physical perfectionism, but a process of research leading to the annihilation

Figure 4.5. Table reading in rehearsal, Oran, Algeria, January 2009. *Left to right*: Moussa, Djalel (filming), Meriem Medjkane, Rihab. Author's collection.

of one's body's resistances" (146). Grotowski called this a *via negativa* or a negative way: "not a collection of skills but an eradication of blocks" (17).

Grotowski's "total act" became the troupe's guiding mantra. If the actors may have been confused about what a total act meant in practice, in theory they agreed that they were engaged in a pursuit that went beyond the mere staging of a play. But although they had been doing rigorous cardiovascular training with Mustapha for three months, some of the actors lacked the extreme level of core strength, the well-developed musculature, and the considerable flexibility that the Grotowski series requires. Yet in the initial Grotowski sessions, the actors attempted to enact the sequence exactly as the book described it, regardless of their own bodies' capacity. Their pedagogical model was to watch as Mustapha demonstrated the exercise and then to try to imitate it. The way they saw it, the actors had to adapt their own bodies to the Grotowski training rather than the other way around.

I never saw Istijmam engage in more advanced aspects of Grotowski's program. For instance, I didn't see them trying to use their voice to "make a hole in the wall . . . to overturn a chair . . . to make a picture fall" (Mitter 1992, 92; see, however, Video 04.01). But they did try to free the body from the laws of gravity. For example, in one of the exercises that Istijmam actors regularly did, the actor is to become a bird, beginning by squatting on the heels and hopping, then raising upright while flapping the arms like wings, and finally taking off and landing (described in Mitter 1992, 93). {**Video 04.04**}

They also worked to transcend their own limits by the way they framed the exercises. They would explain an actor's inability to execute a partic- ular exercise as either "fear" or a lack of proper "imagination." Following Grotowski, Mustapha talked repeatedly about the need to "imagine" the movement first and "concentrate" before executing it. Lack of imagination and concentration would lead to failure. If an actor was afraid of a particular action in her mind, her body would not be able to execute it correctly. "*Imag- iner, concentrer, respirer*" (imagine, concentrate, breathe) became Mustapha's mantra throughout the Grotowski sessions. Locating the key to mastering the Grotowski sequence in the mind seemed to me to discount the level of physical preparation required before an ordinary person could even begin to think about executing most of the exercises. Yet it also highlights a particular configuration of the mind-body relationship in which the body is envisioned as being subordinated to a kind of mental discipline that is itself experienced as a spiritual quest. Fear was given as the other reason for an actor's failure: if an actor was afraid of a particular action, that in itself would be enough to prevent the body from correct execution. If one mastered fear, one should be able to master the exercise. Taking the leap as an example, Jamil explained, "I might do it badly the first time, the second time. The third time, I'm going to get it."[44]

To me, the Grotowski training felt like a kind of boot camp.[45] Maybe a sports team would push themselves to this degree in the United States, but an amateur theater troupe? I could not fathom it. Why did the actors submit to this? I kept asking myself. How did they keep going? What notions of discipline were they working with? I talked about it with the actor who had pulled a ligament the very first night. When that healed, she returned to find the troupe leaping into somersaults from a standing position. She tried but landed twice on her head, winding up with a concussion. Why not say something during the session? I asked her. Why take such a risk of injury? "That's not how it works," she said. If you opted to be a part of it, you went along with what was required. The other choice was to leave. "*Qum wala talqa*" (qūm walla ṭalqa)—do it or divorce— were her words. This display of uniform dedication and commitment to com- mon goals is fairly prevalent in Algerian civic or cultural associations. No one wants to be perceived as falling short or lacking commitment.[46] Displays of unanimity also animated other groups I worked with, though I didn't see any other troupe take up such a challenging physical practice.[47]

For those who stayed in the troupe, the Grotowski program brought together mental imagery, tenacious discipline, and physical force in a way that would enable the actor to be "ready for anything," as Rihab put it. As a laboratory group, Istijmam was particularly drawn to developing a "poor" or "naked" theater in which they were on stage with only their bodies—no stage set. Grotowski gave them the resources to accomplish this. The body became the conduit for the actor's craft. "I didn't want to be limited on stage," Rihab emphasized. "I didn't want fear to limit me." The actor could mobilize her capacity for acting by leaping over a high stack of cushions and landing on her feet—or on her shoulder, as the case may be. Mustapha similarly characterized the training as opening up an energy that was palpable on stage: "You can feel that [Istijmam] has a strong presence . . . even if we make mistakes, we are present, we have this energy," he told me in 2016. "When you go on stage [after a rigorous round of Grotowski exercises], you are like putty . . . the director will sculpt you in his own way."[48]

The actors concurred that strict adherence to the program would free them for spontaneity on stage. Risking injury would allow them to transcend fear. Moving past their bodies' limitations, even through pain, would free up their creative spirits. Accepting a degree of "verbal terror of criticism and rebuke" (Lemon 2004, 320) and a measure of pain seemed a small price to pay for the freedom to act without constraint. Yet Rihab and Moussa—with their thin, lithe, flexible bodies—were initially the only ones able to execute the Grotowski training. It was no surprise that they became two of the actors in *Apples*, nor that Mustapha, initially the trainer, moved into the role of the third actor.

To be fair, Istijmam is hardly the only troupe to have implemented Grotowski's program as an outside-in form of discipline. The program itself was designed in that way.[49] As Open Theater's Joseph Chaikin notes, "Theaters like those in Poland . . . go in for a very heavy external discipline in order to call on a corresponding inner control" (Chaikin 1972, 80). Yet many troupes, including Open Theater, elected not to go this route. Others, like Double Edge Theatre or HartBeat Ensemble, drew on Grotowski's approach but modified his program to their own ends. Istijmam's scrupulous engagement with the Grotowski program exactly as he created it some fifty years earlier contrasts with the ways the Double Edge and HartBeat companies talked about their own uses of Grotowski.

RIGORS AND UNCERTAINTIES

Midway through the US tour, we arrived at the Double Edge complex. Following a shared dinner featuring fresh produce from Double Edge's farm, the Istijmam actors sat with several company members and interns. Jeremy Eaton—an actor and associate director with Double Edge since 2005—was our host. The two companies compared notes about how they practiced. It was one of those unanticipated rich moments when I unfortunately didn't have my recording equipment with me, so I cannot reconstruct the full conversation. But I clearly recall the way the actors from Double Edge emphasized how they adapted materials to their own ends. They might start out with a Grotowski exercise, for instance, but then redirect it to what they sensed their bodies needed in the moment, a kind of inside-out discipline. They might push some exercises in new directions while omitting others. I recall the Istijmam actors listening with interest but without much commentary. I knew from watching their practice that they did not tailor the sequence. To the contrary: during the rehearsal residency in 2016, Jamil remarked that the actors seemed to have gotten the Grotowski exercises out of order. The next day, they showed up with their photocopies of the chapter in hand, consulting them throughout the session.

Double Edge framed their training around an inner sense of what they needed, modifying it to suit their individual development. Similarly, the HartBeat Ensemble's Brian Jennings had described how he put Grotowski together with tai chi and chi gong, drawing from these three sources to develop his own approach to movement in theater. {See Video 03.12} What made the precise sequence of exercises that Grotowski had developed more than a half century earlier so attractive to Istijmam? I suggest two possibilities. The first involves styles of disciplinary pedagogy resonant with those found in contemporary Islamic practices of self-discipline as well as in the Algerian public schools. The second, which is more amorphous, may be the most telling: an attempt to counter a pervasive sense of uncertainty in Algerian social life.

Moussa told me in 2009 that he experienced the Grotowski training as being "like the Quran" in the rigor, commitment, and respect that a full engagement required. This reminded me of what Saba Mahmood suggested about Islamist practices in Egypt, wherein self-valorization is achieved via willing submission to a strict disciplinary regimen (Mahmood 2005). Here, the disciplinary impulse seems to work from the outside in, rather than vice versa. Similarly, Samuli Schielke (2015, 70, 79) has noted that the contemporary market for religious texts in Egypt tends to feature a "manual-like approach" that offers firm, clear guidelines alongside an emphasis on personal responsibility and self-discipline as paths to self-realization. Perhaps there are also parallels with the kind of discipline that is practiced during Ramadan, the Islamic month of fasting, where the ability to control the impulses of one's body indexes one's commitment and moral fortitude. An uncompromising mastery of the body's drives and desires is viewed as a mark of strength, whereas the inability to discipline one's body is perceived as a weakness. This outside-in pedagogy may also align with models of authority and discipline in the Algerian public schools. When I was talking about Istijmam's discipline in 2009 with one of the actors who later left the troupe, she told me that the public schools imposed a punitive outside-in discipline—she gave the example of being forced to sit for an hour with your hands on your head.

Yet if Istijmam's training intersected with Islamic forms of discipline and public school pedagogical practices, wouldn't other Algerian associations have displayed a similar commitment? In fact, it was quite the opposite. In the other four theater troupes that I worked with regularly, rehearsals almost never started on time, actors didn't always show up, and performances could be booked and then cancelled at the last minute. Starting rehearsal an hour or even two hours late was not at all unusual. Once, I accompanied a troupe that arrived via rented bus to a performance over a day from their home only to find that the local organizers had no knowledge that we were coming (they managed to put on the show regardless—hours after it had been scheduled, though with a reduced audience).

Might Istijmam's rigorous practice of self-discipline also be understood, then, as a response to this kind of uncertainty and lack of rigor? Uncertainty permeates many aspects of life in Algeria. There is the unpredictability of infrastructure: the worker who turns off the water to your neighborhood for maybe an hour or maybe a week without informing you; the fragile electrical or internet connection that may or may not work; the cellular network that goes dark without warning. It's in the flight that is delayed for hours, with no explanation other than "We don't know." It's in consumption practices—the brand of imported coffee (or, in my case, dark chocolate) that you always found in that one store until it disappeared, and no one knew when it would be back. It's in cultural life, in the movie that might start two hours late because the bulb in the projector blew out, and it took that long to scour the town for a replacement. The sense that things don't work as they should is so pervasive that it was imagined to affect even those in authority, as playfully evidenced in one of Istijmam's early improvisations in the 2016 rehearsal residency. A police officer (enacted by Lila) tried to fire on a terrorist. But her rifle didn't work, and she ended up being gunned down herself. Not even a police officer could be protected if she was relying on a state-issued weapon. {Video 04.05}

On another level, uncertainty is located in social attitudes surrounding time and discipline: the meeting you scheduled knowing that it might or might not take place; the hours you spend waiting for someone who might or might not come. Perhaps most strikingly, uncertainty surrounded who was running the country during the six years that Algerian president Bouteflika was incapacitated by a stroke. From June 2013 to April 2019, he remained in office and was even reelected in 2014 despite being partially paralyzed and unable to speak. Bouteflika was again a candidate for the 2019 elections, but this time Algerians had had enough, and widespread demonstrations throughout the winter and spring of 2019 forced him to resign on April 2 after two decades of rule.[50] From 2013 to 2019, however, Bouteflika was president in name only. Who was working in the shadows behind him? Was he even alive? No one knew for sure. Although forms of precarity—of a life without guarantees or predictability—characterize contemporary times under neoliberalism, they may take a particular shape under the "government of crisis" that characterized Algeria in the Bouteflika period, where permanent instability was the norm (Serres 2019).[51]

In this regard, Istijmam's rigorous program can perhaps be understood as an attempt to counter a wider societal sense of uncertainty and lack of rigor. Rihab said as much in an interview in 2009.

It's true that we [in Algeria] have a hard time with discipline, that we tend to arrive late, to let things go, to leave things for the next day—"Yes, we're going to do it, but we'll do it when we get around to it." We have this tendency. What we wanted to set up in the troupe was a certain discipline. This is very complicated for someone who isn't disciplined at all. So to be even a little disciplined, we have to go overboard, we have to overdiscipline ourselves just to get to a "normal" level of discipline. . . . The Grotowski work, it's as if it pushes us, because you cannot do this work without a discipline. It's almost impossible. You have your work, you have things you have to do. You have to have a "datebook." [She laughed, inflecting the word to indicate its foreignness.] We're not used to having a datebook! "Tomorrow, what are you doing?" "Oh, tomorrow I have this, and that, but at what time, I don't know." So, our rehearsal, we come a half hour before, then we start work with Mustapha, one hour. Then a five-minute rest, then an hour with Jamil. And with that [schedule], you have to organize the rest of your time, have a certain organization in your life. It's as if this work brings us together and pushes us to have a certain organization.[52]

When members started leaving the troupe in the weeks surrounding the introduction of the Grotowski training, those who remained became even more disciplined. They took a short break to regroup and then issued an invitation to all former members to rendezvous at the train station on a particular day and time for a trip together to the south of Algeria. Those who showed up could rejoin the group, no questions asked. On the appointed day, Jamil, Rihab, Djalel, Moussa, and Mustapha appeared. Together they traveled to Tamanrasset, where they did some local performances. When they returned to Oran, they decided to put on *Et-Teffeh* (*Apples*). They gave themselves one weekend to memorize the script (in its original Arabic). They then mounted the play in a month, working together for up to eight hours a day. (Some, like Moussa, then went to other jobs at night.) They told me that this rigorous schedule would not have been possible without the Grotowski training. Istijmam's discipline paid off in then unanticipated ways, because one of the qualities they had to demonstrate for the Center Stage selection committee was the ability to be self-disciplined—and I had no hesitation in recommending them!

In the end, the Grotowski program became so integral to Istijmam's practice that it was among their first activities at each stop on the tour. By 2016, it had become internalized, like a meditation, a practice that would ground the actors and allow them to "imagine, concentrate, breathe" so that they would be able to transcend themselves on stage. The fact that their metapragmatic engagement with this training foregrounded adherence to a strict external discipline might have constituted a point of exchange with the troupes and audiences they met in the United States. But the nature of rehearsal, located behind the scenes, makes these practices invisible almost by definition. Rehearsal is not on the roster of topics that are typically engaged in cultural encounters. Moreover, it would be hard to package rehearsal practices into the kind of cultural scenario typically aspired to on a tour. What becomes visible, then, in the encounters on tour are highly curated performances in which differences in training and approach are not brought to the fore.

If their Grotowski training was based in rigorous conformity to a program, Istijmam's improvisation work would seem at first glance to be quite the opposite. Improvisation, after all, is intended to foster a generative, playful spontaneity. Yet the two practices were linked. "For improvisation, the body has to be ready," Mustapha told me back in 2010. "Grotowski is a tool for us."[53] As with the Grotowski program, Istijmam trained for spontaneity through a disciplined engagement with the practices outlined in a text, in this case Christophe Tournier's *Manuel d'Improvisation Théâtrale*.

TRAINING FOR SPONTANEITY: IMPROVISATION
AS DISCIPLINARY PRACTICE

August 4, 2016. As the actors ran around the rehearsal space in a circle, Djalel asked them to repeat the principles of improvisation that they had been learning, in order. He interrogated them as they ran. "What is the second principle?" he asked.

Lila, running, replied, "Listen (*écoute*)."

"Have your eyes on everything (*Aie l'oeil à tout, enregistre*)," Rihab added.

"Very good," said Djalel. "What does it mean, 'have your eyes on everything'?" Rihab shouted out an answer, and someone else added to it: "There are some who watch, others who observe. It's not the same thing." Djalel concurred. "There are some who listen, others who hear." He then read from his notebook, a stopwatch around his neck, asking the actors questions as if they were at an oral exam as they continued jogging. Eventually, he went back to the first principle, "Accept."

The actors called out the subprinciples: "Never say no" and "Yes, and."

"Very good," Djalel said. He continued to fire off questions as Jamil watched from the side of the room. "*Et quelle est la base la plus importante*, the most important rule in improvisation?"

Lila offered an answer: "*Acceptation* (Acceptance)."

"No," Djalel replied. "That's one principle. But the most important, *la plus importante*?"

"Don't ask any questions," said Moussa. That, too, was one principle, Djalel said, but not the most important.

Lila tried again: "*L'écoute*? (Listen?)."

Djalel said no.

Rihab took another stab, in English: "To play, take pleasure." The others interjected possible responses, but it was not what Djalel was looking for.

"Faster," he said, urging them on. He repeated, "The most important rule in improvisation is . . ." At one point, feeling hot in the August afternoon, he opened the window next to him, and Rihab said "To be open" in English. Then Djalel supplied the answer he was looking for: "Yes, and . . ." {**Video 04.06**}

—∞—

August 22, 2016. Djalel began the session at a whiteboard, where he had written the six principles of improvisation that they had learned up to that point. The principles were in black marker down one side of the board; they were broken down into subprinciples in red along the right side. Rihab, Mustapha, and Moussa sat on the floor facing the board. Djalel used a pointer, going down

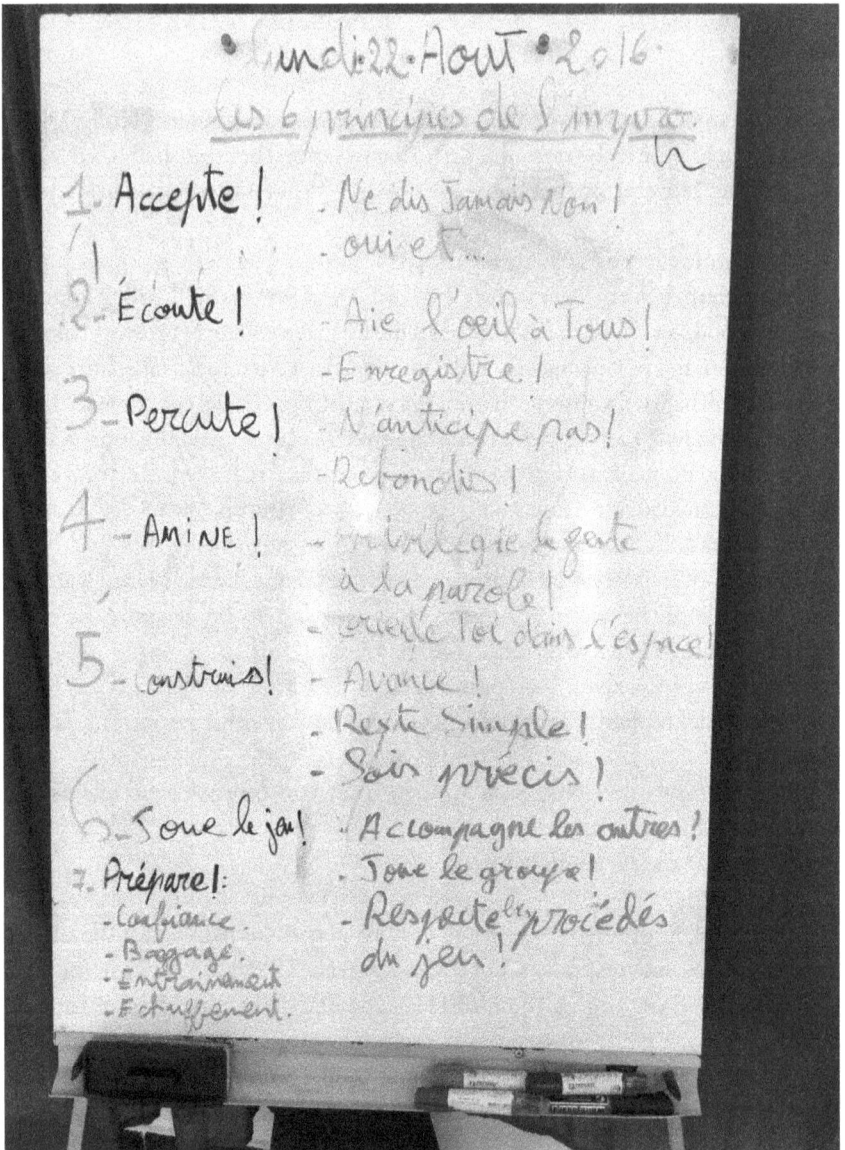

Figure 4.6. Tournier's first seven principles of improvisation, posted by Djalel, Oran, Algeria, August 2016. Author's collection.

the board and pointing to one principle at a time. He called out a principle, and the actors read the text below it aloud in unison, in the kind of monotone voice a class uses to recite together. Sensing that this could be of interest, I started filming at the sixth principle.

"Six!" Djalel called out.

The actors responded in unison: "Play the game. Accompany the others. Play the group. Respect the procedures of the game."

He stopped to see if they were following, asking, "Do you understand these?" The group answered yes in unison. He repeated the question: "And you understand these?" The group again replied yes in unison. He persisted: "Nothing is missing from the board? Everything has been corrected?" Here, it became clear to the others that they had missed something. Rihab and Moussa shared a moment of mirth and a high five, but Djalel looked at them severely, and they became silent. He chastised them: "Are you in nursery school?" He asked once again: "There is nothing missing on the board? There is one more mistake." He then asked them to identify errors in the board that he had apparently deliberately planted. Spelling errors. Punctuation errors. He pointed out that an exclamation point was missing after one principle. Then he displayed the seventh principle, which he had previously hidden under a sheet of paper: "Prepare!" He went over its meaning: "Confidence"; "techniques [of acting, *bagage*]." "Do you understand?" he again asked.

"Yes," replied the actors together.

"Questions?"

"No."

Then Djalel gave a mini quiz on what he just presented.

Djalel: "What are techniques [*bagage*]?"
Moussa: "The principles of improvisation."
Djalel: "And?"

The actors were initially silent. Djalel snapped his fingers to get them to respond more quickly.

Rihab: "Confidence."
Djalel: "No, within 'bagage.' The techniques of improvisation. The techniques." He wanted the actors to understand that there were the principles of improvisation, but there were also the techniques that develop through practice. He pointed to the third bullet under "Prepare."
Mustapha: "Training."
Djalel: "Training is during the improvisation exercises . . . Before I go on stage, I repeat [the principles], I train." He pointed to his head.

Figure 4.7. Djalel writes on the whiteboard, Oran, Algeria, August 2016.
Photo credit: Istijmam Culturelle.

"Concentration is a form of training. Emptying out one's head is a form of
training. . . . I prepare myself. To be able to improvise in the moment, it's
training." He seemed to want people to respond, asking if they thought he
was talking to the chairs. They finally said yes. He pointed to the fourth
bullet under "Prepare." "And?"
Moussa: *"Echauffement"* [warming up]
Djalel: "I warm up before going on stage. . . . I warm up. Not I hang out and
go straight on stage. . . . To warm up, I review the principles: accept,
listen, never say no. . . . I concentrate, I warm up . . . I repeat all of that
in my head. . . . I start observing the stage. The wings. My fellow actors,
how they're dressed, the details. All of that is warming up. . . . That
allows you to concentrate more. You don't go into the trivial details of
questions, looking at yourself, what you're wearing, what you're doing,
what people are around." He then switched gears. "I am going to read
you a very important short text. You have to remember it. 'Confidence is
essential before going onto the stage.' Are you listening?" He went on to
explain that only when the actor masters every aspect of his role can he
improvise—and only then if the atmosphere lends itself to improvisation.
He concluded: "Did you understand? Is it clear?"

Moussa: "Yes."

Djalel: "When I have confidence, techniques, training, warming up . . . then I can improvise on stage with my fellow actors."

Toward the end, Djalel made clear the shift in footing that characterized this session, with him in the role of the teacher and the others as students. In an exchange with Rihab, Djalel addressed her with the common girl's name Zoulikha to indicate that he saw her as his pupil. "What's going on with you, Zoulikha?" he asked. "You aren't having problems at home (*fi-ddar*)?" Moussa responded playfully with a rhyme: "She's having problems at the bar (*fi-lbar*)" (where, of course, a young girl would never set foot). "Thank you, professor," Mustapha exclaimed as the session came to an end. Rihab, now fully assuming the role of student, went up to correct other errors in spelling and grammar on the white board. {**Video 04.07**}

—∽∿∾—

In the summer of 2016, Djalel led the actors through the ten principles of improvisation outlined in Christophe Tournier's book.[54] He presented them in the numbered form that Tournier used: (1) Accept! (2) Listen! (3) Strike! (4) Animate! (5) Build! (6) Play the game! (7) Prepare! (8) Innovate! (9) Have fun! (10) Dare![55] Tournier broke down each principle into subsections, which Djalel presented with lowercase letters (the subsections are set off in boldface in Tournier's book but are not lettered). For instance, Djalel taught the first principle, "Accept," with two subheads: "lowercase a" (*"petit a"*) "Never say no!" and "lowercase b" "Yes, and . . .". Throughout the improvisation sessions, Djalel would drill the actors on the principles and their components as he introduced activities designed to provide practice with each of them.

When I first started watching Istjmam's improvisations, I was focused on their contents. Improvisations, I thought, were sites that could foster what I saw as spontaneous and sometimes critical play with social expectations and societal dilemmas. But I gradually came to see that the metapragmatic framing—that is, the way they taught improvisation—was just as culturally significant as the material in the sketches. Metapragmatic or "how to" discussions like the ones above structured the improvisation sessions during the monthlong rehearsal residency in August 2016. While working methodically through the Tournier book, Djalel would present a principle and then introduce exercises Tournier had targeted to that principle. They referenced the principles in almost every session.

In looking at the actors' metapragmatic talk about improvisation—that is, their discussion about how to approach improv and carry it out—it appears to be modeled on a style of discipline resonant with their Grotowski work. Again, they used a kind of discipline that one might find in the Algerian public schools, with a demand for exact reproduction of the text and unison student responses. Djalel styled himself as a strict primary school instructor, and the actors assumed with ease the roles of obedient students. Istijmam is hardly alone, of course, in taking public school pedagogies into their theatrical practice. Catherine Cole has described how Ghanaian concert party artists would also use "an educational vocabulary of instruction and correction" as their improvised plays got closer to performance (Cole 2001, 115).[56] But for Istijmam, this form of instructional pedagogy constituted the frame itself for their improvisatory work.

I later learned that the troupe had explicitly agreed to adopt this model. There wouldn't have been time, Rihab explained to me by email, to allow for collective process in all the areas they needed to work on.[57] So they decided to rotate leadership in relation to the actors' different areas of expertise: Moussa would be in charge of music, and Djalel would head up improvisation and lighting. Jamil handled artistic direction, designed the mise-en-scène, and ran rehearsals; Lila was charged with administration. As Rihab put it, Djalel and the actors were all taking on roles, playing the parts of instructor and students as they enacted that style of pedagogical relationship. "It's as if the residency was a permanent role-play," she said. "The teacher-student relationship is the one that requires the most discipline and rigor," she added, "which we consider very precious during this workshop. It works well, it makes the task more enjoyable and the objectives more accessible."

The metapragmatic frame itself, then, modeled on a strict instructional hierarchy, was made into part of Istijmam's theatrical practice: they were acting to create both the frame and the exercises within it. This instructional hierarchy was sometimes repeated inside the improvisations themselves. For instance, in one sketch, Rihab played the instructor, and Mustapha and Moussa were the students. As Rihab wrote on the board, uttering nonsense syllables, the two men sat on the floor in front of her. When they started to act out, she came over and pretended to hit them. It was all in good fun, and it occasioned much laughter among the actors and Djalel, but the repetition of the disciplinary model of teacher-student is striking. {Video 04.08}

In another exercise, the actors stood with their eyes closed, deep in focused concentration. Djalel led them into a meditation, telling them to imagine that they were "like a needle, pointed in my concentration." Then he recalled the seven principles of improvisation they had learned thus far. Next he gave them a series of basic phrases or questions that they had to answer in one voice, without opening their eyes. The first: "The last name of Jane is . . .". They responded together: "Goodman."

"I am a needle," he repeated. Then he would give them part of a proverb or another common figure of speech and ask them to finish it in unison. "When all three of you speak correctly and on the same pitch, that is a needle," he explained. Or he might ask them to supply the correct answer in a common phrase: "The symbol of peace is a ___ dove."

"White," they responded (in Arabic, *dove* preceded *white*, so there was no blank in the sentence).

If they were not in unison, he would point this out: *"Attention!"* he said at one point. "The needle is starting to move." At one point, Rihab laughed. *"Attention,"* Djalel said again, sternly. "I remain professional. I stay concentrated. I remain professional. Laughter is not among the principles of improvisation." {**Video 04.09**}

The nature of Istijmam's instructional or metapragmatic frame comes further into focus when compared with approaches to improvisation exercises advocated by troupes in other parts of the world. Laurie Frederik has described how the Cuban troupe Teatro de los Elementos worked implicitly with well-known improvisation principles such as "saying yes" or "giving and receiving" without explicitly referencing them by name. Both the director and the actors would incorporate new elements into the mix, forming a "collective animal" that would initially "chang[e] its form in every improvisation" (Frederik 2012, 133). Even when the improvisations developed more continuity, they did so around particular characters that evolved from one exercise to the next. Of course, this troupe was using improvisation to devise their own plays, whereas for Istijmam, improvisation prepared them for greater responsiveness on stage but did not form the substance of their play itself. For Istijmam, improvisation was first and foremost a discipline of rehearsal, not a forum for creation.

Istijmam's approach to improvisation also contrasts with the approach of the practitioners who developed the exercises. Christophe Tournier, author of the work Djalel used, drew a number of the exercises from such luminaries of improvisation as Viola Spolin, Keith Johnstone, and Del Close, among others. Spolin's foundational work *Improvisation for the Theater* (1983) was taken up by many laboratory-style troupes, including Open Theater. Quotations from Spolin, translated into French, serve as epigraphs for many of Tournier's chapters. In her writings, Spolin urged a "shift away from the teacher as absolute authority" (1983, 9). "True personal freedom and self-expression," she wrote, "can flower only in an atmosphere where attitudes permit equality between student and teacher. . . . Judging on the part of the teacher-director limits his own experience as well as the students'" (Spolin 1983, 8). Tournier did not take up this quote directly, but his discussion of the pedagogy of improvisation opened with a contrast between improvisation and school learning (Tournier

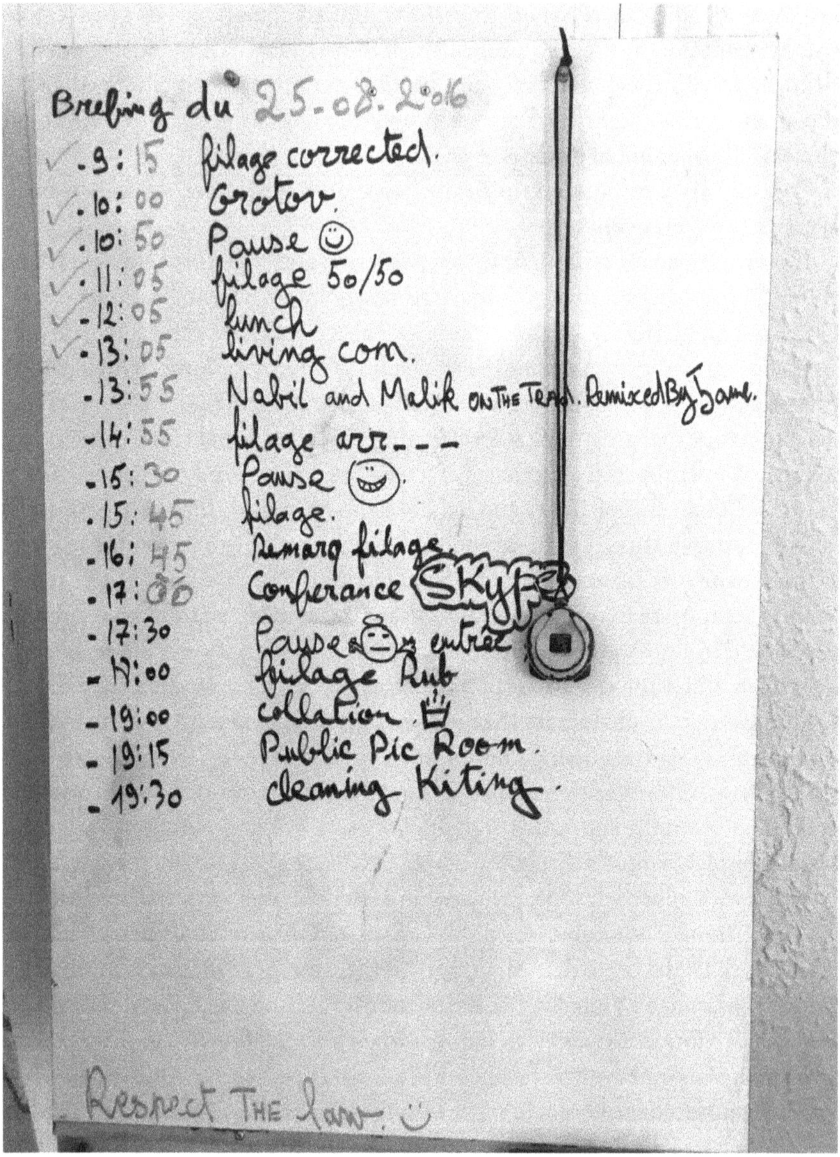

Briefing du 25-08-2016

✓ - 9:15   filage corrected.
✓ - 10:00   Groton.
✓ - 10:50   Pause ☺
✓ - 11:05   filage 50/50
✓ - 12:05   lunch
✓ - 13:05   living com.
- 13:55   Nabil and Malik on the Team. Remixed By Jame.
- 14:55   filage arr.----
- 15:30   Pause ☺.
- 15:45   filage.
- 16:45   Remarq filage.
- 17:00   Conference SKYPE
- 17:30   Pause ☺ entrez
- 18:00   filage Pub
- 19:00   collation ☐
- 19:15   Public Pic Room.
- 19:30   cleaning Kiting.

Respect the law. ☺

Figure 4.8. Rehearsal schedule, Oran, Algeria, August 2016. Author's collection.

2003, 51). Tournier also presented an eleventh rule of improvisation—"Forget the rules!" (72). Djalel had alluded to but never presented this eleventh rule (at least not in my presence), saying only that "they would see about it later." This could well have been due to the time pressure of the short rehearsal residency. From what I know of Istijmam's practice, they would always be ready to say that ultimately there were no rules, but (in agreement with other improv specialists) they would add that that getting to the state where no rules were necessary nonetheless required solid knowledge of and practice with the rules.

Again, then, Istijmam set the principles of improvisation into a metapragmatic frame that emphasized discipline, conformity, and submission to the authority of the text—much as they did for the Grotowski training. But as with their Grotowski work, for Istijmam, this did not mean a lack of creativity. To the contrary: it was in accepting authority that creativity and spontaneity could best be fostered. The authoritative, metapragmatic frame allowed for a playful imaginativeness in the actors' practice of improvisation.

If the Istijmam actors did not question the use of Tournier's principles as a scaffolding for their work, they did sometimes challenge Djalel about how to implement them. For instance, about halfway through the rehearsal residency, they were experimenting with the sixth principle, "Play the game," and its two subprinciples, "Accompany the others" and "Play the group." The objective was to support another actor's vision of an improvisation, not to undermine it by trying to change direction. In this scene, Moussa was leading the action. He was pretending to film a scene enacted by Rihab and Mustapha, hoping to enter the film into competition and win prizes, "even an Oscar." The scene unfolded among the three actors. Then they exited, and Djalel came out, the Tournier book in hand. First, he reminded them of the principle they were working on, "*Accompagner les autres*" (Accompany the others). He added, "*Je respecte les principes de l'impro, et j'écoute les autres*" (I respect the principles of improv, and I listen to the others). Then he snapped his fingers and asked them what this entailed.

Mustapha replied in time to his snaps: "What, who, why, when (*quoi, qui, comment, quand*)" in a sing-song format that lent itself to memorized recitation.

Then they discussed the improvisation itself. Djalel reiterated that the point of this principle was to play together as a group, not to try to be the star. They discussed what they had done in the scene at some length. Djalel thought that at one point, Rihab had sought to change or "sabotage" the sketch. She listened to his feedback attentively and then said that she disagreed. She had wanted to do so, she said—she had lots of ideas—but she vetoed them in order to support Moussa's vision. At the same time, she added, "That's improv. You strike (*percuter*). . . . Now, if Amine (Moussa) proposes, if he comes with an idea, he already brings a lot to the group so we can all play together. . . . He brings him in as a character, he brings me in as a character, he asks us to do something. But it will become flat if there aren't some little . . . you see?"

Djalel affirmed: "I take up the first act of my friend, and I support it, I don't anticipate . . . I don't tell myself that my poor friend is in trouble. No, I have to tell myself that my friend is acting."

Rihab pushed back again. "No, it isn't that he is in trouble . . . there are small things that can be added, even in the [midst of the] action."

After trying for several minutes to explain her course of action to Djalel, Rihab said she would give him an example of what it would look like if she had tried to undermine the scene or change the direction. They went offstage, entered, and replayed the scene. But this time, she did not try to support Moussa but rather introduced her own action, coming in later than anticipated and failing to take account of an imaginary character that he had added into the scene.

This is a small example, but it speaks to the energetic collaboration and animated discussion that took place inside what appeared as an authoritative pedagogical frame. The metapragmatic teacher-student model went only so far. Still, Djalel closed the improv by asking them to repeat the sixth principle of improvisation. "Come on, go!" he exhorted them.

"Play the game," Mustapha said.

"Small a?" Djalel asked.

"Play as a team," Rihab called out.

"Have confidence," Mustapha added.

"Accompany the others," Djalel reminded them, walking toward the actors with his arms outstretched. "Small b?"

"There is no star," said Mustapha.

"Very good. Continue."

"Stay alert," said Rihab.

"Small b—Play the group," Djalel said, eventually supplying the answer he wanted. He went back to the book. "'There is a telepathic exchange between one and another [on stage],'" he read. "The more this sense is developed, the greater the spontaneity," he added, citing an epigraph by Jacob Levy Moreno (Tournier 2003, 34). The session ended by repeating and explaining the principles. Again, Djalel snapped his fingers to get the actors to respond: "Play the game; Accompany the others; Play the group." {**Video 04.10**}

In the workshops in the United States, the metapragmatic framing largely fell away. Metapragmatic orientations to theatrical practice are generally not considered part of cultural exchange. The script of the play, the traditions of marketplace performance that it comes from, and the social situations that it references are shared as elements of culture. But the "how to" of rehearsal practice remains behind the scenes. Yet it is perhaps in rehearsal where cultural relationships to pedagogy, discipline, and authority are most visible.

DISCIPLINING INTUITION

Rihab, Moussa and Mustapha stood in a horizontal line, arms at their sides. Slowly, tuning in to the energy among them, they raised their right arms in unison. They then moved their right hands to their hearts in a sweeping gesture. "*Oui, et . . .*" they exclaimed together in French. "Yes, and . . ."—one of the key principles of improvisation. {**Video 04.11**}

All of Istijmam's improvisation rehearsals began and ended with the actors in line, exclaiming "*Oui, et . . .*" in this way. They were rehearsing a theatrical technique that Alaina Lemon (2018) has called phatic intuition—that is, they were trying to collectively or "telepathically" sense the energy flowing between their bodies and respond to it as one. Many of the improvisation exercises in rehearsal were focused on generating this sense of phatic intuition. In effect, all of improvisation works this way: actors need to be continuously attuned to energy shifts so they can play off each other. Phatic intuition is especially palpable during exercises that do not involve a verbal component. Djalel was getting at this when he said that "there is a telepathic exchange among actors on stage." It was like a ping-pong game, he added, demonstrating with his body how one needed to be able to follow the ball.

One of the exercises Istijmam used to cultivate phatic intuition was the "mirror," an exercise that Tournier borrowed from Viola Spolin (Tournier 2003, 103). Two actors are to mirror each other's movements. One leads, but it should appear to those watching that they are moving together. When used in a group, this exercise is called "the monkey" and resembles the dancelike improvisation that Mustapha did with the Sarah Lawrence students. {**Video 03.05**} In an exercise Tournier calls "Count to Twenty," the actors are to stand in a line and try to count, in order, from one to twenty without overlap or without uttering a number together (Tournier 2003, 112). For example, Rihab might lead off, saying "one," Moussa might add "two," Mustapha might say "three," and then someone would have to utter "four" without overlapping with anyone else. Two actors could not speak at the same time, or they would have to start over. (Istijmam never got beyond twelve in the sessions I observed.)

The metapragmatic framing of the improvisation workshops in the United States both drew on and differed from what took place in the rehearsals in Algeria. The backstage component—the troupe's metapragmatic orientation to the exercises as a form of discipline—utterly fell away. No principles were presented.

No techniques were discussed. The Tournier book was absent. Teaching the principles clearly wasn't the point in a two-hour workshop. Instead, Istijmam introduced exercises that playfully cultivated phatic intuition. For instance, in a workshop with a dance troupe in Portland, Maine, everyone was seated in a large circle. One person—and only one—could stand up at a time. They all had to sense the energy and try to stand when no one else did. This resulted in many moments of mirth when more than one person tried to get up. {Video 04.12}

The work of phatic intuition is to bring people together into a shared flow of energy, dissolving both interpersonal and cultural boundaries. It depends on an absence of reflection and an attunement to group connectivity. In foregrounding phatic intuition over other forms of improvisation, the workshops in the United States were designed to downplay difference. The focus was understandably on creating an embodied encounter in which everyone could participate. It was clearly not the place for the kind of self-reflexive discipline that Istijmam used in their own training. This meant, however, that one of the troupe's basic orientations to theatrical practice—an element that might have elicited keen discussion—was not seen or shared in the United States. Again, the structure and expectations of this kind of tour—in other words, the metapragmatic orientation of the tour itself—worked to foreclose even the possibility for such an exchange.

HORIZONS OF POSSIBILITY, REVISITED

Istijmam's embrace of the authority of the text—whether Grotowski or Tournier—articulates in some ways with wider formations of discipline and pedagogy in Algeria. It also gave them a structured way to counter some of the lack of structure in Algerian society. But their reliance on these texts may above all be related to access. While researching theater as a novice in the field myself, I could search online for titles, order what I liked, charge the books to my university research account, and have them delivered to my front door the next day. I could search the online catalogue of my excellent university library, request as many books as I wanted with the press of a button, and pick them up at my office. In Algeria, one cannot go into a bookstore and find these texts. One cannot peruse the stacks of Algerian university libraries—and even if one could, there is little likelihood that these books would be there. One cannot go online and order a book to be delivered to one's doorstep in a day or two. There is nothing like Amazon.com in Algeria, where even the national postal service is barely operative. Moreover, one cannot sign up for a workshop with Tournier or with one of Grotowski's students. These experts do not travel in circuits that include Algeria. What the actors had access to were texts or, in some cases, photocopies of texts that someone had brought back from France. Consider that Djalel was trained as an accountant. He taught himself improvisation, with Tournier (and to a degree, Jamil) as his guide. Above all, then, Istijmam's sustained engagement with training through texts underscores Jamil's repeated point—that there is no actor training in Algeria. For Istijmam, these texts became primary supports in their own autodidactic training. They had to figure it out for themselves because there was no other choice. Cultural models of discipline aside, it makes sense that Istijmam accepted the authority of these texts. This was the material they had to work with. Alongside discrepant horizons of temporality, then, this points to disjunctive horizons of access. For them, "poor theater" wasn't just a theatrical trend—it was a socioeconomic reality. In this sense, the question of whether discipline comes from the outside or the inside—a question I had asked them directly in 2010—is the wrong question. The question is what resources they had available. Jamil put it this way: "At the beginning, we started from the book. It was a book. We didn't have Grotowski in front of us doing the postures."[58]

Recall that the name *Istijmam* refers to a space of relaxation after a long day's work. Since their beginnings in 2007, Istijmam developed an extraordinary discipline through specific rehearsal practices. During the 2016 residency, they worked all day, every day, with at most a single day off each week. They developed professionalization through their own autodidactic training. The Actor in the play couldn't find a place to rehearse other than the Restroom, hidden away from the world, a place where no one wants to linger despite the Attendant's utopian vision. Istijmam's primary resources were a rehearsal space and a couple of guide books. With only these to go on, they disciplined themselves to rehearse day and night to develop their acting chops, never suspecting that one day they would find themselves in the United States.

NOTES

1. We translated *wardrobe* as *closet* for the English language performance for ease of comprehension by US audiences.

2. HartBeat called this their Neighborhood Investigative Project. For more information on HartBeat, see https://www.hartbeatensemble.org/, accessed February 16, 2020.

3. Christophe Tournier began practicing improvisation in 1991 in Geneva with the Fédération d'Improvisation Genevoise. He has also practiced with the Troupe des Tripotés and the Théâtre Tout-Terrain in Haute-Savoie.

4. Along with the tramway, big box home improvement stores cropping up outside the city meant that people no longer shopped as much at the local lighting stores that remained.

5. Outside of cultural associations or cooperatives, the state-supported Houses of Culture (*Maisons de Culture*), located in every wilaya, may also sponsor theater troupes, as can universities.

6. Artistic troupes must find their own rehearsal spaces. Troupes associated with organizations that had their own physical locales, such as the Numidya or the Sidi El Houari cultural associations in Oran, use their association's space. Troupes associated with city initiatives may use city-owned spaces, such as a youth center administered by the office of the mayor. The Regional Theater of Oran (TRO) was available only to its own professional troupe or to troupes who were contracted to perform in that space. Though it was named after Abdelkader Alloula, the TRO had no formal relationship with the Alloula family or with Istijmam. As an independent theater troupe, Istijmam was free to enter into contract with the TRO for a particular performance, as they did when they performed Alloula's *El Ajouad* in March 2019. At that point, they could use the TRO for a limited number of rehearsals, as contractually specified.

7. Amazigh or Berber refers to the peoples who inhabited North Africa before the arrival of Arabs in the seventh and eleventh centuries. With the rise of Arab nationalism in the twentieth century came an accompanying subnational movement to include the emerging nation's Amazigh history and language (Tamazight). See Goodman 2005; Maddy-Weitzman 2011. The city of Oran is primarily Arabophone, but it has a small Amazigh/Berber population who emigrated to the city primarily from the Kabyle region.

8. Thanks to Mohamed Yabdri for information in this section.

9. Cheniki (2006, 211–54) provides a detailed annotated bibliography on the history of Algerian theatrical production.

10. Baffet (1985) develops a history of state theater in Algeria and includes a series of appendices that provide some of the official documents of the time. Rouchard (1980) provides a brief account of the five national theaters. Djellid (1982) provides a brief history of children's theater at the Regional Theater of Oran, alongside a wider history of theater in Algeria. Kali (2005, 67–82) discusses the creation of and the relationship between the TNA and the regional theaters.

11. The Tripoli Program was drafted by the Comité National de la Révolution Algérienne (CNRA) in Tripoli, Libya, between May 25 and June 7, 1962, just prior to independence. See the Programme du Front de Libération National Adopté à Tripoli par le CNRA en juin 1962, Annuaire de l'Afrique du Nord 1962, 683–704 (FLN 1962). See also McDougall 2017, 240–44.

12. From Decree 65-1 of January 8, 1963, concerning the organization of Algerian theater, reproduced in Baffet (1985, 187).

13. Baffet (1985, 62–68, 191) refers to an unpublished 1962 report by Mustapha Kateb and Mohammed Boudia, both prominent men of theater, called

"De l'Orientation." This document apparently spelled out the role of theater and the TNA in the new Algerian nation.

14. Ordonnances 70.38 and 70.39 of June 12, 1970, reorganized the theatrical infrastructure, decentralizing the TNA and creating the regional theaters (Kali 2005, 68; Baffet 1985, 194). The formal creation of the TRO as a regional theater was accomplished via decree 73.74 on April 24, 1973 (Baffet 1985, 194). Kali (2005, 73–75) discusses the creation of the regional theaters including the TRO. On the decentralization of the TRO, see also Sehaba 1997 and N. Kh. 1997.

15. République Algérienne Démocratique et Populaire, Secrétariat d'Etat à la Culture et aux Arts Populaires. Bilan Critique: Analyse Quantitative du Secteur de la Culture à Travers les Trois Précédents Plans Nationaux de Développement. 73 pages. No further publication information is available.

16. The five initial theaters were located in the cities of Algiers, Oran, Constantine, Annaba, and Sidi-bel-Abbes (Baffet 1985, 189). As of this writing in June 2019, state theaters are also found in Saïda, Mascara, Djelfa, Tizi-Ouzou, Bejaïa, Skida, Guelma, and Souk Akhras. In Laghouat, Tamanrasset, and Tlemcen, there are state troupes but no dedicated theater building as of this writing. I am grateful to Mohamed Yabdri for this information.

17. The information in this paragraph is drawn from Kali 2005, 75–80.

18. Kali does not provide specific documentation of this account other than his personal knowledge, but he does cite Selim Merabia, director of the Regional Theater of Constantine, who opined that "the impotence and failure of the administrative management of theater . . . reveal an attempt to subjugate the men [sic] of the profession. When the artist receives a salary and experiences a 'dumbing down' (nivellement par le bas) . . . how do you want talent to flourish and how can an artist [i.e., actor] create and manage his career. . . . It's not for no reason that some just gave up while others left the profession." Kali cites "an interview that appeared in 2001" but does not provide the source of that interview (2005, 76).

19. According to the Archives of the Festival of Mostaganem, the Mostaganem Festival of Amateur Theater was run under the auspices of the Muslim Scout Association from 1967 to 1974. From 1975 to 1990, it was organized by the Union National de Jeunesse Algérienne (UNJA). From 1991 to 2003, it operated under the auspices of the Association Culturelle du Festival National du Theatre Amateur. Since 2004, it has been organized under a festival Commissariat. For a comprehensive (but unpublished) dissertation on amateur theater in Algeria, see Djellid 1984–85. On amateur theater, see also Cheniki 2006, 225–38; Kali 2005; Salhi 1998.

20. Kamal Salhi (1998) also discusses the blurred boundaries between so-called amateur and professional actors. Algeria is hardly alone in this regard; on Yorùbá popular theater, see Barber 2000.

21. Personal interview, August 2016, Oran.

22. Loi n° 12-06 du 18 Safar 1433 correspondant au 12 janvier 2012 relative aux associations. The law may be viewed here: https://www.joradp.dz/FTP/JO -FRANCAIS/2012/F2012002.pdf, accessed February 16, 2020.

23. Law 87-15 of July 21, 1987, had for the first time granted the right to form locally based nonpolitical associations without prior governmental authorization. Law 90-31 of December 4, 1990, extended this right to national organizations. On civic associations in Algeria, see Liverani 2008.

24. On resistance to Law 12-06, see https://euromedrights.org/publication /memorandum-assessment-of-law-12-06-of-12-january-2012-on-associations, accessed June 6, 2018. See also https://www.amnesty.org/en/latest/news/2013 /05/algeria-new-law-on-associations-used-to-stifle-civil-society, accessed June 5, 2018, and https://www.algerie-focus.com/2014/01/loi-sur-les-associations, accessed June 29, 2018.

25. Personal interview, March 5, 2009, Oran.

26. Hadj Miliani, interviewed by Mohamed Kali for a story in *El Watan*, April 4, 1996 (Kali 2005, 56).

27. Omar Fetmouche, interviewed by Mohamed Kali for a story in *El Watan*, April 4, 1996 (Kali 2005, 57).

28. A national center for theatrical training had been established in 1964 in Bordj El Kiffan but was not active by the time Istijmam members would have sought training. See introduction, note 6, and Baffet 1985, 191–92.

29. In Grotowski 2002, 147–73.

30. Blog post, March 31, 2008, http://istijmam.canalblog.com, accessed June 17, 2019. The blog was developed and written by Leila Bibouche, one of the original troupe members, with the troupe's approval. Her posts cover occasional moments in the troupe's theatrical journey between March and September of 2008. She left the troupe in January 2009.

31. A similar laboratory approach characterized the work of the Pilobolus Dance Theater; see Royce 2018.

32. In the Open Theater Papers housed at Kent State University, reference is made to a "Mid-East tour" during August 8–17, 1971 (Box 5, File 6). Open Theater archives at Kent State are indexed here: https://www.library.kent.edu/special -collections-and-archives/open-theater-papers-1, accessed April 11, 2018. Open Theater apparently followed the Mid-East tour with an appearance at the 1971 Mostaganem Festival of Amateur Theater in Algeria, which took place during August 22–28, 1971. Open Theater's performances in Algeria are discussed in Bendimered 1971.

33. On Schechner's approach to theater, see Harding and Rosenthal 2011; Schechner 1985.

34. Personal interview, June 22, 2010, Mostaganem.

35. Personal interview, August 28, 2016, Oran.

36. President Boumediene and his entourage launched the programs known as the "Révolution agraire" (agrarian revolution) and the "Gestion socialiste des entreprises" in 1972. See Stora 2001. See also McDougall 2017, 256–60.

37. This was moderator Stephen Davis's translation from Arabic for the audience. Jamil talked about how the goual worked to get the spectator to participate via a dialogue in the imagination.

38. See also chapter 2. Alloula's experience at El Meïda is described in Ouazani and Hadj Slimane 1997. The material in this paragraph on the El Meïda performance comes from this article.

39. Grotowski 2002, based on a sequence of physical actions that Grotowski had developed from 1959 to 1962.

40. Group interview with Istijmam, June 24, 2010, Oran.

41. "Actor Training" can be found in Grotowski 2002, 133–46. See Wolford 2010 for a clear overview of the Grotowski method.

42. In 2019, this actor returned to the troupe for an appearance in Alloula's *El-Ajouad*.

43. Personal interview, March 5, 2009, Oran.

44. Personal interview, January 8, 2009, Oran.

45. Alaina Lemon (2004, 316) similarly characterized the first-year directing and acting course at the Russian Academy of Theatrical Arts as "art boot camp." However, the small number of students in this elite program had passed a rigorous screening program and were preparing for professional careers.

46. Participants' personal commitment to rigor alongside their conviction that they deserved strict discipline resembles how Alaina Lemon characterized students in the training program of the Russian Academy of Theatrical Arts. She went so far as to call these methods "verbal terror" (Lemon 2004).

47. See Goodman 2013a on public displays of unanimity as a common practice in Algerian cultural associations from the 1930s to the 1950s.

48. Personal interview, August 28, 2016, Oran.

49. See, for instance, Lendra 1991.

50. https://www.washingtonpost.com/world/africa/algerias-abdelaziz -bouteflika-submits-resignation-ending-two-decade-rule/2019/04/02/11d9680a -557b-11e9-814f-e2f46684196e_story.html?utm_term=.e4654918ee53, accessed June 7, 2019.

51. On precarity as both a political-economic condition associated with neoliberalism and the embodied and affective experience of living in this condition, see (among many others) Berlant 2011; Butler 2004. On precarity and performance, see Ridout and Schneider 2012.

52. Personal interview, March 5, 2009, Oran.

53. Personal interview, January 22, 2009, Oran.

54. Tournier draws inspiration for the principles and exercises from internationally recognized experts including Viola Spolin, Robert Gravel, Del Close, Keith Johnstone, Jacob Lévy Moreno, and Louis Jouvet.

55. My translation from French.

56. Ghanaian concert party artists engaged in a less explicitly marked improvisational practice, combining and embellishing stock plots and characters from everyday life. See Cole 2001, chapter 5.

57. Personal communication via email, October 25, 2017.

58. Group interview with Istijmam, June 24, 2010, Oran.

FIVE

—m—

ENCOUNTERS IN TRANSLATION

How *Et-Teffeh* Became *Apples*

"WHEN YOU SEE THE SAME words in another language you see them differently. This is the first time we are performing *Apples*. We have performed *Et-Teffeh* since 2009. But now we're performing *Apples*, and it's another thing." Jamil was responding to an audience member's question about how the play had changed in translation.[1] His reply points in two directions. First, the source or original text starts to look different when held up against the linguistic conventions and cultural understandings of another language. Second, translation of a theatrical script is geared to performance—to a new material and embodied encounter with the text. *Apples* would live differently than *Et-Teffeh* in the actors' mouths and bodies. Yet as the audience question suggests, the translation process—like the rehearsals—was part of the behind-the-scenes labor that was invisible on tour. This chapter goes backstage to tell some of the stories of how *Et-Teffeh* became *Apples*.

For the actors and for me, the translation process emerged as one of the most compelling moments in cultural exchange. Finalizing the translation of *Apples* for performance in the United States constituted one of the major components of the rehearsal residency. On a basic level, we wanted to refine the English text to improve flow, accuracy, and suitability for the stage. More broadly, we sought to create what the actors referred to as a "bilingual" script (*version bilingue*) that would restore some of Arabic—enough to retain an Algerian flavor without sacrificing meaning. In asking ourselves what would need to change in order for the play to be reasonably accessible to US publics, we were doing what some translation scholars call "domesticating" the text, or making it more comprehensible to the target audience. But we were also "foreignizing" it by retaining some of the Algerian Arabic.[2] For the actors, *bilingual* did not mean that the play would actually be delivered in two languages via some form of simultaneous translation. Rather, it meant that the script would move between domesticating and foreignizing moments in a way that would make it both accessible and foreign, both familiar and strange.

The actors' desire to create a bilingual script points to a key difference with conventional translation practices. Most translations are oriented to the target audience. The terms *domesticate* and *foreignize* are themselves imagined from the target audience's vantage point. But the actors also wanted to orient the translation to Algerians in the United States (who were a small but regular contingent in the US audiences) and to make the play feel Algerian to themselves as performers. After all, they were the ones who would be performing *Apples*. In this case, foreignizing the text for one audience meant domesticating it for the other, and vice versa. This oscillation between foreignizing and domesticating may be what Jamil meant when he characterized Istijmam's translation process as "destabilizing . . . in a good way."

For the actors and me, creating the bilingual script was a collaborative, emergent, and indeed destabilizing undertaking. As I convey something of how our translation process unfolded, I am not assessing the validity of the translation of *Et-Teffeh* into *Apples* via an extended comparison of the Arabic and English scripts. Rather, I develop an account of our translation process itself.

STAGES OF TRANSLATION

Translating *Et-Teffeh* into *Apples* was unconventional from the beginning. Whereas in literary translation, the translator is usually a native speaker of the target language, here that was not the case. In fact, no one on the translation team was fluent in both Arabic and English. When Istijmam was accepted by Center Stage with a promise to perform in English, the troupe commissioned two credentialed friends to translate the play, Malik Bourbia and Nabil Taibi. Malik was at the time working on a master's degree in translation and had excellent command of Arabic and good knowledge of English. Nabil had been studying English since 1996, earning a bachelor's degree (*licence*) in English teaching. He had subsequently taught English in Algeria in settings that included high school, university, and private school. Malik and Nabil were rap artists in their spare time, which gave them a good sense of the poetic play of language in performance.[3] Nabil had surrounded himself with American and British friends and had done a lot of listening to colloquial English. Both Nabil and Malik were fluent native speakers of Darija (Algerian Arabic), of course, but Nabil had not worked as much in classical (Modern Standard) Arabic as

Malik had. Malik had the stronger Arabic as well as training in translation; Nabil had the stronger English. Both were well versed in Abdelkader Alloula's work. Their task was to take Alloula's text *Et-Teffeh*, which was written in artistic colloquial Arabic (more cultivated and poetic than street Darija but far from Modern Standard Arabic), and translate it into English.[4]

Malik and Nabil delivered their translation to Istijmam in December 2015. Rihab emailed it to me, asking me to take a quick look before they sent it on to Center Stage. I read through the English version as a native speaker, not a translator, attending to how it would likely sound to US audiences. I did a quick edit for grammar, flow, and fluency and sent it back to Rihab. She and Jamil liked what I had done, saying that it felt "lighter." I then made an audio recording for them as a reference for pronunciation. This version, which I call the working text, was the one they worked with from December 2015 to August 2016. In the first months of 2016, each actor met in daily Skype sessions with Jamil, where they were accountable for memorizing a new line each day. In April, the troupe came together in Paris to begin putting the play together. By then, they had their parts mostly memorized.

The actors and I revisited the translation during the first two weeks of the August 2016 rehearsal residency in Oran to refine the English and to develop what they called the "bilingual version." We would arrive at the Alloula homestead at 9:00 a.m. (on many days, the actors had already gathered at 7:00 a.m. to run laps on a local track). We would take our coffee or tea to the terrace, where we sat looking out over the city and the sea, waking up to the day, and breathing in the coolness of the morning air. After a few minutes, we would move into the *salon* (living room), Abdelkader Alloula looking down from his picture hanging on the wall above us. Jamil, the three actors (occasionally joined by Djalel), and I took our places around the long oval table in seminar style: texts in front of us, pens in hand, and smartphones at the ready for dictionary and thesaurus consultation. Each session started with the actors reading aloud their lines from the passage under consideration that day. We then worked through the passage line by line and word by word, sometimes spending the entire hour on a single reply. The sessions closed with another table reading of the passage as we had revised it. For all five of us, French was the strongest second language: my French was better than my Arabic, and their French was better than their English. Rihab and Jamil had essentially native fluency in French; Rihab, with a master's degree in translation and considerable university study of English, had the greatest mastery of all three languages. Our encounters with the text, then, were from the beginning mediated through three languages.

Although we worked collaboratively, my position was closer to the typical anthropological role of native informant. I was able to tell the actors what would (and would not) sound right and what US audiences would (and would not) be likely to understand. As the native informant, I also had a sense of what kinds of cultural understandings surrounded particular words and phrases when they were translated into English. In short, I was able to "recontextualize" the script for the actors in relation to how I thought US audiences would interpret it (Bauman and Briggs 1990). But I was rarely the final authority. The actors often had a better sense than I did of what would sound best on stage. After all, the actors themselves were to be the media of translation: it would take place in their mouths and through their bodies.

CULTURAL MATTER

As the actors and I moved slowly through the script, we did not realize that our conversations touched on virtually every debate in translation studies. We engaged with questions that scholars of translation have long been asking (using different terms at different moments), such as whether to aim for denotational (word for word) equivalence with the source text or instead seek corresponding contextual or functional meanings in the target language.[5] We certainly ran up against one of the thorniest problems in translation: how to take into account the poetics of language (its sounds and rhythms). In retrospect, our work articulated strongly with debates about whether to domesticate or foreignize a translation, but we did not use these terms. Nor did we have an overarching philosophy or "ethics" (Venuti 2012, 499) of translation that we sought to implement. Rather, we started from a nitty-gritty engagement with the text itself, fueled by the two sometimes competing desires captured by the term *bilingual*. We wanted the play to be accessible to US publics, and we also wanted it to feel Algerian. This led to different decisions at different moments, informed by a combination of discussion and "feeling" (as Jamil would put it).

Of course, cultural understandings need not be located exclusively around what are considered to be separate cultures, typically understood in national terms. The notion that a source text contains an inherently stable or fixed meaning is in part created through the translation process itself (Benjamin 1969; Crapanzano 2004). Any performance of a text is going to entail some degree of recontextualization; otherwise, there would be no desire to repeat the classics over and over again. *Et-Teffeh* itself no doubt underwent changes in interpretation between its first performance in Algeria in 1994 and its subsequent performances by Istijmam between 2009 and 2011 (though unfortunately, I do not have specific data on how the interpretation might have transformed). That said, the explicit process of translating a text into a new language for an entirely different public does entail a highly self-reflexive process—one that Istijmam took to heart.

As the actors and I worked line by line through the translation, we encountered various kinds of "cultural matter" (Silverstein 2003, 75). Cultural matter refers to the broad set of implicit understandings about context and usage that exceed and sometimes even subvert the denotational (literal or dictionary) meaning of a word or phrase. Cultural matter is what opens a text to multiple interpretations, allowing audiences to recontextualize it in relation to the concerns and conventions of their own times. It includes the chains of associations, or "indexical penumbras" (Silverstein 2003, 89), that words carry in one cultural context but not another. Even if a translated term is identical to the source in its denotational meaning, it can take on a different charge because the surrounding cultural matter is so different. Cultural matter also points to usage (or metapragmatic) conventions specific to particular times, places, and social situations. In short, cultural matter infuses words with contextual, social, and historical associations that can supplement and exceed their denotational meanings.

Translating cultural matter can entail reworking the text in ways that may change its form, a process that Silverstein calls transduction. As he puts it, in the material world, transduction occurs when one form of energy is converted to another form (such as when the force of water is converted to electricity through a hydroelectric generator). In the linguistic world, transduction occurs when cultural matter from one language takes a different form in another language (Silverstein 2003, 83). By Silverstein's definition, most of what we did entailed transduction. Occasionally, we resorted to what Silverstein calls transformation, moving more radically away from the Arabic text so that the translation would make cultural sense to US audiences.

Ever present with us around the table was the imagined US audience, and we continually grappled with what words and phrases might mean in a US context. We had to make decisions about cultural matter that did not readily translate from Arabic to English. Said differently, we were engaged in what Deborah Kapchan calls the "play between what can be cited (words) and the unspoken cultural and affective depths associated with them" (2020, 6). Would we try to explain a term's "indexical penumbra" via an explanatory gloss, would we clarify through gesture and stagecraft, would we find a different term with similar associations in English, or would we omit it altogether? We encountered cultural matter in the form of language ideologies, or beliefs about the relative social values of particular languages and language varieties. We encountered cultural matter in the form of metapragmatic conventions in one language that had to change form to be understood in another.[6] Perhaps above all, we encountered the materiality of language itself: the ways the English words sounded to the ear, felt in the mouth, and would resonate on stage.

Indexical Penumbras

We hit our first indexical penumbra in the play's opening lines.[7] Recall that the Customer comes out on stage with a hand plastered over his mouth, emitting sounds but no words. The Attendant wonders why the Customer won't speak and initially decides (in the Arabic version) that he must be mute. Our working text read, "I think you are looking for the Home for Deaf-Mutes." In Algeria, the actors told me, the Arabic term (Dār el-Bakākīsh) had no pejorative connotations. But I thought that it could trigger negative associations in the United States, and I felt bound to let the actors know about this. First of all, I said, the idea that people with hearing or speaking challenges should be placed in a home apart from society was no longer accepted. Second, the term *mute* itself was seen as pejorative and was no longer in common usage. I proposed changing "Home for Deaf-Mutes" to "School for the Deaf."[8] In Algeria, the actors countered, there was no pejorative association to the term *mute*, and what were called houses for deaf-mutes in fact functioned as schools. The word *house* was not problematic at all, they added, raising the example of the "Houses of Culture" found in every city (Maison de Culture, Dār el-Thaqāfa)—of course, *home* and *house* do not have quite the same associations in English, but we didn't get into that. Second, the actors thought that *mute* more accurately reflected the plight of the Customer than *deaf* did, because he was unable to speak (but apparently able to hear) when he entered the Restroom. As we discussed the phrase, though, Jamil ended up acknowledging that talking about someone living in a house for deaf-mutes did indicate that they were marginalized.

Moussa then raised a key issue that would come up more than once. "There are many things in the text that will contradict an American way of seeing things," he said, "and that is good. We shouldn't take out every word that contradicts. . . . After, there will be a space for discussion. . . . That's the kind of exchange we can do." How far would we go, continued Moussa, in changing lines that made sense in one culture but were not acceptable in the other? In other words, how much were we going to domesticate the text to make sure it did not offend US audiences? Would we start taking out passages like one in Alloula's famous play *El-Ajouad* that showed people publicly displaying a white cloth with the red blood of the bride after she had been deflowered on her wedding night? What would we do with material like this, material that was subject to different kinds of cultural evaluation, material that might give US audiences a negative impression of Algeria? In short, what would we do with the "milieu" in which a text arose, with "the vibrations of a territory, formed by the stories that have lived there" (Kapchan 2020, 17, drawing the term "milieu" from De-leuze and Guattari)? After much consideration, the troupe took my suggestion to change "Home for Deaf-Mutes" to "School for the Deaf." For the troupe, denotational accuracy was not worth encountering a penumbra of discomfort and unease in the opening moments of the play. The Arabic script did not create discomfort among spectators, they agreed, so the English one should not either. They went for equivalence in function over denotational accuracy, adapting the text to avoid a negative indexical penumbra.

We encountered another penumbra around a phrase that the Attendant uttered early in the play, when he initially refused to let the Customer use the Restroom to release his pent-up frustration and fury. "The law is the law," our working script read. Rihab pointed out that in the original Arabic script, the word *here* started the phrase: "Here (hnā), the law is the law." We asked ourselves what the *here* referred to. Was it Algeria? Was it the public restroom as an institution? If the latter, was the Attendant contrasting his orderly rest-room with the lawlessness of the larger society? As an indexical shifter, *here* was a term designed to take its meaning from context, and in this case, the context that *here* pointed to was ambiguous. Our conversation evoked a larger dichotomy between societies perceived as operating under the "rule of law" (like America) and those that were not (like Algeria). "It's true that [in the US] all the laws are respected," said Rihab. That was hardly the case, I countered, but I did acknowledge differences between the United States and Algeria. More to the point, I said, when people entered a public institution in Algeria, they could usually see posted on the wall the *"règlement intérieur"* (internal regula-tions) that governed that establishment. In America, at least in a restroom, that was not typically the case. And whether or not we included *here*, the moment would go by so quickly, I added, that it wouldn't offer audiences much if any room for reflection.

If *here* was meant to refer to the Restroom's regulations, I asked, how about having the Attendant say, "The rules are the rules"? "No, it's the law (el-qānūn)," Jamil replied. "It's not the same." But he too wondered whether we should include the *here*, agreeing that audiences wouldn't be likely to grasp its meaning. I then became annoyingly literal (I realize in retrospect), suggest-ing that we resolve the penumbral space around *here* with a long explanatory gloss to make clear the meaning the actors wanted to convey: "Even if in the rest of the society there is no law, here, we have the law." (Thankfully they didn't go for this clumsy suggestion, but it does serve to illustrate what we were up against in this passage.) What about adding "Here, in my business, the law is the law," Jamil countered. But Mustapha felt that *here* by itself was sufficient because throughout the play, the Attendant made reference to the importance of the rules in his establishment. This would become clear in context, he thought.

In the end, the actors concurred that the meaning of *here* was not crystal clear even in the Arabic text. It could refer to the restroom, but it could also refer to the country. In the latter case, however, it could only be understood ironically by an Algerian. "If you live in a society like Algeria, and an Algerian comes to tell you that 'here, the law is the law,' either he is corrupted or he isn't right in the head," Jamil said. US audiences wouldn't necessarily grasp that irony. Finally, we decided to add *here* back into the text: "Here, the law is the law." In performance, Mustapha let a sonic space around *here* ring out through a short pause. He also underscored the importance of law in his Restroom with a militaristic salute that a junior officer might give to his superior, bringing his hands crisply to his forehead and punctuating the phrase with his feet. This intersemiotic move, in which he used gesture to mirror discourse, did serve to emphasize the phrase in a way that made it stand out for audiences, though there is no way to know how they interpreted the line. {**Video 05.01**}

A similar conversation arose near the end of the play, around the Attendant's line "We have to structure this business and establish professional relation-ships, rights and duties. And think about how to improve our services and profitability now that we have more hands." For the actors, the word *business* (the English term had been taken up into Darija) signified an informal or black market economy. At the same time, *business* also evoked capitalism for them— that is, a business designed to be profitable rather than to provide a public ser-vice. The Attendant seemed to be pointing to this second definition. "Would an old labor unionist say *business*?" Rihab wondered. I chimed in here, saying that I could feel the arrival of capitalism in words like *profitability*. I thought I remembered that Algeria had signed on to its first restructuring plan with the International Monetary Fund in the early 1990s, when the play was writ-ten.[9] The actors continued talking about Algeria's move toward neoliberalism, contrasting it with the country's socialist past. "We were really socialist, com-munist, with the Russians," Jamil said. "And now we're changing to be with the United States."

"It's like the Customer's scene," added Mustapha, "with the change from the social [to] capitalism, [from] the state-run [to] the private."

Rihab countered that Algeria was still fundamentally a socialist, state-based system, but Jamil disagreed. "We're putting all that in the closet," he said, making reference to the Actor's line about being given the marginal role of a wardrobe in the state theater. In the end, we left in the term, knowing that *business* raised a set of associations for the actors that might not be legible in the same way to US audiences. The terms were identical, but their penumbras were different.

Cultural matter sometimes proved challenging enough that we replaced Arabic words with different terms altogether in English. In the last line of the play, the Attendant was trying to gather together his new team, excited to have the Customer and the Actor join forces with him to run the Restroom. The initial translation read, "And now give me a hand, guys. We have to clean the floor quickly. The '*aşr* prayer is coming soon. It will get crowded in here." At first, the actors decided to repeat the last two sentences in Arabic, in a kind of sonic echoing that we used frequently to develop the "bilingual" script. But as the actors were rehearsing that scene, we discussed the fact that US audiences would not understand what the '*aşr* prayer was nor why it mattered. Rather than leaving it opaque or adding a denotational gloss explaining that '*aşr* prayer came in the late afternoon, Jamil decided to substitute clock time for prayer time to make the text maximally intelligible in English: "At 5 o'clock, it will get crowded in here." They then repeated the Arabic phrase after it (*'and el-'aşr yekter el-zeḥām*), with Arabic constituting the last spoken line of the play. Here, then, the use of American cultural understandings guided the translation, but this domesticating move was offset by the Arabic echo.

Discussions around the '*aşr* prayer pointed to another difference that we encountered in translation. In Arabic, it is common for religious formulas to punctuate ordinary speech. Phrases like "God bless the parents," "God willing," or "God bless you" recur frequently in speech but are not generally meant to be interpreted literally. Rather, these formulaic phrases serve a phatic function, working to maintain channels of connection. They are also indexical, locating people as a part of a shared speech community. In English, however, people are not used to hearing phrases like "God bless the parents," so they can sound heavier and more literal than they do in Arabic. Did the actors want these phrases included, I asked. Moussa liked them. He thought this way of speaking was part of the character of the Attendant. Jamil pointed out that Alloula's plays always had a character whose speech would be full of these kinds of formulaic expressions.

Yet Jamil also recognized that this way of speaking was cultural, not religious. It wasn't because the Attendant was a practicing Muslim who did the five daily prayers that he spoke like this. It was simply part of his sociolinguistic milieu. Similarly, talking about the 'aṣr prayer didn't mean that the Attendant was getting ready to pray—it was merely another way of telling time. Moreover, the actors repeatedly emphasized to me that Alloula was writing for his society. He was not writing to show Americans something of Algerian culture. In that spirit, the actors wanted the play to speak to American society. The Attendant's religiously inflected turns of phrase could make him sound different and distant in the United States—which is quite the opposite of the way this populist character was envisioned in Algeria. "Five o'clock" was more consonant with the Attendant's positioning in Algerian society, in that sense, than "the 'aṣr prayer." Here, then, we eschewed denotational translation altogether.

In the end, we made decisions case by case. Sometimes we took the stock religious formulas out, other times we translated them into English, and sometimes we left them in Arabic only. For instance, after the Attendant told the Customer, "I will even handle your funeral," he muttered to himself, "*Nerbaḥ ma'ak ḥasana*" (I'll get points from God). We left this phrase in Arabic only. In a few places, it seemed that Alloula himself may have been pointing ironically to the use of these formulas. When the Attendant told the Customer that it sounded like he was dying, he said, "You are at death's door. God bless you, in advance." The "in advance" was understood as ironic humor in both the Arabic and English versions, and we left it in.

Sonorities and Transformations

One of the key devices we used to create the bilingual script was to retain Arabic sonorities. In most cases, the actors would deliver the same phrase in both English and Arabic. Sometimes one character would say the word in both languages; more often, one character would utter the line in one language, and a second character would repeat it in the other language. A couple of times, the text was delivered in Arabic only.

Sometimes, Arabic was used onomatopoeically to convey something of the sense of the phrase. The first Arabic sounds audiences heard came out of the mouth of the Customer. He had initially entered the Restroom with his hand over his mouth, afraid to release what was there. When he finally spoke, it was in Arabic: "*Bghīt ninfajer, netgarra', netarteg*," he said, the guttural quality of the words pointing to their meaning ("I want to explode, to vomit"). Leaving the Customer's first lines in Arabic only could create an interesting *décalage*, Jamil said; that is, they could open up a "gap" between what audiences heard in Arabic and what they would then understand from subsequent lines. This gap, wherein the sound rings out before the meaning becomes clear, constitutes a foreignizing device, producing a sense of difference at the very beginning of the play. The "word vomit"—the explosion of words the Customer utters when he finally gets permission to use a stall—presents another use of onomatopoeia. This passage is characterized in Arabic by guttural and pharyngeal consonants whose very sound comes from the back of the throat and the pharynx, evoking a sense of retching. In one line, the letter *gh* is found in eight out of nine substantive words. Rihab wanted to leave this in Arabic, so that she could use the sound to convey the Customer's physical release of pent-up frustration. {**Video 05.02**}

Other examples of using both English and Arabic worked more as sonic echoes, with the Arabic coming right before or after the English text. For instance, when the Customer had located apples at the grocer's and was asking for their price, the Customer's line "How much?" was repeated by the Attendant in Arabic, "*Shḥāl?*" Similarly, when the Customer described the scene after the factory was razed, he first uttered "*el-sraḥraḥ*" and followed it immediately with "emptiness." Rihab felt that the Arabic sonority of "*sraḥraḥ*" conveyed a feeling that was missing in the English *empty*. One phrase that stood out for audiences was a proverb voiced by both actors. Rihab, as the Customer, introduced a line the grocer had uttered, using direct reported speech: "The grocer closed the store, uttering the traditional saying . . ." Then Mustapha, voicing the grocer, uttered the proverb in Arabic: "*El-ḥmār mā yeshim el-qerfa.*" Rihab repeated it in English: "The donkey can't appreciate cinnamon." They momentarily assumed similar positions, their identical postures underscoring that they were uttering the same line. {**Video 05.03**}

Proverbs play with the poetics of language in ways that cannot be easily conveyed in translation. This was also the case for the songs and poems. These constituted some of the most strongly "bilingual" (simultaneously domesticating and foreignizing) moments in the play. The English play opens with Rihab singing, from backstage, the first lines of "Killing Me Softly with His Song" as the Attendant makes as if to turn the dial on a radio. The song had been extremely popular in Algeria via the Fugees' 1996 cover. It was also, of course, an American song made famous by Roberta Flack in 1973.[10] Istijmam's decision to use it to open the play was clearly a domesticating move. (The song was part of Istijmam's mise-en-scène, not specified in Alloula's script.) Later on, however, in one of the most opaque moments of the play for US audiences, the Customer asks the Attendant what he should do about his many dilemmas. "Advise me," he says in English, and then repeats in Arabic: "*E'ṭīnī rai*" (Give me your opinion). "Rai," in Arabic, means *opinion*, but it also refers to one of the most popular musical genres in Algeria—rai music. "Give me some rai," the Customer could also be understood as saying. The Attendant plays on this double meaning, kneeling down and launching into one of the most popular rai songs, made famous by the globally renowned rai singer Cheb Khaled.[11] Algerians in the audience always got the joke. At one of the performances in New York, I heard two Algerians behind me repeating the phrase "E'ṭīnī rai" and laughing. Most people in the audience, however, spoke no Arabic and had no idea why the Attendant had suddenly broken into song. But it was such a fun scene that we could not take it out. It stayed in the play as a moment that audiences enjoyed without quite knowing why.

Another bilingual moment occurs sonically when the Customer, who has been sitting quietly in the cube during the Actor's scene, cries out a string of seemingly disconnected images: *peace, relaxation, rose water and children, musk, sugar, cookies, happy feast, thank god, sweets, I am full, lemonade, you are looking awesome in your new clothes, fried dough with raisins, my shoes are tight, it is painful.* As with the word vomit, this is another quasi hallucinatory scene, but the images here are mostly joyous, many referring to the Muslim holy day ʿeid. In this passage, the troupe made the decision to alternate between English and Arabic, retaining terms in Arabic that had no easy English translation. For instance, "Happy ʿeīd" was left in Arabic (*ṣeḥḥa ʿeīdek*). Other terms we left in Arabic included *sharbāt* (a specific Algerian lemon-based beverage), *ḥelwet miliāna* (sweets), *el-sfenj bi-l-zbīb* (fried dough with raisins), *el-ḥinna* (peace), *mā el-zahr wa-l-awlād* (rose water and children), and *sukkur el-qālib* (raw sugar).

The only time US audiences heard long strings of Arabic text came in the poems at the end of the play. The poems were performed bilingually, with the actors trading Arabic and English lines back and forth. Rihab would deliver a line in English. Moussa would provide the translation of that line in Arabic and then deliver the next line in English, which Rihab would deliver in Arabic. From the actors' perspectives, every line of every poem was translated. But the audience did not necessarily understand that the English and the Arabic mirrored each other. For the actors, including the Arabic lines was both sonically and culturally important. "There are sonorities in Arabic that are really beautiful. I didn't want to lose them," said Moussa. "It's good to have [the US] public hear popular poetry," Mustapha added.

Retaining the sounds of Algerian Arabic was perhaps the key means of making the text "bilingual"—that is, foreignizing the text for US audiences while at the same time domesticating it for the troupe members. They chose the passages to deliver Arabic "by feel" (*"au feeling"*), Jamil said in response to an audience question. These decisions were usually made around the table, but they sometimes came about in rehearsal as the actors experienced how the play felt in their mouths and bodies. To them, the bilingual version would allow for a sensory or synaesthetic (Kapchan 2003, 148) encounter with the sonic qualities of language for both themselves and their audiences. It let the actors bring with them to the US stage some of the "affect that resides in the mother tongue" (Kapchan 2003, 142). At the same time, retaining some phrases in Arabic may have constituted what Lawrence Venuti has called "a dissident cultural practice" (2008, 148), or a way of resisting the hegemony of English-language translation, though the actors did not say this in so many words.

The phrases that we left in Arabic also offer examples of the translational practice that Michael Silverstein (2003) called transformation, wherein a term comes to mean something "substantially or completely different" from what it signified in the initial source text (2003, 91). Silverstein focuses on the transformation that occurs when ethnographers lift a term out of their "field" language and make it symbolize (untranslated) the larger culture as well as the ethnographer's own analysis of that culture. He gives the example of the term "kula," which has become a shorthand way of evoking Bronislaw Malinowski's work in the Trobriand Islands. Whereas in the Trobriands it referred to a particular kind of trading practice, in the scholarly literature it has been transformed in ways that separate it from its context of use: now, it also points to Malinowski's ethnography.

For English-speaking audiences, the Arabic terms in *Apples* are separated in somewhat related ways from both their denotational signifiers and their contexts of use. They point to a cultural location grounded in difference, offering a periodic sonic reminder that the play came from elsewhere. After a post-tour video screening of the play that I held at Indiana University, two participants who had previously seen *Apples* live talked about the inclusion of Arabic. "I was glad to have that Arabic in there, interspersed. I thought it stretched it out, made it larger," one said. "Whatever they're saying specifically that's not in English has a visceral impact on the ear and on my ear, and I feel like it translates the story in such a way that even though I don't speak Arabic, there's something that I connect to with that," added another.

Word Play

Plays on words are highly specific to particular languages and speech communities and are notoriously difficult to translate. We talked at some length about two moments of word play in *Et-Teffeh* that we wanted to try to convey in *Apples*. In the end, we reconfigured them by seeking new words and phrases that worked according to the same poetic principles in both languages, but we did not reproduce the denotational content.

The first moment occurs when the Actor enters the Restroom. He is blown away not only by the acoustics but also by the cleanliness and even the "lovely smells" of the space. For many years, maintaining cleanliness in public rest-rooms in Algeria was no small feat due to nationwide water rationing. That is, water did not run through the faucets twenty-four/seven but would be turned on at intervals ranging from an hour or two a day to a morning once or twice a week. (In some remote regions in the summer, it could be as little as once every three weeks or more.) Flushing toilets without running water is of course prob-lematic. Attendants in public restrooms would need to store water in rooftop tanks or large plastic barrels and bring buckets to the individual stalls. (The Attendant refers to this practice when he says, "I have to go bring some water to a customer.") Having a Restroom with the capacity to store sufficient water was the best case scenario; the worst, well . . .

The Restroom's good hygiene becomes the subject of a play on words. In *Et-Teffeh*, the Actor utters the line "What hygiene," using the French phrase *"quelle hygiène"* (pronounced ee-jen). The Attendant, apparently unfamiliar with this French term, hears the second syllable as *jinn*, an Arabic term referring to a troublesome spirit that can inhabit people. "No sir, there is no jinn," he insists. In Arabic, this always got a laugh. We weren't sure how to convey this moment in English. US audiences wouldn't know what *jinn* meant. I thought the term *genie* might do the trick.[12] We translated the passage like this.

> Actor: What hygiene!
> Attendant: Genie? No, no sir, there is no genie, no evil spirit. May god protect us.

We had the Attendant repeat *genie* and also give the denotational gloss "evil spirit" to make it clearer that he had heard *genie* instead of *hygiene*. It was not as good a match as the French *hygiene* and the Arabic *jinn* because of the added "-ie" on *genie*, but it was all we could come up with. It was never clear to me whether audiences got the joke.

Another play on words involved substituting entirely new terms. In *Et-Teffeh*, the Actor utters a French term, *"magnifique."* The Attendant hears *"fric"* (money, in slang used commonly in both France and Algeria). We translated this by finding a new play on words.

> Actor: Divine!
> Attendant: Wine? No, not wine. He's like this because of the apples.

Again, it was unclear whether audiences picked up on this. The play between *fique* and *fric* might have worked better than that between *divine* and *wine*. What the translation in both cases fails to convey is the relative sociolinguistic status of the characters. For Algerians, it would have been clear that the Actor had a certain level of education: he was obviously someone who knew at least enough French to be able to sprinkle it into his vocabulary. It would also have been apparent to Algerian audiences that the Attendant had had limited exposure to French.

In performance, US audiences discovered another play on words that we did not intentionally create (and that is not found in the Arabic text). The Actor is talking about how he was given a small role in a play just to be "placated." Some audience members appeared to hear this as "play-cated," creating a pun out of the first syllable. The line would get occasional laughter.

Embodied Play

Mirroring or reinforcing text by embodied gesture is, of course, a key form of conveying meaning. Throughout the translation sessions, the actors would repeatedly talk about how *le jeu*, by which they meant the "play" of stagecraft, would help to clarify meanings that did not readily translate. The body, here, becomes a medium of translation. We see this from the moment the Customer starts speaking: "My stomach is up in my throat, my intestines are tied in knots, and my pulse is racing." Rihab, as Customer, embodies each of these statements, her arms and hands first rising, then spinning in circles, then pulsing at her heart. This embodied or intersemiotic mirroring is visible throughout the play. In a particularly humorous example, Mustapha, as the Attendant, tries to explain to the Actor why granting permission to the Customer to enter a stall was still in line with house rules. As Mustapha goes into a headstand, he utters the line, "He's just emptying out—in reverse."

LANGUAGE IDEOLOGY: JULIUS CAESAR
BETWEEN ARABIC AND ENGLISH

Recall that when the Actor enters the Restroom, he is so taken by the acoustics that he starts reciting a famous Shakespearean passage: Brutus's speech to the Romans after the assassination of Julius Caesar. In *Et-Teffeh*, this passage was performed in Arabic translation. Alloula presumably used an available translation of *Julius Caesar* in Modern Standard Arabic (MSA) when he embedded the lines in his script. When they translated *Et-Teffeh* into *Apples*, Istijmam's translators Malik and Nabil put the lines back into Shakespearean English, using standard text from the play found on the No Fear Shakespeare website.[13] The translation of this passage thus required no deliberation on our part. But when the actors rendered the lines in English after performing them in Arabic for years, this passage came to life for them—and for the characters they played—in new ways. As these lines traveled from English to Arabic and back to English, they pointed us to various layers of cultural matter, starting with language ideology.

From a perspective of language ideology—that is, what people believe about how languages operate socially, culturally, and politically[14]—languages are not all valued equally. Different languages may be understood to play competing cultural roles and may be endowed with unequal social or political value. In Algeria, four languages—MSA, Algerian Darija, Tamazight (Berber), and French—constitute the linguistic field. One of the country's major tasks following independence from France in 1962 was to "Arabicize" the population, replacing French, the language of the colonizer, with MSA in the state administrative offices, the courts, and the public education system. MSA was ideologically cast as authentically Algerian even though few Algerians at the time had studied or could speak MSA. Although this was a necessary move in the postcolonial context, it was also seen by some as controversial because it erased the country's African (Amazigh) and francophone heritages. Moreover, whereas Tamazight was politically and pedagogically supported by a significant Amazigh identity movement[15] and eventually came to be taught as an option in some public schools, Darija has never been placed on equal footing with MSA and has not even achieved the limited status that Tamazight enjoys.

In *Et-Teffeh*, the Shakespearean lines, cast in MSA, strongly contrast with the Darija that the rest of the play employs. According to Jamil, when the Actor uttered the Shakespearean passages in MSA, he could have been understood in the Algeria of the 1990s only by a certain category of people that Jamil referred to in French as "arabisants," or a faction of the governing elite who were ideologically committed to an Arabo-Islamic Algeria and who could use MSA fluently. As a practical matter, Arabization in the public schools had been rolled out gradually.[16] This meant that most educated Algerians of Alloula's generation (including Alloula himself) had been schooled primarily in French, not MSA (though Alloula learned MSA on his own). So for Jamil, when Alloula—who usually wrote in an artistic colloquial Darija—inserted a passage in MSA, this had to be understood as an ideological move. As Jamil put it, audiences "are listening to the play and then at a certain moment you put a passage where there's only a single group of people who can understand it, that is on purpose (*'c'est voulu'*)." From Jamil's perspective, Alloula was using these lines to address the ideologues advocating for a monolingual Arabophone Algeria. In other words, Alloula was speaking about the abuses of power in power's own language.

As a form of cultural matter, the language ideology that positions MSA above Darija is configured differently than the ideology surrounding the gap between contemporary spoken English and Shakespearean English. Whereas Shakespearean English marks a historical period and is no longer in use, MSA is a contemporary language. Throughout the Arab world, it is now the language of state, the language of the news media, and the language of the public education system.[17] At home, however, no one speaks MSA: each country or region has its own variety of spoken Arabic. When Rihab initially heard Moussa deliver Brutus's lines in Shakespearean English, she realized that she couldn't feel the difference with ordinary spoken English the way she did in Arabic. "When we performed in Arabic," she said, "given that the rest of the play was in Darija, and here, there was another level of language, so that brings you directly to another attitude. But given that we are not English [speakers], we don't feel this difference in level. We have to double our efforts. . . . That's why he [Moussa] can't be transported [in the passage], because we don't feel English enough. . . . I don't know what we have to do." She initially wanted Moussa to mark it via his performance, by being more "extravagant," more demonstrative with his voice and body. But she then realized that the problem lay in the linguistic economy, where the languages had different relative values.

Language ideology also endows languages with affective charge. Jamil felt that Alloula's use of MSA was more "direct"—to the point of being "blunt"—than was Alloula's usual practice. Jamil reiterated many times to me that Alloula's texts rarely contained direct political messages, that his politics were generally implicit in the stories. "It's genius," Jamil said, "that Alloula used the language of Shakespeare to speak bluntly. When other Algerian playwrights do this [speak bluntly], they lower the level of the language. But here, Alloula raised it by using Shakespeare. And he didn't take just any passage—he took the passage from Brutus after he killed Julius Caesar, who was a dictator, and Brutus speaks to the people."

The difference in language ideology between the Arabic and English texts constitutes an indexical penumbra that is essentially untranslatable. That being said, not all Algerian audiences would interpret Alloula's use of MSA the way Jamil did. For one thing, by the time Istijmam first performed the play in 2009, far more young Algerians had been schooled in MSA than was the case when Alloula wrote the play in the early 1990s. For another, audience members had different understandings of why Alloula had used the Shakespeare passage to begin with. Nevertheless, the MSA–Darija relationship is not at all the same as the relationship between Shakespearean and contemporary English. The gap between these registers has an entirely different cultural and ideological charge in English than it does in Arabic.

Characterization and Affect

Arabic was also used to bring to life minor characters. When Rihab animated the Neighbor who tried to shut up the Customer at the grocer, she first uttered his words in English and then repeated them in Darija with a somewhat different inflection. She also played the Neighbor as an old man, stooped over, his hand shaking, his voice breaking. Creating the social persona of the Neighbor seems to have entailed putting Darija in his mouth even on the US stage. {**Video 05.04**}

Similarly, when Rihab and Mustapha co-animated the court scene, Mustapha stepped outside his primary role as Attendant to take on the role of the group of old women. He gave a voice in Darija to the woman recounting a tale of woe about her husband, who had met with all kinds of indignities at the hands of the courts and ended up dying without proper burial. Here, translation was built into the mise-en-scène in *Apples*, as the woman (Mustapha) gestured to Rihab to translate her words. This self-conscious performance of translation elicited audience laughter in the United States—not only because Mustapha played the woman comically but perhaps also because this was the only scene in the play that made the translation process explicit. It was clearly not part of the Arabic text. {**Video 05.05**}

In both passages, Darija was used to indicate something about the sociolinguistic status of the characters being portrayed. Yet this distance was not linguistically marked in the Arabic script, so in the Algerian performances, the characters could be in direct contact with the spectators. In the English version, they were linguistically bound, fixed in a position as Darija speakers where they could not reach the audience and were thus in need of translation. In Bakhtin's terms, they were "stylized" as representatives of a sociolinguistic type (Bakhtin 1981, 362).

As the script was translated into English, some of the characters themselves underwent transformation. The actors described this as a "softening." Rihab told me that she experienced the Policeman (one of her secondary roles) as more nuanced and multidimensional in English than she had in Arabic. This was noticeable even in some of the sonic echoes. For instance, when the Actor is clearly eager to rehearse the Shakespeare passage in the Restroom, the Attendant finally gives up. In Arabic, the line reads "*el-zar' yinbet*," which the translators rendered as "Tell me exactly what you want right now." This felt heavy, so we changed it to "Okay, go ahead." We decided to retain the Arabic phrase as an echo because the English didn't quite capture the meaning of the Arabic. But in performance, the line gradually began to take on a different charge in Arabic than it had in English. Jamil remarked that when Mustapha delivered the line, it sounded more aggressive and angry in Arabic than the corresponding English phrase. Mustapha softened it to match the affective tone of English.

CULTURAL MATTER AND THE
MATERIALITY OF LANGUAGE

The passage from *Julius Caesar* raised another issue that the actors and I had to contend with throughout the translation sessions: How would the English lines resonate in the mouth and the body? We sought not only to locate a term in English that would best convey the meaning of the Arabic term but to do so in a way that would work for the stage. We were approaching translation through a lens of performance, looking, as Jamil put it, "for the action in the word." Literary translations make use of paratextual devices like prefaces, annotations, and footnotes to situate the text in its larger context. Actors have no access to those devices. They must convey meaning through embodied performance and vocal delivery.[18] This was particularly palpable in the passages from *Julius Caesar*. The meter, rhythm, and prosody of vocal delivery became part of our morning translation sessions.

The passages from *Julius Caesar* are cast in Shakespearean English through a poetic form designed to travel: its parallel phrases, repetitions, and rhythms make the text easily transportable from one context—or one play—to another.[19] But this poetic form was not initially apparent to Moussa. As we did every morning, we began the session with the actors reading the passage aloud. Then we reviewed it line by line.

> Moussa (reciting the text): If then that friend demand why I rose against Caesar, this is my answer: not that I loved . . .
> Jamil (cutting him off): You see, that's fast. Here you have a colon. You were asked why [you rose against Caesar]. This is your response. [You're taking] pronunciation too fast sometimes.
> Jane: I think so as well. In this sentence, it's Shakespearean English, it is not very well understood. You really have to enter into the speech.
> Jamil: We sense that you are looking for a logic in the sentence, whereas you don't know it . . . you are looking for a meaning. You're not sure of it. Mark the colon.
> Moussa: Sometimes I skip (*zapper*) this step, Jamil. Sometimes I go looking for the character (*personage*), the feeling of the character, you see? I try to look for what he feels, and I skip the foundation of the text. Yes, it's true.

This sonic and embodied encounter with the poetics of the text continued into the next passage. Its meaning could emerge only through the actor's ability to emphasize and then break with its parallel structures:

> *As Caesar loved me, I weep for him;*
> *as he was fortunate, I rejoice at it;*

as he was valiant, I honor him:
but, as he was ambitious, I slew him.

The first three phrases each begin with *as*, making the *but* of the fourth phrase stand out, requiring a longer pause around it. Three more parallel structures follow, with abstract nouns (for the most part) grouped on either side of the prepositional clause "for his."

There is tears for his love;
joy for his fortune;
honor for his valor;
and death for his ambition.

These too require a longer pause before the fourth phrase and additional emphasis on the words *death* and *ambition*.

Jamil said, "Do you see the rhythm? 'There is tears for his love; joy for his fortune, honor for his valor.' You feel that there is a rhythm. There are semicolons. That means that there is a rhythm."

The final quoted passage in *Apples* is similarly parallel, structured around three iterations of a question.

Who is here so base that would be a bondman? If any, speak; for him have I
offended.
Who is here so rude that would not be a Roman? If any, speak; for him have I
offended.
Who is here so vile that will not love his country? If any, speak; for him have I
offended.
I pause for a reply.

Jane: "If any, speak"—you need to put in a long pause. You are going too fast. "If any—pause—speak."
Jamil: Even stronger. Excuse me, Jane. "If any—pause—speak—longer pause."
Jane: Yes, that's it.
[...]
Moussa: Okay.
Jamil: Comma after the first [phrase] and semicolon after the second.
Jane: Exactly.

Here, the cultural matter that infused the text with meaning was located in timing and vocal emphasis. It had to be sensed in the body and sonically articulated. As Jamil put it, Moussa had to "feel the question mark in the sentence."

Translating here became a synaesthetic or sensory process, experienced through the senses in the body of the performer (Kapchan 2003, 148).[20]

As Moussa worked on the passage, he gradually came to sense it differently in English than he had in Arabic. "When Alloula wrote it, when he put in the passage translated in Arabic, he didn't put it in Algerian Arabic (Darija). He put it in classical Arabic, in order to have this rhythm, this gap (*décalage*), this shift in tone, this shift in timing, in rhythm. But in English, I feel it as flagrant."

The poetics of language—its meters and cadences, rhythms and rhymes—are among the most difficult (if not impossible) to translate and are most often lost (or at best, transformed) in translation.[21] When Moussa performed the passage in its original English, he had to find the poetics of language through his mouth, voice, and body. When he did, the passage generated an affective charge that had not been present when Istijmam performed the Arabic text.[22] For Rihab, "the passage became even more powerful in English." In one performance in the United States (Indiana University), she was in her usual position during the Actor's scene, occupying a corner of stage (ostensibly in a restroom stall) where she is sitting by the cube, head down. When the Actor reaches the line "Not that I loved Caesar less, but that I loved Rome more," she is supposed to change her position to sit on the cube. But on that night, she found herself bound by the power of Moussa's performance to the point of being unable to move. "Usually I am with my cube, and when I utter a line, it's very precisely timed (*ponctuel*), as Moussa is acting. Me, at that time I'm listening a lot because I'm not facing him . . . and at a certain moment, at the first passage, I'm supposed to change position in my cube . . . and in Indiana, Moussa starts speaking [as Brutus], and there is a force that rises, an emotion that rises. It was very, very strong. I was utterly unable to budge! I did not change positions. Even though it was a stage direction, I didn't change position. . . . I couldn't move. There was an atmosphere so charged, so charged with emotion. . . . It was simply impossible to interrupt that atmosphere. I don't know how to explain it to you. There was something in the air that was extremely strong." Rihab had encountered what Patrick Eisenlohr terms a "sonic atmosphere," wherein the acoustic dimensions of sound intensify the discursive contents of language to produce an experience of being "carried away" (Eisenlohr 2018, 127).

This feeling of "something in the air" that became palpable via what for the actors was an English translation points to how the poetics of language (rhyme, meter, vocal emphasis) were materially constituted through breath, pitch, and resonance. The charge of a text performed anew in translation was similarly felt when Istijmam gave an impromptu run-through of the play for the interns at Double Edge Theatre in Ashfield, Massachusetts. Travis Coe was among them.

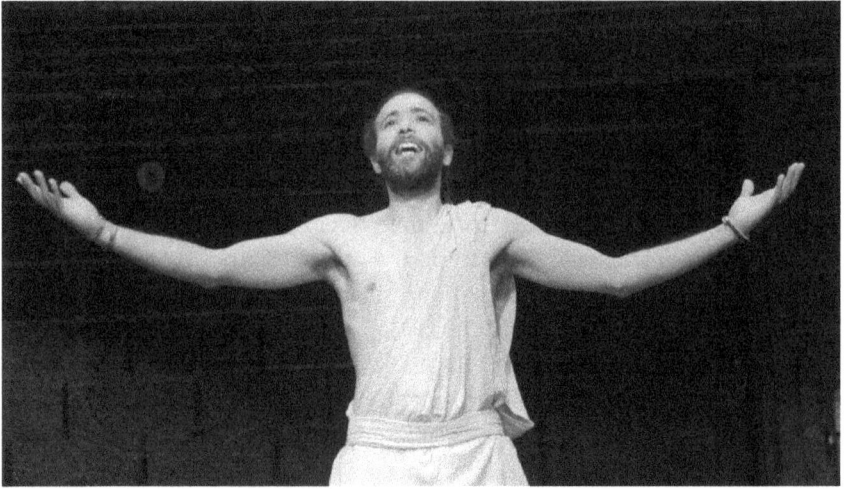

Figure 5.1. Moussa recites a passage from *Julius Caesar*, La MaMa Theater, September 2016. Photo credit: Istijmam Culturelle.

That evening, Travis sat talking about the play with some of us on the porch of the Inn at Norton Hill, where we were lodged. The next day, he and I spoke again. His perspective is worth quoting at some length.

> I feel like we know Shakespeare so well here. And what I was saying last night was that it's very intellectual, our approach to Shakespeare, it's very text based. . . . And so, when I saw it yesterday with the company, I saw it in a whole new way because, and he was doing it in English, you know, the text was brought back to the English language, but I felt it in such a different way, like it wasn't an intellectual conversation with it. It was a passionate conversation with it, a physical conversation with it. . . . And I think what he did was meet the text in a way that was about getting to the core of what the speech was speaking to, instead of being like, "Ah, the rhythms of it and the meticulousness of making sure that I'm breathing at this certain point." It's like, no, drop all that and approach the text from you. Approach the text from a very immediate place. And like I was saying last night, I've never felt Shakespeare be so relevant again. So, contemporary again. . . . It's like this breath of fresh air that sort of punched you in the gut and then slapped you in the face, and then made you, made your eyes water. . . . I hope to always do Shakespeare like that.[23]

In sum, Moussa found an affective or embodied charge in the English text that he had not found in Arabic. This charge was generated when he encountered poetic structures in the English text (parallel phrases, rhythm, and meter) that were not present in the Arabic translation with which he was familiar. Like other forms of cultural matter, poetics cannot be directly conveyed in translation. It was Moussa's very unfamiliarity with Shakespearean poetics in English, and the ways he deviated from more familiar performances of these lines, that enabled audience members like Travis to find something new in translation.

TRANSLATING THE SHADOW PLAY

Embedded texts—or texts that are inside other texts—stand out from the main story of *Apples* in ways that make them particularly accessible for analysis and discussion. Both the Shakespearean passage and what I call the shadow play constitute such embedded texts. Unlike *Julius Caesar*, which is recognized worldwide, the shadow play is an original text, coming from the Actor's (and Alloula's) imagination. I use the term *shadow play* to refer to the play that the Actor has developed on his own and seeks to rehearse in the Restroom. (Note that my use of the term is distinct from the traditional shadow theater or shadow puppetry that is also found in the Arab world.) I call the Actor's play the shadow play for two reasons: it centers around a character with a shadow or negative side, and it shadows the text of *Apples* itself. As a play-inside-the-play, it sketches a picture of a society torn apart by forms of collusion and corruption that perhaps could not be approached directly.

The shadow play features a character whom the Actor describes as split, two-faced, and "schizophrenic." On the surface, he is a "good person"—honest, loyal, and upstanding. He has no vices: "he doesn't even chew gum." But beneath the surface lurks his shadow: a gambler, a smuggler. He writes profanities on the walls. He commits blasphemy during the call to prayer. He steals the policeman's whistle, taking for himself the authority of the state. In short, he violates the very principles that hold the society together. As the play unfolds, the shadow appears to become rehabilitated. He puts on a *chechia*, or headscarf—the kind that pious Muslims in some parts of the world might use to pray. But looks do not tell the whole story. In the context of *Apples*, the shadow play was described by the Actor (Moussa) to the Attendant (Mustapha). As Moussa described the play, he and the Attendant began acting it out. Mustapha, as Attendant, entered into the Actor's fantasy until he suddenly became aware of the subversiveness of the Actor's vision and broke away, reverting to his primary role as the Restroom Attendant.

We spent two full mornings finalizing the translation of the shadow play, lingering over it longer than any other part of the script. It is written in a cryptic, imagistic style that the actors themselves did not claim to fully comprehend. "It is absurd," Rihab said, referring to the genre of theater made famous by

Figure 5.2. Moussa and Mustapha enact the shadow play, La MaMa Theater, September 2016. Photo credit: Istijmam Culturelle.

(among others) Samuel Beckett and Eugène Ionesco. Moussa captured this absurd quality when he called the passage "psychedelic." As we went through the shadow play line by line and word by word, it raised questions about duplicity, collusion, corruption, and the two-faced nature of power that were both anchored in Algerian history and able to transcend time and place. Yet the shadow play was so laden with cultural matter that it often proved difficult to translate. It conveyed images that felt light in Darija but became heavy in English. When we tried to translate or gloss an indexical penumbra surrounding a word or phrase, we repeatedly ran up against a feeling of heaviness and a sense that the aesthetics of the line were being lost.

Because our discussion around this passage was particularly rich and extensive, I use it to conclude this chapter's exploration of the kinds of cultural matter we encountered in translation. Tracking conversations among the actors and me about the shadow play gives a sense of the emergent and dialogical nature of our work around the table. These conversations also shadow the translational work itself, offering an extended glimpse into a form of labor that usually remains unseen.

Shadows in/of Translation

The good character in the shadow play is described in Arabic as someone who "never looks behind himself." Nabil and Malik had translated this as "never looks over his shoulder." While not inaccurate, I didn't think this phrase would mean anything to US audiences. I could not come up with a colloquial equivalent at the time. We discussed it at some length. In what follows, I am translating from French and Darija.

> Mustapha: The person who doesn't look behind himself is a person who has nothing to reproach himself about, who has never had a problem with anyone.
> Moussa: He has no fear that someone will attack him from behind.
> Jamil: He doesn't look behind himself in the sense that he is not afraid of the blows of an enemy. Because someone who looks behind himself, he is always . . .
> Rihab: He fears being attacked because he did something bad. But [here], he hasn't done anything bad.
> Jamil: Even in Arabic, it isn't obvious. And if we say, "He is extremely loyal, he never looks over his shoulder"?
> Jane: I think that it won't be understood very well, "he never looks over his shoulder." . . . We would be more likely to say he "never looks back," but it's not the same thing . . . [it means that] he doesn't question himself, what he has done in the past.
> Jamil: Yes, it can have that meaning. . . . It's true what they said, Amine and Mustapha, about how he doesn't fear enemies because he's only done good . . . but "he doesn't look behind himself " . . . in the sense that he doesn't look back at his past, he doesn't ask himself questions. . . . It's true, it has multiple meanings.
> Jane: What doesn't work is he "never looks over his shoulder." . . . "He isn't rattled by what others think"? . . .
> Jamil: I have the feeling that it's a little heavy. . . .
> Rihab: Can we say "He never hurts someone and is extremely loyal"? . . .
> Jamil: What is very important in this line, it's that the story needs to be very clear. That's very important. In Arabic, it works because we need to have these details, and sometimes, the details are not heavy. . . . But I feel like it becomes heavy [in English] . . . it's as if you are adding something that you don't need. [Jamil then reads aloud the Arabic text, emphasizing its poetic nature.] But in translation, it's unnecessary detail (*du détail en plus*).
> Jane: Yes, it slows down the story, makes it heavier. . . .
> Jamil: "He doesn't even chew gum" . . . "never looks over his shoulder," it's too much.
> {Video 05.06}

Although this is a minor example, it gives a sense of how words that sounded light in the Arabic phrase became heavy when translated into English. The "lighter," more colloquial phrases I suggested in English didn't adequately capture the meaning. In this case, we opted to simply take out the phrase, deciding that the rest of the text conveyed what audiences needed to know about the "good character."

We made a different choice several lines later, with the word *chechia*. As the Actor describes it, the bad character changes into the good character simply by changing his look, by putting on the chechia "like Muslims do in the mosque." The Arabic text does not contain this explanatory phrase about Muslim sartorial practices. Algerians would have known that a chechia referred to a man's head scarf, and they would have known that at the time, it was ideologically associated with a particular brand of piety. But to tell American audiences simply that the man put on a chechia meant nothing. Most wouldn't even recognize the word, let alone what it indexed about one's ideological position in 1990s Algeria. Nabil and Malik had added the denotational gloss "like Muslims do in the mosque." We left the explanation but lightened it further by removing the verb *do*—changing it, Moussa said, from a practice to a description.

The next part of the shadow play was even more difficult to convey. Whereas the bad character seizes power by changing his look, the good character loses his way altogether. Malik and Nabil's original translation hewed closely to the Arabic: "The good character loses his way and gets tattoos on his chest." The Actor (Moussa), playing the lost good character, then breaks into a well-known song about immigration, "Seknet Marseille" ("She lived in Marseilles").[24] No one will know this song, I said. Few would know of the popular rai genre, even though it had put Algeria on the world music map in the 1980s. No one would know the Algerian singer Zohra, who had made it popular in the 1990s. No one would know that it was referring to the heavy Algerian immigration to the French Mediterranean city of Marseilles for most of the twentieth century. Few would even know about Algeria's long colonial relationship with France. No one would know that any Algerians with the means to leave the country in the 1990s were doing so. And no one would know what the tattoos were meant to convey. How could we translate this?

> Jamil: I want to ask the question, why did he do this tattooing, in your opinion? And why "Seknet Marseille" and not another song? Because we have to orient the spectator.
>
> Moussa: For me, the first meaning of the song, it's as if he was drunk, but the second meaning is maybe immigration . . . because at one point the song says, "I will reserve a seat on a boat, for the plane (*avion*) you need *piston* (influence)." It's as if he says to this person who put on a chechia, "I can't stay, I'm leaving the country."

Mustapha: At that time, it was the beginning of the violence in Algeria, 1991, 1992. I think that those who were less serious put on a chechia, and those who were more serious left the country, fleeing to live in Marseilles. [...]

Jamil: The point we agree on is that it's a song that talks about exile. It's important to orient the spectator instead of just leaving the song like that.

Jane: Yes, people won't understand. Are there lines from the song that we could add?

Jamil: Without actually explaining the meaning, because the phrase is "Seknet Marseille." When this song is sung, only Algerians can understand. Even if I tell you, "She lived in Marseilles," that makes no sense.... What I'd like to say is [he tattoos] *on his chest a song that talks about exile.* That's all. Just listen to the tune because ... there is the melody of the song that transports you ...

Rihab: That makes you travel ...

We continued experimenting with various ways to make the scene's meaning more apparent to US audiences. Eventually, we settled on a combination of text, song, and embodied action. Moussa, as the Actor, would describe the lost good character as someone who had tattooed on his chest a song about exile, adding denotational explanation not found in the Arabic script. He would then sing the song while pretending to row a boat on the sea. That way, the embodied action in the mise-en-scène would reinforce the line's meaning. "It's clear," I said, "but will they understand that at the time, everyone wanted to leave Algeria?"

"We don't care," said Jamil. "After, maybe it will come out in the talk-backs. Because if we go there, we won't talk about anything else. The meaning of the line doesn't go there. ... But tattooing on your body a song about exile, that already means that people are going into exile because they are troubled. It's not because they want to leave their country."

The last lines of the shadow play become even more cryptic. The Attendant and the Actor both suspend their primary roles, joining forces to become the characters in the shadow play. The two characters sit on a hilltop pontificating about their society while, above their heads, angels fight with daggers, blood dripping down on them like rain. This passage underwent considerable re-translation from Nabil and Malik's initial English version. Who were these characters? What were they talking about? What authorized them to speak? What were they doing?

Conversation spun out around the verb *yeftī*, which shares a root with *fatwa* and relates to the issuing of religious opinions or orders.[25] Nabil and Malik had chosen to add denotational text to bring out the meaning of the Arabic text. Their translation read, "The two characters are sitting on the top of a hill leaning on each other, doing the work of the mufti, issuing Islamic fatwas to the society." "Issuing fatwas, that is not mentioned [in the Arabic text]," Rihab said. For US audiences, the translators had added this explication of what the work of the mufti, or the religious leader, was about. Jamil wanted to take it out, contending that the larger point was that "they were speaking about the negative aspects of the nation" and proffering judgments. "But they were poorly placed to give fatwas, that's what needs to get brought out," Rihab added. "We need to find a verb that gives a sense that they were philosophizing about their society even as they were noting [what was happening] and judging—all of that is in yeftī, it's strong, this verb."

We struggled to find an equivalent in English. I threw out several possibilities: philosophize, deliberate, examine, contemplate, moralize. Nothing quite worked. At first, we settled on *moralizing*, but I wasn't happy with it. The verb *pontificate* came to me that evening. I liked its religious (albeit Catholic) overtones and the sense that those who pontificated were speaking not from within but from outside their society, a bit out of touch, looking down from above without actually being engaged. The cultural matter around *pontificate* was not an exact match for yeftī, but it seemed closer.

Counter-Strike

When we tackled the final part of the passage, I admitted that I simply did not understand it. Angels fighting with daggers? Blood dripping down on them like rain? We batted the images around a bit. How to understand this person on the mountaintop who is talking with his shadow, and then there are angels? Was it the good angel on the right shoulder and the bad angel on the left? But angels weren't supposed to fight in Islam. Jamil thought it showed the darkness into which society had fallen: Was it a sign of the shaky times we were living in that even angels were fighting? Rihab countered: "It's an absurd image, isn't it?" At one point she wondered aloud, "If we're sitting around the table [discussing this] and asking ourselves questions, what will it be like for the spectator?"

At the end, the shadow play dissolves into brief phrases that the two characters volley back and forth.

> "Did you know that the newspaper colludes with the intelligence services?"
> "The intelligence services collude with illusion."
> "Citizens without hope."
> "The price of cannabis rises."

"Religious leaders sell out to foreign interests."
"This Imam is doing illegal business."
"Political leaders steal from thieves."
"The builder's house is in ruin."
"The doors and the windows of the boss's house are made of steel."
"The roof of ivory."
"The floor of marble, and so on."
{Video 05.07}

For Moussa, these images evoked the first-person shooter game *Counter-Strike*.

> There were musicians, philosophers, playwrights killed, and it wasn't
> just by terrorists. There was also a settling of scores. That's why I call the
> Dark Decade the decade of *Counter-Strike*. *Counter-Strike* . . . you start the
> game, you take up a weapon, and you start killing. For me, that's the Dark
> Decade. . . . It was senseless, it didn't mean anything, it was psychedelic. If
> "angels are fighting with daggers," it's all over: the image of peace, serenity,
> purity . . . and now the angels are making war. . . . It's the apocalypse. It's an
> apocalyptic image. We could say that the apocalypse was born in Algeria. . . .
> Because today in Algeria, we have no philosophers, we have no playwrights,
> we have no filmmakers.

On stage, these harsh images are thrown out so quickly that it's hard for
a spectator to hang on to them. They lack the memorable poetic ring of Brutus's speech. Yet the shadow play does convey something of the ambivalent
performances of power, the ways it can reveal one face while hiding a more
nefarious face beneath it. It puts into play the ways good and evil coexist, in
tension, in the same person, the same community, the same country, in how
they simultaneously inhabit power, making it always two-faced, always hard
to pin down. From the schizophrenic character who dresses evil in piety to
cryptic images of collusion, false intelligence, corrupt leaders, a press that
sells out to foreign influence, theft by those in power . . . It is no wonder the
Attendant fears that he will lose his job if he lets the Actor stage the shadow
play in the Restroom.

FROM TEXTUAL TO "ROUGH" TRANSLATION

Our exercise in translating the text line-by-line and word-by-word points with
fascinating specificity to the kinds of cultural matter that we encountered as *Et-
Teffeh* became *Apples*. In effect, the cultural exchange that Istijmam anticipated
may have taken place around the table perhaps even more than in the United

States itself. By bringing our conversations into this account, I am opening up the considerable backstage labor that the troupe and I took on in preparation for the US tour.

On tour, the actors and audiences engaged in a different kind of transla-tion exercise—an exercise that I am calling "rough translation" after the NPR podcast of the same title.[26] The podcast asks, "How are the things we're talking about being talked about somewhere else in the world?" Rephrased to remove from the center a presumed North American *we*: How do debates and questions raised in one time or place spark or speak to similar debates in another time or place?[27] On the one hand, the translation process enabled the Algerian actors to look back at their own society some twenty-five years earlier. At the same time, they looked across the sea to the United States. Following *Apples* as it has circulated (and continues to circulate via video) among US audiences reveals how, like a halqa, it has opened up various stories with which both Algerians and Americans grapple: from the conundrums of late capitalist modernity to the connections between art and politics.

NOTES

1. New York, La MaMa Theater, September 29, 2016.

2. On domesticating and foreignizing moves in translation, see especially Venuti 1998, 2013.

3. Azpak n.d.

4. Because I was not present for their translation process, I do not discuss it here.

5. Venuti 2012 offers a comprehensive history of the debates in translation theory.

6. As Michael Silverstein (2003) explains, in the material world, transduction occurs when one form of energy is converted to another form, such as when the force of water is converted to electricity through a hydroelectric generator. In the linguistic world, transduction occurs when cultural matter from one language takes a different form in another language.

7. My use of the term "indexical penumbra" is somewhat expanded from Silverstein's usage. He describes it as the "tone . . . of a word or expression" (2003, 89). I include in that "tone" the "sociocultural contextualization" (86) and metapragmatic dimensions of meaning (which, for Silverstein, are part of what is taken into account in transduction).

8. I am grateful to Leila Monaghan for discussing this with me over email. "School for the Deaf" was her suggestion.

9. In fact, Algeria signed onto two IMF restructuring programs, in 1989 and 1991, per Nashashibi et al. 1998, 5–6.

10. "Killing Me Softly with His Song," lyrics by Lori Leiberman in 1971, composed by Lalo Shifrin. The Fugees covered it as "Killing Me Softly," a recording that won the 1997 Grammy award for Best R&B Performance by a Duo or Group with Vocal: https://www.grammy.com/grammys/artists/fugees, accessed May 28, 2018.

11. The song is "Lazrag Se'ani" by Cheb Mami. It can be heard here: https://www.youtube.com/watch?v=Hfp1XwG2__s, accessed July 4, 2018.

12. The English term *genie* derives from the French term *génie*, derived in turn from the Latin *genius*. Even though they are etymologically unrelated, the French *génie* was used to translate the Arabic *jinni* (singular of *jinn*) in a French translation of *Arabian Nights*, and in English, *genie* has retained the sense of some sort of nonhuman being or spirit. https://www.etymonline.com/word/genie, accessed May 28, 2018.

13. http://nfs.sparknotes.com/juliuscaesar, accessed July 4, 2018.

14. For a succinct discussion of language ideology, see Irvine 2012, http://www.oxfordbibliographies.com/view/document/obo-9780199766567/obo-9780199766567-0012.xml, accessed October 19, 2017.

15. On the Amazigh or Berber identity movement in Algeria, see Goodman 2005 and Maddy-Weitzman 2011, among others.

16. On the language question in Algeria, see Benrabah 2013; Taleb-Ibrahimi 1995.

17. In linguists' terms, MSA is almost far enough from Darija to be considered a different code rather than register.

18. Some translators have called for an encyclopedic corpus of footnotes or annotations to be read alongside the translation. Vladimir Nabokov, for instance, wrote that he wanted to see "translations with copious footnotes, footnotes reaching up like skyscrapers to the top of this or that page so as to leave only the gleam of one textual line between commentary and eternity" (2012, 125).

19. On decontextualization and entextualization, see Bauman and Briggs 1990; Briggs and Bauman 1992.

20. As Kapchan has noted, "A successful translation makes the images come alive—visually, aurally, olfactorily and gustatorily. These senses blend together in the body of the performance as they do in the body of the performer" (2003, 148).

21. On translating poetics, see Jakobson 1959.

22. On "the way affect resides in language," see Kapchan 2003, 142.

23. Personal interview, September 21, 2016, Ashfield, Massachusetts.

24. A video of the song with images from immigration in Marseilles can be viewed here: https://www.youtube.com/watch?v=JQJv2aqDIbk, accessed July 2, 2018.

25. John Bowen (2012, 138–39) discusses the various meanings of terms that share the trilateral root f-t-y.

26. https://www.npr.org/podcasts/510324/rough-translation, accessed June 4, 2018.

27. The project of using anthropological research to critique aspects of US society has long been one focus of the discipline. It was formulated in terms close to those of the 2017 NPR podcast by George Marcus and Michael Fischer in their now classic *Anthropology as Cultural Critique* (1986).

—ɯ—

EPILOGUE

Apples in America

A DOZEN STUDENTS FILED INTO Dr. Kate Bredeson's Theater History class at Reed College on an unusually snowy February day in Portland, Oregon. After taking their places around tables arranged in a rectangle, the students were prepared to talk about the video of *Apples* that they had seen during an open screening I had hosted the night before. Dr. Bredeson began the class by asking the students to write thoughts, impressions, and questions they had about the play on large whiteboards that lined three walls of the classroom. Once the students had made their own comments, they then circulated around the room, reading what others had written and adding their own ideas. Within a few minutes, the whiteboards were full of quotes from the play, remarks about the aspirations and activities of particular characters, inquiries about specific aspects of the mise-en-scène, and wider reflections on the role of theater in contemporary societies. When the students got back to their seats, Dr. Bredeson asked a couple of them to summarize comments from the various boards. She then opened the floor for what became one of the most animated discussions I witnessed following a video screening of *Apples*.

Had the members of Istijmam been present for this event, they almost certainly would have called it a halqa. In referring to such an event as a halqa, the Istijmam actors do not mean that spectators are directly participating in the story as it unfolds on stage. In Istijmam's halqa, spectators do participate in the play, but they do so in their imaginations. Audiences actively constitute the work as they watch and again in postperformance reflection and conversation. Jamil had said as much during a panel discussion at Yale University's Pierson College: "The spectator in Algerian theater participates in the play. He participates via his imagination. In the marketplace halqa, the goual would

213

work with spectators to get them to participate. For us, the interaction of the spectator during the play is very important." He went on: "After the play, the spectator is going to reflect on it, maybe find solutions, maybe not, but at least reflect." From these remarks, it is clear that Jamil would have included post-performance discussions of the kind that took place at Reed as part of a halqa. He had already used the term to characterize other postperformance conversations (see chap. 2).

The halqa that unfolded in Dr. Bredeson's Reed College classroom in 2018 provides a compelling model for how to approach the various discussions around *Apples* in the United States. Taking up the range of commentary the play generated as it moved from live audiences in 2016 to video audiences in the two years following the tour, I put together a series of tableaux, drawing together the English definition of tableau as a pictorial representation with the French definition of tableau as a chalkboard. The tableaux, like Dr. Bredeson's whiteboards, both give a sense of the kinds of discussions *Apples* has sparked and serve as generative points of engagement through which current viewers may continue talking.

In Dr. Bredeson's class, the students connected the various conversations by drawing arrows from one to another with multicolored markers. They also extended the conversations by drawing lines that spiraled out toward new areas of inquiry. Here, I draw a virtual set of lines and arrows by grouping together commentary from different audiences around similar topics or questions. Commentary comes from four live, postperformance talk-backs with the actors (at Indiana University, the University of New Hampshire, the Denmark Maine Arts Center, and La MaMa Theater in New York), from one extended conversation following a rehearsal at Double Edge Theatre in Ashfield, Massachusetts, and from eight video screenings that I organized after the tour (one at Reed College, one at a community center in Acton, Massachusetts, and six at Indiana University, each for a different audience).[1] At three of these events, audiences already had broad exposure to avant-garde theater (Double Edge Theatre and theater classes at Reed College and Indiana University). Two of the Indiana University screenings were with people who had seen the play live in 2016 and had indicated on a postperformance survey that they would be interested in further discussion. In the final tableau, I also draw in commentary from the actors themselves as we engaged in our own halqa during the rehearsal residency.

—⁓—

A halqa, the actors repeatedly emphasized, speaks first and foremost to society. They never tired of explaining that Alloula's mission was to create a new form of halqa: he was writing plays that would tell stories about and for ordinary Algerians. Would Americans understand these stories? I raised this question throughout the rehearsal residency. I was worried that most Americans had no context for making sense of *Apples*. The actors and I talked about how Americans would know little or nothing about Algeria. Most would know nothing of its 132 years under French colonial rule. They would not have known of its twenty-five years as a socialist republic. They would not have known that Algeria had had significant street protests in 1988 that eventually led to the resignation of the president, more than twenty years before the 2011 uprisings that swept much of the Arab world. They would not have known about the Dark Decade of the 1990s, with its massacres, assassinations, and disappearances, nor of the generalized climate of insecurity and fear that had gripped the country. The program notes would take care of some of this, but did we need more framing?

With my students in mind, I thought we did. Wearing my teacher's hat, I raised the idea with Istijmam of providing a short, spoken introduction before the play that would furnish some context about the time when it was written. It would talk about what else was going on in Algeria as Alloula was writing *Apples*. Knowing about the country's neoliberal turn away from its socialist past in the late 1980s could help audiences to make sense of the Customer's quest for apples, the vanishing factory, and the Attendant's attempt to make a go of it as an entrepreneur after spending his life in the labor union. Knowing about the 1990s assassinations of artists and intellectuals, including the playwright himself, would add poignancy and power to the Actor's quest for rehearsal space and artistic expression. Jamil was skeptical: the play, as a work of art, should speak for itself, he thought. But gradually he realized that above all, like Alloula, he wanted the play to be understandable to its new audiences. He envisioned an introductory voice that would start in the dark and would end as the Attendant (Mustapha) came out on stage. Mustapha would stand for a few seconds in silence, holding the cube in tribute to the fallen artists. Then the play would begin.

I drafted a short text, and we went so far as to record it. I did not protest (though I should have) when Jamil chose me as the speaker. Lila emailed the audio file to Lisa Booth and Deirdre Valente, the tour organizers, who were not in favor of it but were willing to respect the troupe's wishes. The night before the opening show at the Kennedy Center, I had a sinking feeling in my stomach. I should not be helping to frame the play for audiences. The play was not just some sort of anthropological record of Algerian society in the 1990s (though it was also that). It was up to the spectators—not the anthropologist—to make meaning of it. Perhaps for the first time, I understood what it meant for a play to be a halqa—an event that generated imaginative engagement, an event that sparked questions, not answers. Happily, we pulled the offstage voice. The play would speak for itself.

The discussions the actors and I had about how much to situate the play in its own historic context also played out among some spectators. Consider an exchange between two advanced undergraduate students at Indiana University. Both had seen the play live in 2016 and had attended a video screening and discussion some twenty months later, in May of 2018. The first student was majoring in Middle East studies; the second, in theater and international studies.

> Student 1: I feel like the context of Algeria in this neocolonial era is really important to our reading of the play. And these general ideas about class struggle or whatever, I feel like they need to be, we need to put them into context.
>
> Student 2: I feel like as an audience member, for me, I was obliged to see how the play connects to me and my life and my circumstances. And I think that while it is potentially important to recognize context in Algeria during the time the play was written, I don't think that is why they're performing it now. I think that they're performing it now because of modern sensibilities and because it's relevant in a modern context.

The first approach is more classically anthropological: this student sought to situate the play in its larger socioeconomic, political, and cultural contexts. He was not alone: a number of audience members also approached the play as a way to inform themselves about Algeria. This kind of inquiry is of course critical for developing cross-cultural understanding (and is addressed in chap. 1). But it can also be a subtle form of othering that locates the works of African creators as ethnographic documents rather than artistic products.

The second student, while acknowledging the importance of historical work, approached the play as a marketgoer might enter a halqa. That is, a marketgoer would most likely not be analyzing the historical circumstances that gave rise to whatever story he was hearing. He would not be approaching the story as a cultural document. Instead, he would be appreciating its value as a contemporary aesthetic production. The storyteller in the halqa might indeed take up a tale from the past, but he would fashion it not to give a history lesson but to speak with artistic flair and a measure of humor to the current moment. A successful goual would create an experience of el-furja, that sense of pleasure that a live performance can elicit.

Of course, these approaches are hardly mutually exclusive. Stories told at a halqa are inextricable from wider political and economic contexts. The politics of halqa storytelling are inseparable from the storyteller's artistic prowess. Poetics and politics have long been understood to be interconnected (e.g., Bauman and Briggs 2003; Bowen 1991; Clifford and Marcus 1986). But as the actors never tired of telling me, a play was not an ethnographic document. It was an emergent engagement with a work that was never finalized.

This kind of split came up at more than one event. An audience member at the HartBeat panel wanted to talk about art and decolonization, seeking to locate Istijmam's work in relation to Algeria's postcolonial experience. She wanted the "wisdom" that Algerians might be able to impart about that experience. For her, art should "help people see that history." Jamil took issue with her question: "Theater really needs to speak to society. . . . Let's leave the work of history to the historians and speak directly to society. . . . We want to educate a generation. . . . But maybe young people don't need to know what France did in Algeria. They need to know what we can do now." Jamil might have added, Let's leave the work of anthropology to the anthropologists. {**Video Epilogue 01**}

In a similar vein, one audience member at the Yale Pierson event asked Istijmam, "How much of the job that you do in the States is about educating people about modern Algeria?" He went so far as to ask them to quantify: "What percentage of your work is education for the audience?"

Jamil deflected the question: "We start in a dynamic of wanting to learn, not to teach (*d'apprendre, pas de faire apprendre*). . . . We want to learn from ourselves first, and to learn from the people who surround us. For us, learning and listening are primordial. We hope to live this at 100 percent, but it's almost impossible." {**Video Epilogue 02**}

These exchanges help to crystallize some of the key tensions of the tour. Was Istijmam in the United States to represent Algerian culture, or to create a shared experience that transcended cultural boundaries? Was the halqa a cultural representation of an Algerian theatrical form, or an ephemeral experience of el-furja that worked to bring actors and audiences into a shared space of pleasure, promise, and potential (a "utopian performative," in Dolan's terms [2005])? On some level, of course, the encounters on tour contained elements of both of these perspectives. For Istijmam, the cultural history of the halqa was a touchstone that they readily and repeatedly accessed, as they had done in UNH classes or at the end of their workshop with the HartBeat Ensemble (chap. 3). But as Jamil's remarks make clear, Istijmam leaned toward the second of these perspectives, evoking the halqa as an emergent artistic experience rather than a signifier of cultural difference.

Moreover, in their discussions of *Apples* with audiences, Istijmam foregrounded the issues and problems that all societies confront. For them, the halqa was not a static piece of Algerian heritage but a living artistic form that could bring actors and audiences into a shared space of connection. The troupe repeatedly invited discussion of how *Apples* could also speak to Americans. As a living artistic form, the halqa raises a question related to that posed by the NPR podcast *Rough Translation*: How do issues from one time and place speak to similar issues in another time and place?[2] Just as a marketplace goual might have made a traditional story resonate with contemporary issues, so does *Apples* bring the stories of Algeria of the early 1990s into relation with the present-day United States. Using the stories from one place to illuminate what transpires elsewhere is part of the old but still timely mandate to use anthropology not just to understand other places but also to engage in "cultural critique" of the ethnographer's own society (Marcus and Fischer 1986).

"I would love for this play to meet Americans," Mustapha had said to a gathered audience at the University of New Hampshire. He elaborated: "The day when we gave the first performance [in Algeria], it was as if the play had been written in 2009, because we performed it in 2009. And we put it on here, in the United States [in 2016], and based on the reactions of the public, it is as if the story had been written a month ago. We are acting now in relation to your situation, the vote, the elections [of 2016], capitalism, and so on. So we can say that maybe it is a universal text that can be performed everywhere . . . really, there are passages or stories where we find our contemporary lives." Rihab made a similar point during a conversation with the audience following the performance of *Apples* in Denmark, Maine: "When we came here, we knew that we came with an Algerian story, with Algerian problems, with our own culture . . . but we were fairly surprised to learn that the play, even though it was written in 1991, resonates in America today. . . . People came [after the performances] to tell us that 'it is the same thing here.' So, in the end, human beings suffer from the same problems. It's what makes the work even more open to the world and to universality." **{Video Epilogue 03}**

As the play "meets Americans" and "transforms" via the video and this book, I invite current viewers of *Apples* to engage in "rough translation" by developing and extending the conversations launched on the tableaux below. As in a halqa, these tableaux are meant—like Dr. Bredeson's whiteboards—to serve as springboards, juxtaposing perspectives and generating questions rather than providing definitive interpretations. The final tableau, centered on the passage from *Julius Caesar*, brings back the actors as they talked at some length about what this passage in a play from the early 1600s was doing in an Algerian play in the 1990s and how it continued to speak as they toured the United States in 2016.

TABLEAU: APPLES, DEMOCRACY, SCARCITY, VANISHING

In a talk-back after the performance of *Apples* in Denmark, Maine, Rihab linked the Customer's story to larger questions about democracy, desire, and scarcity. Even if the three characters come together at the end of the play, she said, the problem isn't resolved: "The play itself asks questions about democracy, about lack, about how to satisfy desire—it's the question of the whole play. It continues, and it continues here [in the US] as well."

Jamil concurred: "It's not just about the ability to buy apples, it's about desire, to desire democracy, to desire acting, to desire creating, and this is the same problem in the world."

Many US spectators could relate to the Customer's quest. They asked, What are the "apples" in today's world? Who can get them, and who can't? Some linked the Customer's struggles to those of coal miners and others left behind. Others saw resonances with the Black Lives Matter movement.

I felt the intensity of this reaction to economic and political struggles; I feel that living here in America I find some of the same things. . . . One thing I really resonated with was the idea of freedom, but if you're free and you have these things like apples that no one can afford, what is the price of freedom? Are you really free? (September 20, 2017, Double Edge Theatre post-rehearsal discussion)

All the talk of modernity and getting left behind, I think that that's a universal thing. . . . Everyone kind of expects to move forward together, and then when it doesn't happen—you know, we hear about coal miners and then it's like, well, times are changing, you know, you're not going to have a job . . . those kind of universal narratives it seems like they happen everywhere, and repeatedly. (June 29, 2017, Indiana University Summer Language Program)

Here's a guy who's an attendant in a restroom, certainly not much of a job, and he, so many times, talked about how important it was for him to keep his job. If he did this, he'd lose his job. If he did that, he'd lose his job. . . . I do feel like that's a little bit what's going on in our country, people just following the status quo, and worried about the future and worried about losing things. And the idea of going out on a limb and risking and not worrying about that is lost. (July 30, 2017, Acton, Massachusetts)

The despair, not just the wanting of the apples and not just the wanting to be able to make a living, but the despair that was brought on by those in power who could keep it from him, the man who was trying so hard to get the wife the apples and to go to his work and to do what made him the family man, and that despair and anguish that came with that when it was taken from him through no fault of his own. (May 8, 2018, Indiana University screening)

I have privileges to food and to certain things like that, so I don't see apples as being that. I see it as, like I was saying about what's happening with this Black Lives Matter movement right now, it's like the apple for me is, can I survive? Survival is one of those apples right now. It's like having that idea of "am I allowed to even get to, reach the apple to survive, or am I going to get shot in the head?" Especially as a person of color, you know? It's something that you think about constantly right now. (September 20, 2016, Double Edge Theatre post-rehearsal discussion)

Audiences also took up the question of disappearance—of jobs, but also of basic rights that were there one day but gone the next.

You walk in and say, "this was a building yesterday and today it's not." And his whole life crumbled and it was really just very, very sad. (July 30, 2017, Acton, Massachusetts)

I saw the show in September 2016 and it has a completely different meaning now [March 2018] than it did then. Particularly because of the political moment that we're in. That was two and a half months before Trump was elected president. And particularly the moment where the gentleman is going to work, is commuting to work, and then he sees nothing, he can't find his place of employment, so he retraces his steps and then he realizes, "No, this *is* where I'm supposed to work and it's not here anymore." So just this idea of senselessness that we have something and then we don't. Like tweeting that, and I'm not trying to get political here, but tweeting that trans people can no longer serve in the military for instance, one moment it's fine and then the next moment it's not, and we don't have an explanation for it. . . . So [the play] speaks differently to me now than it did then, and it's only, what, a year and a half apart. (March 28, 2018, Indiana University theater class)

Overall [the play] was interesting, especially in this cultural context, for example the health care bill happening. So it feels like there are similar conversations going on, of what is the value of democracy, and would democracy guarantee equality? What is the balance . . . do we want to not see apples at all, or do we want to have apples that we can just watch? (June 29, 2017, Indiana University Summer Language Program)

I came from a somewhat impoverished family that felt the weight of the society that was around us bearing down because we were dealing with things that were financially difficult, and we didn't have the means to participate in the keeping up with the Joneses sort of conversations. And I think when you're in that kind of community, you feel that kind of pressure, the weight of financial burden is heavy. . . . I think that when you live the life where your small, low-end job could be taken away from you, even though you're working for survival because someone with millions and millions of dollars bought some piece of property and turned it into something else. . . . The struggle, that you have no control really, even if you work yourself to death, you still could be just completely disregarded, thrown to the side and told "well, sorry about it, find something else." We don't get the higher fruits. We get the lower fruits. . . . And I think this play is a small reminder of that kind of struggle. (May 8, 2018, Indiana University screening)

Some participants related to the sense of needing a place to scream, to release:

I had so many moments where even if I couldn't put my finger on it, there were things that were almost universal about what we were seeing, with someone not being able to access apples, and there's all these rules that are coming out of nowhere. You can't figure out what's going on with the government. You say the wrong thing, you have to go into a bathroom to scream. (March 28, 2018, Indiana University theater class)

TABLEAU: "DEMOCRACY DROVE YOU CRAZY"

The question of democracy permeates *Apples*. The Attendant talks to the Customer about how, under democracy, he is "free to do as he liked" and "could even break dance" if he wanted to. Democracy was literally on everyone's lips, a "word in motion" (Gluck and Tsing 2009) that had finally reached Algeria in the late 1980s. But the Customer is fed up with the word. Who cared about democracy when he couldn't even afford an apple? The Attendant tells the Actor that "democracy drove you crazy." He attributes to "democracy" the gibberish that spews from the Actor's mouth. But what is democracy? Who benefits from democracy? For whom is it just an illusion?

Maybe this bathroom attendant hasn't actually been visited by anyone, and this is all just something that's happened in his head. And I think as a fired union worker, on some level, if he is a union worker and if that memory was a real thing, this is something that could be a delusion, democracy as a delusion, a sort of abstraction that doesn't actually make sense or doesn't actually exist. It's just an illusion. . . . And I see that as a metaphor for democracy as an illusion as well. (May 8, 2018 Indiana University screening)

The idea of democracy, what is democracy, how do we see ourselves in democracy if we're not a police officer or not in the courts in some way . . . Is democracy made for us, the general public, or is it just for the people with

power, the gamblers with a lot of money, who can buy all the apples, steal all
the apples for themselves? (September 20, 2017 Double Edge Theatre post-
rehearsal discussion)

What I experienced was the absurdity of where we are, where democracy
is coming and now all of a sudden our lives are in complete disarray. We're
afraid. People are, our neighbors are turning us in and you don't know who to
trust anymore. And your livelihood is gone, and the simple things in life, you
have a craving, you want to be able to go out and buy an apple and you can't.
(July 30, 2017, Acton, Massachusetts)

Along similar lines, the courtroom scene was memorable for many audiences,
perhaps because it satirized the familiar image of Lady Justice. Recall that in
this scene Mustapha, sitting on the cube in the center of the stage, initially
posed with his two hands equally positioned at his shoulders to indicate a balanced scale; then he dropped one hand and changed his smile to a frown when
Rihab said, "No, the *court*."

When the policeman was talking about the people who were living under
the stairs and how they had been evicted and then how, by the same courts
who gave the permission for them to be evicted, they are there now, asking
for a place to live and that the courts are somehow doing them a favor by
pretending that they don't see them. That idea of trying to find help through
the system when the system is what has put you there in the first place. (May
8, 2018, Indiana University screening)

The realization of just how incredibly corrupt our own government is maybe
wasn't so much a part of our national discourse [at the time of the September
2016 performance]. And now it seems like that's something we have in
common with a lot of other countries. This government that we've thought
was working so well and held to this really high ideal, well, no, actually it's
just as corrupt and horrible as everywhere else. (March 28, 2018, Indiana
University theater class)

TABLEAU: "AND HOW DOES IT END?"

"And how does it end?" the Attendant asks the Actor about the play he hoped
to put on. But the question is of equal interest with regard to the ending of
Apples itself. Indeed, the play's ending was one of the most frequent topics of
discussion following performances and screenings. Recall what happened:
The Actor and the Attendant had started to enact together the Actor's vision
of the play he wanted to put on, which I have called the shadow play because

it shadows *Apples* itself and because the main character has a dark or shadow side (chap. 5). At one point, the Attendant broke away, asking, "And you want to put on this play here? Do you want me to lose my job?"

"No, no," the Actor replied. "I only want to rehearse it here, that's all." Satisfied, the Attendant allowed himself to reenter a utopian fantasy, envisioning the Restroom as a space for culture. He and the Actor started to imagine what they could do with the Restroom. It could become a space for art, for music, for poetry. At the mention of poetry, the Actor and Customer began reciting traditional poems. Then they both exited the stage, but the Attendant's reverie continued: he called on them to work with him to develop the business "now that we have more hands." He sat down on the cube as, offstage, the song that opened the play began again (with the voices of Rihab and Moussa). Startled, the Attendant leapt up, disoriented and confused, realized he was hearing music, made as if to turn off a radio, and exited, stumbling and disoriented.

What did audiences make of this ending? Did this story really happen, or was it a dream that took place inside the Attendant's mind? And if it was a dream, did that matter to how audiences understood the play? Was this a hopeful ending, or did it leave audiences in confusion or even despair?

Three perspectives emerged in consecutive comments following the Reed College screening:

What I read in the whole piece is a kind of world-building idea that in theater, we can create community even in a public washroom, right? And the lines at the end, "culture soothes, dramatic arts is a good idea" . . . I feel like certainly there's a lot about it that's specific to the moment in which it was created, but it also feels like the celebration of theater as a form, in a way that I ultimately find very hopeful, which really isn't specific to the context in which it was created. (Reed College, February 19, 2018)

I found that to be really interesting also, but then, it feels like that ending kind of undercuts that hope, because the end leaves me to imagine that this is a dream that the Restroom Attendant is having, and suddenly he is awoken from this reverie. So to me, there's this hope, and then it's undercut by this final ending. (Reed College, February 19, 2018)

I understood the ending completely differently. I thought it was saying that in this moment of ostensible democracy, initially, the person who has these problems with finding the things he and his wife need, and then the person who just wants to practice theater and build this world, the only place they can find these things is in a toilet. That was the opposite of what they [the previous commenters] were saying. This isn't democracy; the only space we know of for a democracy is in a toilet. (Reed College, February 19, 2018)

Dr. Bredeson followed up this conversation in her class the next day. Was the setting in the public toilet a message of hope—that one can form connections anywhere—or of despair—that one can be free only in a restroom? The conversation among Reed students echoed comments raised in other discussions.

> The starting image and the ending image are almost the same. That we've gone through this arc, and we've ended up in the same place, which for me made it feel like this play could be repeated, with different characters, and just kind of cycled in and out, which read pessimistically to me. Because whatever they're creating in the bathroom is disconnected from the outside world and almost outside of time. And so it may be very beautiful, and it may be very moving, but it can only exist right here in this loop and not travel beyond it. (February 20, 2018, Reed College)

> I saw it, kind of, as "Well, we have to take the arts to the bathroom, we have to take complaining to the bathroom, if we have problems, we have to take them to the bathroom, we have to take them to the shithouse." And it just seemed like everything was falling apart. And there was no place to go but the shithouse. And that was hard, actually, to take in. (July 30, 2017, Acton, Massachusetts)

> Our public bathrooms wouldn't be big enough. (July 30, 2017, Acton, Massachusetts)

TABLEAU: BRUTUS'S ADDRESS TO THE ROMANS

A halqa, in the larger sense of an imaginative encounter with a work of theater, can take place even among the actors. A halqa opened up among the actors and me after we finished our final translation session in August of 2016. When we reached the last line of the play, first we clapped for ourselves to celebrate the moment. Then, gathered in a circle in Istijmam's sunny rehearsal room, we talked about how the play spoke to us as we were preparing to leave for the United States. At the same time, we talked about what the author, Abdelkader Alloula, might have been trying to accomplish back in the early 1990s when he was writing the play. In other words, we turned the play backward and forward—seeing it simultaneously as a response to the moment it was written and an invitation to future audiences to encounter it from their own vantage points. In this sense, the play served as a "looking-glass" (Herzfeld 1987) through which contemporary social life—both Algerian and American—could be newly illuminated.

What were lines from *Julius Caesar* doing in *Apples*? Brutus's famous address to the Romans after the assassination of Caesar was one of the passages most discussed by actors and audiences. The Shakespearean passage lends itself to commentary because it is packaged to travel: parallel phrases, repetitions, and rhythms make the text stand out from the rest of the play. It is easy to extract or "decontextualize" this kind of passage from one context—or one play— and embed or "recontextualize" it in another.[3] The passage has also acquired considerable cultural weight over the four centuries of its performance. For most audiences, it is almost instantly recognizable. Not all spectators might know that it comes from *Julius Caesar*, but many would be able to say that it sounded like Shakespeare. Even those who do not identify the passage with Shakespeare know that it stands out from the rest of the play from the way the Actor performs it: changes in pitch, volume, prosody, timing, and corporal expression all set it apart.

Such passages are particularly amenable to being taken up in rough translation precisely because they stand out. If rough translation is concerned with how one historical moment may speak to another, here a four hundred-year-old passage is being made to speak to contemporary times. What did it say to actors and audiences?

How people interpreted the Shakespeare passage depended on whether they took *Julius Caesar* or *Apples* (or some combination) as their point of reference. Usually, when a text is embedded within another text, the second text—in this case, *Apples*—supplies the primary interpretive frame (Briggs and Bauman 1992). But in this case, the passage from Shakespeare is so well-known that its meaning in *Julius Caesar* can spill over into *Apples*. In this case, the storyline of *Apples* temporarily recedes, and Shakespeare jumps to the forefront.

Those who took *Apples* as their primary frame of reference subordinated the Shakespeare passage to the Actor's story. The Actor needed a place to rehearse; this familiar passage from Shakespeare was simply what came out of his mouth. It almost could have been any well-known passage that could testify to the Actor's professional chops. At this point in the play, the Attendant clearly had not understood what the Actor was asking of him. Perhaps, the Actor thought, showing the Attendant that he knew these classic lines could convince the Attendant that he was in fact a true actor.

The thing that I enjoyed was the fact that the Actor character is exploring what this space means in terms of him being a performer. . . . And so with the lines it seemed a real way for him to chew on, and to taste the different words that he has in the monologue and be able to enjoy them, not just in how they sound in the space, [but also] what they mean and what that feels like and what this added space does to what he is saying. (March 28, 2018, Indiana University theater class)

A lot of the Actor's problem in that part of the play was finding a place to do what he loved, to make his art. He wasn't able to do that in any other space, so a lot of what he's doing in performing is justifying himself. Like when he was performing the monologue in front of the Attendant, the Attendant was like, "You know the demon, you need to get out of here, get that checked out." [The Actor] was like, "No, it's Shakespeare." So a lot of it is him justifying himself within the space of the bathroom. (March 28, 2018, Indiana University theater class)

For others, the lines from Shakespeare raised broader questions about what to do when faced with an authoritarian ruler like Caesar. Sometimes, this understanding emerged (as in the first comment below) in postperformance conversation.

I'm just thinking for the first time that this is Brutus saying, "Oh, I killed Caesar because I love my country." . . . And it does make me think the story, the play is maybe more of a call to action than I thought it was. . . . It's about a modern democracy and modern activism and it does compel you to think about what your role is in the system and how you might recognize injustice and do something about it. Not necessarily murder the person in charge, but I don't think that's too extreme in some situations for some people around the world who are dealing with these, with these kinds of circumstances. And I mean, I think we do deal with American government, with Donald Trump as the president of the United States . . . a bizarre world that I never thought I'd live in, and here I am. (May 8, 2018, Indiana University screening)

Others, like the student of Middle Eastern studies quoted earlier, wanted the historical and cultural knowledge to make sense of how this passage might fit with Algerian history:

I love *Julius Caesar*, but I didn't know if one needed to know more Algerian history to know if currently there was someone with too much ambition and who was, who had to be slain. (July 30, 2017, Acton, Massachusetts)

I was thinking about who Brutus could be in this situation and Algeria. And if it really was the Actor trying to express themselves as somebody who's concerned for his country or if it possibly could be that he's making a jab at the people who are in control of a new neocolonial regime who want to take over the country for the sake of the people of the country. (May 8, 2018, Indiana University screening)

When we have the [Customer's story], as that storyline goes on, it becomes more and more specific to the time and place and setting of the play, of it being in 1990s Algeria. . . . When [the Customer] is vomiting up, we've reached this point of intensity with the present, with the present setting of the play. . . . The Shakespeare monologue starts to make it a lot more universal and a lot broader. (February 20, 2018, Reed College)

The Istijmam actors themselves had a range of perspectives on the Shakespeare passage. Rihab initially saw the passage through the frame of the Actor's story—he needed a place to develop his theatrical skills. But for most of the other actors, the passage was so strong that it exceeded the boundaries of the Actor's story. Was Brutus right to participate in the killing of Julius Caesar? When was assassination a proper response to power gone rogue? Did Alloula mean to use a text about slaying a dictator to say something about 1990s Algeria?

> Moussa: This is Alloula's point of view, how could a dictator be left to live while people live as slaves?
> Mustapha: He [Brutus] killed him [Julius Caesar]—he didn't just say it, he killed him. He gave the solution. There is a solution.
> Moussa: This is more or less what's happening today with the Arab Springs. Khaddafi [former president of Libya] died in this way.
> Jamil: Exactly. It's also very strong because at the end, he says, "I pause for a reply." And you will see that in the original text [of *Julius Caesar*], there are other scenes that take place . . . Alloula poses the question: Is this the solution? Then nothing happens in *Apples*.
> Moussa: Alloula was also an Algerian citizen, so maybe for him, the solution was really to remove the president—that is, the dictator—and to radically change it.

Jamil countered that Alloula's position wasn't clear: "Because while Brutus is offering a direct message, his words are taken up in *Apples* as an indirect message. After all, the text doesn't say that Alloula is thinking of changing the system. Instead, he puts on stage a character who killed a dictator and at the end of the passage, he says he will 'pause for a reply.'" For Jamil, this was classic Alloula: to raise a question but never answer it, to leave the questions hanging, the endings open.[4] Jamil complicated any easy attempt to find in the passage a clear indication of Alloula's political judgment about Brutus's action or issues it might open up about Alloula's own times. The actors were getting at the very question posed by rough translation: How can texts from other times and places be used to comment on contemporary issues?

Citing a text can be a slippery move. An author can drop in another text and then back off, attributing it to the first author while leaving their own intentions ambiguous. Cited passages in theater are doubly distanced, standing apart not only from the actors but also from the characters. The character of the Actor provides an ideal way for Alloula to play with the ambiguities of embedding texts within the larger script of *Apples*. After all, who is an Actor, if not someone who puts on other faces and cites the words of others? Between Istijmam's performance of *Apples* and the Shakespearean passage are at least four layers of citation: Shakespeare as he wrote the passage; Brutus, who recited the lines in *Julius Caesar*; the Actor as he utters the lines in *Apples*; and Moussa, who performs as the Actor. Then there was the living Brutus who may or may not have delivered this kind of speech. Any one of these, except the living Brutus, could back away, saying that they were repeating someone's else's lines. The passage becomes a literary hot potato, thrown back and forth among actual and virtual players. The *I* at the origin of the intention of the words is never clear (Urban 1989).

In *Apples*, the Attendant listened to the passage and then told the Actor, "Democracy drove you crazy!" But the Actor could simply attribute the text to Shakespeare: "I'm just using it to rehearse, that's all." In Goffman's terms, the Actor here was claiming to be the animator, but not the author or principal. As animator, he was only reciting a line that someone else had written. He couldn't be held accountable for its content. Alloula, as the playwright, could claim that he was using this text because any actor would have to know it. Shakespeare had written it, not him. Perhaps, as Mustapha suggested, Alloula was hinting at something darker. Perhaps he was asking whether assassination might be the way to address the abuses of political power in his own society. But his use of an embedded quotation made it impossible to know what his own perspective was.[5] Tragically, he himself would be assassinated before he could speak to this question.

The summer after Istijmam's US tour, Shakespeare's *Julius Caesar* became newly controversial in the United States. At the time, the play was being staged by companies across the country, affording "a way to chew over politics, power, democracy, and authoritarianism at a moment when a populist leader with a fondness for executive power has moved into the White House."[6] The New York Public Theater's performance in its 2017 Shakespeare in the Park series became particularly controversial because the actor who played Caesar had been cast as a Trump look-alike. When the dictator was slain, the audience saw a body appearing very much like that of the US president lying, bloodied, on stage. The images went viral, generating heated altercations within and around the theater space. Some corporate sponsors, including Delta Airlines and Bank of America, pulled their funding; others, like American Express and the National Endowment for the Arts, posted announcements to the effect that their sponsorship of the Public Theater did not fund or condone the production.[7] In his opening remarks before the show, director Oskar Eustis made it clear that the Public Theater was not putting on *Julius Caesar* to portray another history but rather to use that history to speak to "what happens when you try to preserve democracy by non-democratic means" and about "the danger of a large crowd of people manipulated by their emotions, taken over by leaders who urge them to do things that not only are against their interests but destroy the very institutions designed to preserve and protect them."[8] In other words, Eustis was offering the play as an exercise in rough translation. {Video Epilogue 04}

The play resonated in similar ways for the actors as they looked back at 1990s Algeria. At the time, Algerians had been confronting a populist Islamist party that had explicitly stated that once it won, there would be no further elections. It would install a sharia-based state that would put an end to multiparty pluralism (seen as an imposed western import) once and for all. In other words, a democratic election would be used to end democracy and install a state that would base itself instead on the principles of Islam (as Algeria's Islamist leaders understood them at the time). In the halqa after our final translation session, the actors talked about this paradox.

> Moussa: They made the revolution in Egypt, they chased out the president. And after, the Egyptian people voted for the Muslim Brotherhood candidate. The Muslim Brotherhood. And they won! What does this say about democracy? It is fundamentally nonexistent. Democracy does not exist. This thing does not exist.
>
> Jamil: Like in Algeria.
>
> Moussa: The Egyptian people voted for the Muslim Brotherhood candidate [Mohamed Morsi]. He took power. Then something happened, or the Americans intervened, they took him out, put in another. But the first one, the people voted for him! In the most democratic way possible. So, who do they take people for?
>
> Jamil: It's like in Algeria. Algeria was the first victim of this movement.
>
> Mustapha: Of the Arab Spring [referring to Algeria in 1988].
>
> Jamil. Yes. The FIS, it was that. The Algerian people voted for the FIS, and there was the army, the Algerian army that came out.
>
> Mustapha: It's the same scenario. Even in Libya, it's the same thing. . . . Some won at the ballot box, and they weren't given [the election].

Was it legitimate for the Algerian ruling cabal to stage a coup in order to take out a party elected with twice as many votes as its closest competitor, if that party was vowing to close down pluralist democracy? Should the United States have supported Algeria's Islamic Salvation Front, which legitimately won the election? Or should the United States instead have thrown its weight behind the subsequent coup, which prevented the democratically elected Islamists from taking power? In other words, was it more democratic to endorse a fair election that would ultimately undermine the principles of democracy, or to attempt to put an end to what, from a democratic perspective, would have constituted a usurpation of rights? Although *Et-Teffeh* did not open up the kind of controversy that the New York Public Theater performance did, it did pose the question of what to do when power becomes so corroded that it undermines the very system that put it in place.

As Jamil suggested, "I pause for a reply" may be the most democratic response of all.

NOTES

1. Screenings and discussions held at Indiana University were as follows: African Studies Program (January 27, 2017), Center for the Study of the Middle East (April 7, 2017), Arabic Flagship summer language program (June 29, 2017), Dr. Jennifer Goodlander's graduate theater seminar (March 28, 2018), and two screenings for people who had attended the 2016 live performance and indicated that they were interested in being contacted for follow-up via a survey that I administered following the 2016 performance at Indiana University (May 8, 2018; June 1, 2018).

2. The podcast *Rough Translation* is hosted by Gregory Warner.

3. On decontextualization, recontextualization, and entextualization, see Bauman and Briggs 1990, Briggs and Bauman 1992.

4. Jamil's comments resonate with those by the *New York Times*'s Michael Cooper. See https://www.nytimes.com/2017/06/12/theater/julius-caesar-shakespeare-donald-trump.html, accessed November 1, 2017.

5. On the politics of citational practices, see Goodman, Tomlinson, and Richland 2014.

6. https://www.nytimes.com/2017/06/12/theater/donald-trump-julius-caesar-public-theater-oskar-eustis.html, accessed November 1, 2017.

7. https://www.nytimes.com/2017/06/12/theater/donald-trump-julius-caesar-public-theater-oskar-eustis.html, accessed November 1, 2017.

8. https://www.nytimes.com/2017/06/12/theater/donald-trump-julius-caesar-public-theater-oskar-eustis.html, accessed November 1, 2017.

WORKS CITED

Abdoun, Rabah. 1989. "Les déséquilibres de l'économie algérienne." In *L'Algérie et la modernité*, edited by Ali El-Kenz, 133–49. Dakar, Senegal: Codesria.

Ag Youssouf, Ibrahim, Allen D. Grimshaw, and Charles S. Bird. 1976. "Greetings in the Desert." *American Ethnologist* 3, no. 4: 797–824.

Agar, Michael. 1994. *Language Shock: Understanding the Culture of Conversation.* New York: William Morrow.

Agha, Asif. 2005. "Voice, Footing, Enregisterment." *Journal of Linguistic Anthropology* 15: 38–59.

Aït-Aoudia, Myriam. 2015. *L'expérience démocratique en Algérie (1988–1992).* Paris: Sciences Po.

Allalou, Selali Ali. 1982. *L'Aurore du théâtre algérien (1926–1932).* Oran, Algeria: Université d'Oran.

Allison, Anne. 2013. *Precarious Japan.* Durham, NC: Duke University Press.

Alloula, Abdelkader. 1995. *Les généreux, les dires, le voile.* Translated by Messaoud Benyoucef. Arles, France: Actes Sud.

———. 1997. "La représentation du type non-Aristotélicien dans l'activité théârale en Algérie." In *En mémoire du futur: Pour Abdelkader Alloula*, edited by Malek Alloula, 119–29. Arles, France: Actes Sud.

———. 2002. *Les sangsues, suivi de le pain, la folie de salim, les thermes du bon dieu.* Translated by Messaoud Benyoucef. Arles, France: Actes Sud.

Alloula, Malek, ed. 1997. *En mémoire du futur: Pour Abdelkader Alloula.* Arles, France: Actes Sud.

Alloula, Rihab. n.d. "Al-Daʿaiya." Unpublished script.

Amine, Khalid. 2001. "Crossing Borders: Al-halqa Performance in Morocco from the Open Space to the Theatre Building." *The Drama Review* 45, no. 2: 55–69.

Amine, Khalid, and Marvin Carlson. 2012. *The Theatres of Morocco, Algeria and Tunisia: Performance Traditions of the Maghreb*. New York: Palgrave Macmillan.

Anderson, Ben. 2016. "Neoliberal Affects." *Progress in Human Geography* 40, no. 6: 743–53.

Ansari, Emily Abrams. 2012. "Shaping the Policies of Cold War Musical Diplomacy: An Epistemic Community of American Composers." *Diplomatic History* 36, no. 1: 41–52.

Appadurai, Arjun. 1996. *Modernity at Large: Cultural Dimensions of Globalization*. Minneapolis: University of Minnesota Press.

———. 2013. *The Future as Cultural Fact: Essays on the Global Condition*. London: Verso.

Arnaudiès, Fernand. 1941. *Histoire de l'Opéra d'Alger: Épisodes de la vie théâtrale Algéroise, 1830–1940*. Algiers, Algeria: Ancienne Imprimerie V. Heintz.

Auslander, Philip. 1999. *Liveness: Performance in a Mediatized Culture*. New York: Routledge.

Azpak. n.d. *Azpak: Fécondation in Micro*. Algiers, Algeria: Verclam.

Bachetarzi, Mahieddine. 1968. *Mémoires 1919–1939*. Algiers, Algeria: Société Nationale d'Edition et de Diffusion.

Baffet, Roselyne. 1985. *Tradition théâtrale et modernité en Algérie*. Paris: L'Harmattan.

Bakhtin, M. M. 1981. *The Dialogic Imagination*. Edited by Michael Holquist. Translated by Caryl Emerson and Michael Holquist. Austin: University of Texas Press.

Bakhtin, M. M., and P. N. Medvedev. 1978. *The Formal Method in Literary Scholarship*. Translated by Albert J. Wehrle. Baltimore, MD: Johns Hopkins University Press.

Barber, Karin. 2000. *The Generation of Plays: Yoruba Popular Life in Theater*. Bloomington: Indiana University Press.

———. 2007. *The Anthropology of Texts, Persons and Publics: Oral and Written Culture in Africa and Beyond*. Cambridge: Cambridge University Press.

Baudrillard, Jean. 1994. *Simulacra and Simulation*. Translated by Sheila Faria Glaser. Ann Arbor: University of Michigan Press.

Bauman, Richard. 1992. "Contextualization, Tradition, and the Dialogue of Genres: Icelandic Legends of the *Kraftaskáld*." In *Rethinking Context: Language as an Interactive Phenomenon*, edited by Alessandro Duranti and Charles Goodwin, 125–45. Cambridge: Cambridge University Press.

———. 2004. *A World of Others' Words: Cross-Cultural Perspectives on Intertextuality*. Malden, MA: Blackwell.

———. 2012. "Performance." In *A Companion to Folklore*, edited by Regina F. Bendix and Galit Hasan-Rokem, 94–118. Malden, MA: Wiley-Blackwell.

———. 2016. "Projecting Presence: Aura and Oratory in William Jennings Bryan's Presidential Races." In *Scale: Discourses and Dimensions of Social Life*, edited by E. Summerson Carr and Michael Lempert, 25–51. Oakland: University of California Press.

Bauman, Richard, and Charles Briggs. 1990. "Poetics and Performance as Critical Perspectives on Language and Social Life." In *Annual Review of Anthropology* 19, 59–88.

Bauman, Richard, and Charles Briggs. 2003. *Voices of Modernity: Language Ideologies and the Politics of Inequality.* Cambridge: Cambridge University Press.

Bauman, Richard, and Joel Sherzer, eds. 1989. *Explorations in the Ethnography of Speaking*, 2nd ed. New York: Cambridge University Press.

Belhadad, Salah. 1997. "Alloula: Expression différente." In *Alloula ou le théâtre vivant, Revue de presse 1959–1995*, 101–5. Montpellier, France: SAFA, Mediterrama–France Liberté. Originally published in *El Moujahid*, October 13–14, 1989.

Ben Achour, Bouziane. 2002. *Le théâtre en mouvement: Octobre 88 à ce jour.* Oran, Algeria: Editions Dar El Gharb.

———. 2005. *Le théâtre algérien: Une histoire d'étapes.* Oran, Algeria: Editions Dar El Gharb.

Bencheneb, Rachid. 1977. "Allalu et les origines du théâtre algérien." *Revue de l'Occident Musulman et de la Médit́érrannée* 24: 29–37.

Bendimered, Kémal. 1971. "Quête à l'échelle d'un art." *Algérie Actualité*, August 22–28.

Bendix, Regina. 1997. *In Search of Authenticity: The Formation of Folklore Studies.* Madison: University of Wisconsin Press.

Benjamin, Walter. 1969. *Illuminations.* Edited by Hannah Arendt. New York: Schocken Books.

Bennoune, Karima. 2013. "Algeria Twenty Years On: Words Do Not Die." Open Democracy. opendemocracy.net, accessed May 30, 2018.

Bennoune, Mahfoud. 1988. *The Making of Contemporary Algeria, 1830–1987: Colonial Upheavals and Post-Independence Development.* Cambridge: Cambridge University Press.

Benrabah, Mohamed. 2013. *Language Conflict in Algeria: From Colonialism to Post-Independence.* Bristol, UK: Multilingual Matters.

Bereksi Meddahi, Lamia. 2012. *Abdelkader Alloula: Culture populaire et jeux d'écriture dans l'oeuvre théâtrale.* Paris: L'Harmattan.

Berlant, Lauren. 2010. "Cruel Optimism." In *The Affect Theory Reader*, edited by Melissa Gregg and Gregory J. Seigworth, 93–117. Durham, NC: Duke University Press.

———. 2011. *Cruel Optimism.* Durham, NC: Duke University Press.

Berrechid, Abdelkrim. 1985. *Hududu Al-Kaini Walmumkini fi Al-Masrah Al-Ihtifali* [*The Limits of the Given and the Possible in Festive Theater*]. Casablanca, Morocco: Dar Athaqafa.

———. 1999. "Morocco (Overview)." In *World Encyclopedia of Contemporary Theater, Volume 4: The Arab World*, edited by Ghassan Maleh and Farouk Ohan, translated by Khaled F. Refai, 179–91. New York: Routledge.

Bigenho, Michelle. 2012. *Intimate Distance: Andean Music in Japan*. Durham, NC: Duke University Press.

Bolter, Jay David, and Richard Grusin. 1999. *Remediation: Understanding New Media*. Cambridge, MA: MIT Press.

Bouzar-Kasbadji, Nadia. 1988. *L'émergence artistique algérienne au XXe siècle: Contribution de la musique et du théâtre algérois à la renaissance culturelle et à la prise de conscience nationale*. Algiers, Algeria: Office des Publications Universitaires.

Bowen, John R. 1991. *Sumatran Politics and Poetics: Gayo History, 1900–1989*. New Haven, CT: Yale University Press.

———. 2012. *A New Anthropology of Islam*. Cambridge: Cambridge University Press.

Briggs, Charles. 1993. "Metadiscursive Practices and Scholarly Authority in Folkloristics." *Journal of American Folklore* 106, no. 422: 387–434.

Briggs, Charles, and Richard Bauman. 1992. "Genre, Intertextuality, and Social Power." *Journal of Linguistic Anthropology* 2, no. 2: 131–72.

Bruner, Edward M., and Barbara Kirshenblatt-Gimblett. 2005. "Maasai on the Lawn: Tourist Realism in East Africa." In *Culture on Tour: Ethnographies of Travel*, edited by Edward M. Bruner, 33–70. Chicago: University of Chicago Press.

Butler, Judith. 2004. *Precarious Life: The Powers of Mourning and Violence*. New York: Verso.

Campbell, Jennifer L. 2012. "Creating Something Out of Nothing: The Office of Inter-American Affairs Music Committee (1940–1941) and the Inception of a Policy for Musical Diplomacy." *Diplomatic History* 36, no. 1: 29–39.

Carlson, Marvin, ed. 2008. *Four Plays from North Africa*. New York: Martin E. Segal Theatre Center Publications.

Carr, E. Summerson, and Michael Lempert. 2016a. "Introduction: Pragmatics of Scale." In *Scale: Discourse and Dimensions of Social Life*, edited by E. Summerson Carr and Michael Lempert, 1–21. Oakland: University of California Press.

Carr, E. Summerson, and Michael Lempert, eds. 2016b. *Scale: Discourse and Dimensions of Social Life*. Oakland: University of California Press.

Caton, Steven. 1990. *"Peaks of Yemen I Summon": Poetry as Cultural Practice in a North Yemeni Tribe*. Los Angeles: University of California Press.

Chaikin, Joseph. 1972. *The Presence of the Actor*. New York: Atheneum.

Chapple, Freda, and Chiel Kattenbelt, eds. 2006. *Intermediality in Theatre and Performance*. Amsterdam, The Netherlands: Rodopi.

Cheniki, Ahmed. 2000. "Le syncrétisme résiduel: L'expérience de Abdelkader Alloula." In *Premières rencontres Abdelkader Alloula*, 11–18. Oran, Algeria: Fondation Abdelkader Alloula.

———. 2002. *Le théâtre en Algérie: Histoire et enjeux*. Aix-en-Provence, France: Edisud.

———. 2006. *Vérités du théâtre en Algérie*. Oran, Algeria: Editions Dar El Gharb.

Cheurfi, Achour. 2007a. "Alloula Abdelkader (1939–1994)." In *Dictionnaire encyclopédique de l'Algérie*, edited by Achour Cheurfi, 78. Rouiba, Algeria: Editions ANEP.

———. 2007b. "Kaki Ould Abderrahmane (1943–1995), homme de théâtre." In *Dictionnaire encyclopédique de l'Algérie*, edited by Achour Cheurfi, 653–54. Rouiba, Algeria: Editions ANEP.

Clifford, James, and George E. Marcus, eds. 1986. *Writing Culture: The Poetics and Politics of Ethnography*. Berkeley: University of California Press.

Cole, Catherine M. 2001. *Ghana's Concert Party Theatre*. Bloomington: Indiana University Press.

Crapanzano, Vincent. 2004. *Imaginative Horizons: An Essay in Literary-Philosophical Anthropology*. Chicago: University of Chicago Press.

Crow, Brian. 2009. "African Brecht." *Research in African Literatures* 40, no. 2: 190–207.

Dahmane, Hadj. 2011. *Le théâtre algérien: De l'engagement à la contestation*. Paris, France: Orizons.

Davis, Stephen. 1993. *Jajouka Rolling Stone: A Fable of Gods and Heroes*. New York: Random House.

Dejeux, Jean. 1978. *Djoh'a: Héros de la tradition arabo-berber*. Sherbrooke, Canada: Naaman.

Dillman, Bradford L. 1992. "Transition to Democracy in Algeria." In *State and Society in Algeria*, edited by John Entelis and Philip C. Naylor, 31–51. Boulder, CO: Westview Press.

———. 2000. *State and Private Sector in Algeria: The Politics of Rent-Seeking and Failed Development*. Boulder, CO: Westview Press.

———. 2001. "Facing the Market in North Africa." *Middle East Journal* 55, no. 2: 198–215.

Djaout, Tahar. 2002. *The Watchers*. Translated by Marjolijn De Jager. St. Paul, MN: Ruminator Books.

Djeghloul, Abdelkader. 1984. *Eléments d'histoire culturelle algérienne*. Algiers, Algeria: ENAL.

Djellid, M'Hamed. 1982. "Pour un théâtre national de l'enfance: Histoire et sociologie de l'expérience du T.R.O." *Document de travail* 16. Oran, Algeria: Université d'Oran.

———. 1984–85. "L'Activité théâtrale en Algérie 1945–1980. Essai d'approche sociologique des tonalités groupales, expressives et superstructurelles." MA thesis, Institut des Sciences Sociales, Université d'Oran.

———. 1997. "Abdelkader Alloula parle des Généreux, du théâtre..." In *Alloula ou le théâtre vivant, revue de presse 1959–1995*, 9–23. Montpellier, France: SAFA, Mediterrama–France Liberté.

Djemai, Abdelkader. 1997. "Alloula ou la folie saine." In *Alloula ou le théâtre vivant, revue de presse 1959–1995*, 69–70. Montpellier, France: SAFA,

Mediterrama–France Liberté. Originally published in *La République*, December 23, 1971.

Dolan, Jill. 2005. *Utopia in Performance: Finding Hope at the Theater*. Ann Arbor: University of Michigan Press.

Doshi, Neil. 2013. "Brecht in Algeria: On the Question of Influence in Kateb Yacine's Late Theater." *Research in African Literatures* 44, no. 3: 72–86.

Eisenlohr, Patrick. 2018. *Sounding Islam: Voice, Media, and Sonic Atmospheres in an Indian Ocean World*. Oakland: University of California Press.

Entelis, John P. 2012. "Sonatrach: The Political Economy of an Algerian State Institution." In *Oil and Governance: State-Owned Enterprises and the World Energy Supply*, edited by David G. Victor, David R. Hulls, and Mark Thurber, 567–609. Cambridge: Cambridge University Press.

Fabian, Johannes. 1983. *Time and the Other: How Anthropology Makes Its Object*. New York: Columbia University Press.

———. 1990. *Power and Performance: Ethnographic Explorations through Proverbial Wisdom and Theater in Shaba, Zaire*. Madison: University of Wisconsin Press.

Faier, Lieba, and Lisa Rofel. 2014. "Ethnographies of Encounter." *Annual Review of Anthropology* 43: 363–77.

Fanon, Frantz. 1963. "On National Culture." In *The Wretched of the Earth*, 206–48. New York: Grove Press.

Feld, Steven. 2012. *Jazz Cosmopolitanism in Accra: Five Musical Years in Ghana*. Durham, NC: Duke University Press.

Fosler-Lussier, Danielle. 2012. "Music Pushed, Music Pulled: Cultural Diplomacy, Globalization, and Imperialism." *Diplomatic History* 36, no. 1: 53–64.

Fondation Abdelkader Alloula. 2000. *Premières rencontres Abdelkader Alloula: Actes des journées d'étude*. Oran, Algeria.

Frederik, Laurie A. 2012. *Trumpets in the Mountains: Theater and the Politics of National Culture in Cuba*. Durham, NC: Duke University Press.

Front de Libération Nationale (FLN). 1962. "Programme du Front de Libération Nationale adopté à Tripoli par le C.N.R.A. en juin 1962." *Annuaire de l'Afrique du Nord* 1: 683–704.

Front de Libération Nationale (FLN). 1964. *La Charte d'Alger: Ensemble des textes adoptés par le Premier Congrès du Parti du Front de Libération Nationale*. Algiers, Algeria: FLN Commission Centrale d'Orientation.

Fuegi, John, et al., eds. 1989. *Brecht in Asia and Africa (The Brecht Yearbook XIV)*. Hong Kong: The International Brecht Society.

Ganti, Tejaswini. 2014. "Neoliberalism." *Annual Review of Anthropology* 43: 89–104.

Gienow-Hecht, Jessica C. E. 2012. "The World Is Ready to Listen: Symphony Orchestras and the Global Performance of America." *Diplomatic History* 36, no. 1: 17–28.

Glasser, Jonathan. 2016. *The Lost Paradise: Andalusi Music in Urban North Africa.* Chicago: University of Chicago Press.

Glick Schiller, Nina, and Andrew Irving. 2015. *Whose Cosmopolitanism: Critical Perspectives, Relationalities and Discontents.* New York: Berghahn.

Gluck, Carol, and Anna Lowenhaupt Tsing, eds. 2009. *Words in Motion: Toward a Global Lexicon.* Durham, NC: Duke University Press.

Goffman, Erving. 1981. "Footing." In *Forms of Talk,* 124–59. Philadelphia: University of Pennsylvania Press.

Goodman, Jane E. 2002. "Writing Empire, Underwriting Nation: Discursive Histories of Kabyle Berber Oral Texts." *American Ethnologist* 29, no. 1: 86–122.

———. 2005. *Berber Culture on the World Stage: From Village to Video.* Bloomington: Indiana University Press.

———. 2013a. "Acting with One Voice: Producing Unanimism in Algerian Reformist Theater." *Comparative Studies in Society and History* 55, no. 1: 167–97.

———. 2013b. "The Man Behind the Curtain: Theatrics of the State in Algeria." *Journal of North African Studies* 18, no. 5: 779–95.

———. 2017. "Before the Ruins: Love, Death and the Unmaking of Place in Neoliberalizing Algeria." *American Ethnologist* 44, no. 4: 632–45.

Goodman, Jane E., Matt Tomlinson, and Justin B. Richland. 2014. "Citational Practices: Knowledge, Personhood, and Subjectivity." *Annual Review of Anthropology* 43, 449–63.

Grotowski, Jerzy. 2002. *Towards a Poor Theater.* Edited by Eugenio Barba. New York: Routledge.

Haddad, Youssef Rachid. 1982. *Art du conteur, art de l'acteur.* Louvain-la-Neuve, France: Cahiers Théâtre Louvain.

Hammoudi, Abedellah. 1993. *The Victim and Its Masks: An Essay on Sacrifice and Masquerade in the Maghreb.* Chicago: University of Chicago Press.

Hanks, William F. 1987. "Discourse Genres in a Theory of Practice." *American Ethnologist* 14, no. 4: 668–92.

Hannerz, Ulf. 2005. "Two Faces of Cosmopolitanism: Culture and Politics." *Statsvetenskaplig Tidskrift* 107, no. 3: 199–213.

Hannoum, Abdelmajid. 2000. "The Storyteller." *Mediterraneans / Méditerranéennes* 11, no. 42: 189–93.

———. 2010. *Violent Modernity: France in Algeria.* Cambridge, MA: Harvard University Press.

Harding, James M., and Cindy Rosenthal, eds. 2006. *Restaging the Sixties: Radical Theaters and Their Legacies.* Ann Arbor: University of Michigan Press.

Harding, James M., and Cindy Rosenthal, eds. 2011. *The Rise of Performance Studies: Rethinking Richard Schechner's Broad Spectrum.* New York: Palgrave Macmillan.

Harvey, David. 1990. *The Condition of Postmodernity: An Enquiry into the Origin of Cultural Change.* Malden, MA: Blackwell.

Hastings, Adi, and Paul Manning. 2004. "Introduction: Acts of Alterity." *Language and Communication* 24: 291–311.

Herzfeld, Michael. 1987. *Anthropology through the Looking-Glass: Critical Ethnography in the Margins of Europe.* Cambridge: Cambridge University Press.

———. 1996. "National Spirit or the Breath of Nature? The Expropriation of Folk Positivism in the Discourse of Greek Nationalism." In *Natural Histories of Discourse,* edited by Michael Silverstein and Greg Urban, 277–98. Chicago: University of Chicago Press.

Holquist, Michael. 2002. *Dialogism: Bakhtin and His World.* London: Routledge.

Hymes, Dell. 1989. "Ways of Speaking." In *Explorations in the Ethnography of Speaking,* edited by Richard Bauman and Joel Sherzer, 433–51. Cambridge: Cambridge University Press.

Irving, Andrew. 2015. "Chance, Contingency and the Face-to-Face Encounter." In *Whose Cosmopolitanism? Critical Perspectives, Relationalities and Discontents,* edited by Nina Glick Schiller and Andrew Irving, 65–73. New York: Berghahn.

Ivy, Marilyn. 1995. *Discourses of the Vanishing: Modernity, Phantasm, Japan.* Chicago: University of Chicago Press.

Jakobson, Roman. 1959. "On Linguistic Aspects of Translation." In *On Translation,* edited by Reuben Brower, 232–39. Cambridge, MA: Harvard University Press.

———. 1960. "Closing Statement: Linguistics and Poetics." In *Style in Language,* edited by Thomas A. Sebeok, 350–77. Cambridge, MA: MIT Press.

Jay, Cleo. 2016. "Performance and Social Activism in Morocco: The Legacy of Fatima Chebchoub." *International Journal of Cultural Studies* 19, no. 5: 549–62.

Jiancun, Yu, and Peng Yongwen. 2011. "Richard Schechner and Performance Studies in China." In *The Rise of Performance Studies: Rethinking Richard Schechner's Broad Spectrum,* edited by James M. Harding and Cindy Rosenthal, 98–117. New York: Palgrave Macmillan.

Kali, Mohammed. 2005. *Théâtre algérien, la fin d'un malentendu.* Algiers, Algeria: Editions Ministère de la Culture.

———. 2014. *Théâtre de marionettes en Algérie et ailleurs.* Algiers, Algeria: Dar al-Kitab al-Arabi.

Kaouah, Abdelmadjid. 2014. "La 'Halqua': Un théâtre complet." In *Abdelkader Alloula: Vingt ans déjà!* Edited by Nourredine Saâdi, 17–31. Algiers, Algeria: Les éditions Apic.

Kapchan, Deborah. 1995. "Performance." *Journal of American Folklore* 108, no. 430: 479–508.

———. 1996. *Gender on the Market: Moroccan Women and the Revoicing of Tradition.* Philadelphia: University of Pennsylvania Press.

———. 2003. "Translating Folk Theories of Translation." In *Translating Cultures: Perspectives on Translation and Anthropology,* edited by Paula G. Rubel and Abraham Rosman, 135–51. Oxford: Berg.

———. 2007. *Traveling Spirit Masters: Moroccan Gnawa Trance and Music in the Global Marketplace*. Middletown, CT: Wesleyan University Press.

———. 2008. "The Promise of Sonic Translation: Performing the Festive Sacred in Morocco." *American Anthropologist* 110, no. 4: 467–83.

———. 2014. "Intangible Rights: Cultural Heritage in Transit." In *Cultural Heritage in Transit: Cultural Rights as Human Rights*, edited by Deborah Kapchan, 1–22. Philadelphia: University of Pennsylvania Press.

———. 2014a. "Intangible Heritage in Transit: Goytisolo's Rescue and Moroccan Cultural Rights." In *Cultural Heritage in Transit: Intangible Rights as Human Rights*, edited by Deborah Kapchan, 177–93. Philadelphia: University of Pennsylvania Press.

———. 2020. "Introduction: On Translation and Ethnography." In *Poetic Justice: An Anthology of Contemporary Moroccan Poetry*, translated and edited by Deborah Kapchan, with Driss Marjane, 1–47. Austin, TX: CMES Series in Modern Middle East Translation.

Kh., N. 1997. "La décentralization et l'expérience du TRO." In *Alloula ou le théâtre vivant, revue de presse 1959–1995*, 73–77. Montpellier, France: SAFA, Mediterrama–France Liberté. Originally published in *La République*, December 25–26, 1974.

Kirshenblatt-Gimblett, Barbara. 1998. *Destination Culture: Tourism, Museums, and Heritage*. Berkeley: University of California Press.

Klein, Debra L. 2007. *Yorùbá Bàtá Goes Global: Artists, Culture Brokers, and Fans*. Chicago: University of Chicago Press.

Kurin, Richard. 1997. *Reflections of a Culture Broker: A View from the Smithsonian*. Washington, DC: Smithsonian Institution.

———. 1998. *Smithsonian Folklife Festival: Culture Of, By, and For the People*. Washington, DC: Smithsonian Institution.

Ladenburger, Thomas. 2010. *Al-Halqa: In the Storyteller's Circle*. New York: Taskovski Films.

Lemon, Alaina. 2004. "'Dealing Emotional Blows': Realism and Verbal 'Terror' at the Russian State Theatrical Academy." *Language and Communication* 24, no. 4: 313–37.

———. 2018. *Technologies for Intuition: Cold War Circles and Telepathic Rays*. Oakland: University of California Press.

Lempert, Michael. 2016. "Interaction Rescaled: How Buddhist Debate Became a Diasporic Pedagogy." In *Scale: Discourses and Dimensions of Social Life*, edited by E. Summerson Carr and Michael Lempert, 52–69. Oakland: University of California Press.

Lendra, I. Wayan. 1991. "Bali and Grotowski: Some Parallels in the Training Process." *The Drama Review* 35, no. 1, 119–39.

Lepselter, Susan. 2016. *The Resonance of Unseen Things: Poetics, Power, Captivity, and UFOs in the American Uncanny*. Ann Arbor: University of Michigan Press.

Liverani, Andrea. 2008. *Civil Society in Algeria: The Political Functions of Associational Life*. London: Routledge.

Al-Madani, Izzidine. 1999. "Tunisia (Overview)." In *World Encyclopedia of Contemporary Theater, Volume 4: The Arab World*, edited by Ghassan Maleh and Farouk Ohan, translated by Maha and Tony Chehade, 262–73. New York: Routledge.

Maddy-Weitzman, Bruce. 2011. *The Berber Identity Movement and the Challenge to North African States*. Austin: University of Texas Press.

Mahmood, Saba. 2005. *Politics of Piety: The Islamic Revival and the Feminist Subject*. Princeton, NJ: Princeton University Press.

Mandell, Joan. 1998. "Cultural Resilience through Change: Finding the Theme for *Tales from Arab Detroit*." *Visual Anthropology* 10: 189–208.

Marcus, George E., and Michael M. J. Fischer. 1986. *Anthropology as Cultural Critique: An Experimental Moment in the Human Sciences*. Chicago: University of Chicago Press.

Martinez, Luis. 2000. *The Algerian Civil War 1990–1998*. Translated by Jonathan Derrick. New York: Columbia University Press.

———. 2012. *The Violence of Petro-Dollar Regimes: Algeria, Iraq, and Libya*. New York: Columbia University Press.

Martinez, Luis, and Rasmus Alenius Boserup, eds. 2016. *Algeria Modern: From Opacity to Complexity*. Oxford: Oxford University Press.

Massumi, Brian. 2002. *Parables for the Virtual: Movement, Affect, Sensation*. Durham, NC: Duke University Press.

Mazzarella, William. 2017. "Sense Out of Sense: Notes on the Affect/Ethics Impasse." *Cultural Anthropology* 32, no. 2: 199–208.

McDougall, James. 2017. *A History of Algeria*. Cambridge: Cambridge University Press.

Merdaci, Abdelmadjid. 2008. *Dictionnaire des musiques citadines de Constantine*. Constantine, Algeria: Les Editions du Champ Libre.

Mitter, Shomit. 1992. *Systems of Rehearsal: Stanislavsky, Brecht, Grotowski and Brook*. London: Routledge.

Morad, G. 2009. "El-Istijmam dans la pure tradition de la halqa." *La Voix de l'Oranie*, June 28.

Moreh, Shmuel, and Philip Sadgrove. 1996. *Jewish Contributions to Nineteenth-Century Arabic Theatre: Plays from Algeria and Syria*. Oxford: Oxford University Press.

Morris, Pam, ed. 1994. *The Bakhtin Reader: Selected Writings of Bakhtin, Medvedev, Voloshinov*. London: Arnold.

Mostefa, Abderrahmane, and Mansour Benchehida. 2006. *Kaki: Le dramaturge de l'essentiel*. Algiers, Algeria: Editions Alpha.

Muñoz, José Esteban. 2009. *Cruising Utopia: The Then and There of Queer Futurity*. New York: New York University Press.

Nabokov, Vladimir. 2012. "Problems of Translation: Onegin in English." In *The Translation Studies Reader*, edited by Lawrence Venuti, 113–25. New York: Routledge.

Nashashibi, Karim, et al., eds. 1998. *Algeria: Stabilization and Transition to the Market (Occasional Paper 165)*. Washington, DC: International Monetary Fund.

Noyes, Dorothy. 2014. "Heritage, Legacy, Zombie: How to Bury the Undead Past." In *Cultural Heritage in Transit: Intangible Rights as Human Rights*, edited by Deborah Kapchan, 58–86. Philadelphia: University of Pennsylvania Press.

Ouazani, Cherif, and Brahim Hadj Slimane. 1997. "La quête des dires: Rencontre avec Abdelkader Alloula." In *Alloula ou le théâtre vivant, revue de presse 1959–1995*, 95–99. Montpellier, France: SAFA, Mediterrama–France Liberté. Originally published in *Algérie Actualité*, January 14–20, 1988.

Pahwa, Sonali. 2020. *Theaters of Citizenship: Aesthetics and Politics of Avant-Garde Performance in Egypt*. Evanston, IL: Northwestern University Press.

Pais, Anna. 2017. "Almost Imperceptible Rhythms and Stuff Like That: The Power of Affect in Live Performance." In *Theorizing Sound Writing*, edited by Deborah Kapchan, 233–50. Middletown, CT: Wesleyan University Press.

Power, Cormac. 2008. *Presence in Play: A Critique of Theories of Presence in the Theatre*. New York: Rodopi.

Prochaska, David. 1990. *Making Algeria French: Colonialism in Bône, 1870–1920*. Cambridge: Cambridge University Press.

Puchner, Martin. 2006. "The Performance Group Between Theater and Theory." In *Restaging the Sixties: Radical Theaters and Their Legacies*, edited by James M. Harding and Cindy Rosenthal, 313–32. Ann Arbor: University of Michigan Press.

Rahal, Malika. 2017. "1988–1992: Multipartism, Islamism and the Descent into Civil War." In *Algeria: Nation, Culture and Transnationalism, 1988–2015*, edited by Patrick Crowley, 81–100. Liverpool, UK: Liverpool University Press.

Reynolds, Dwight. 1995. *Heroic Poets, Poetic Heroes: The Ethnography of Performance in an Arabic Oral Epic Tradition*. Ithaca, NY: Cornell University Press.

———. 1998. "From the Delta to Detroit: Packaging a Folk Epic for a New Folk." *Visual Anthropology* 10: 145–64.

Richards, Thomas. 1995. *At Work with Grotowski on Physical Actions*. London: Routledge.

Ridout, Nicholas, and Rebecca Schneider. 2012. "Precarity and Performance: An Introduction." *The Drama Review* 56, no. 4: 5–9.

Roberts, Hugh. 2003. *The Battlefield, Algeria 1988–2002: Studies in a Broken Polity*. New York: Verso.

Rose, Jacqueline. 2015. "Wounded Cosmopolitanism." In *Whose Cosmopolitanism? Critical Perspectives, Relationalities and Discontents*, edited by Nina Glick-Schiller and Andrew Irving, 41-48. New York: Berghahn.

Rosenberg, Jonathan. 2012. "America on the World Stage: Music and Twentieth-Century U.S. Foreign Relations." *Diplomatic History* 36, no. 1: 65–69.

Rosenthal, Cindy. 2011. "Joan MacIntosh: Interview." In *The Rise of Performance Studies: Rethinking Richard Schechner's Broad Spectrum*, edited by James M. Harding and Cindy Rosenthal, 196–212. New York: Palgrave Macmillan.

Roth, Arlette. 1967. *Le théâtre algérien de langue dialectale, 1926–1954*. Paris: François Maspero.

Rouchard, François. 1980. *Le théâtre national algérien (document à diffusion restreinte)*. Paris: UNESCO.

Royce, Anya Peterson. 1984. *Movement and Meaning: Creativity and Interpretation in Ballet and Mime*. Bloomington: Indiana University Press.

———. 2018. "'Being Curated by a Divine Force': The Forty-plus Year Success of the Pilobolus Dance Theater." In *Psycho-Cultural Analysis of Folklore: In Memory of Prof. Alan Dundes* 2, edited by P. Chenna Reddy and M. Sarat Babu, 347–60. Delhi, India: BR.

Rukaibi, Abdallah El. 1999. "Algeria (Overview)." In *World Encyclopedia of Contemporary Theater, Volume 4: The Arab World*, edited by Ghassan Maleh and Farouk Ohan, translated by Maha and Tony Chehade, 55–68. New York: Routledge.

Salhi, Kamal. 1998. "Post-colonial Theatre for Development in Algeria: Kateb Yacine's Early Experience." In *African Theatre for Development: Art for Self-Determination*, edited by Kamal Salhi, 69–96. Exeter, UK: Intellect.

———. 2004. "Morocco, Algeria and Tunisia." In *A History of Theatre in Africa*, edited by Martin Banham. Cambridge: Cambridge University Press.

Schechner, Richard. 1985. *Between Theater and Anthropology*. Philadelphia: University of Pennsylvania Press.

Scher, Philip W. 2014. "The Right to Remain Cultural: Is Culture a Right in the Neoliberal Caribbean?" In *Cultural Heritage in Transit: Intangible Rights as Human Rights*, edited by Deborah Kapchan, 87–109. Philadelphia: University of Pennsylvania Press.

Schielke, Samuli. 2015. *Egypt in the Future Tense: Hope, Frustration, and Ambivalence Before and After 2011*. Bloomington: Indiana University Press.

Schutz, Alfred. 1944. "The Stranger: An Essay in Social Psychology." *American Journal of Sociology* 49: 499–507.

———. 1967. *The Phenomenology of the Social World*. Translated by G. Walsh and F. Lehnert. Evanston, IL: Northwestern University Press.

Schuyler, Philip D. 1984. "Berber Professional Musicians in Performance." In *Performance Practice: Ethnomusicological Perspectives*, edited by Gerard Béhague, 91–148. London: Greenwood Press.

———. 2000. "Joujouka/Jajouka/Zahjoukah: Moroccan Music and Euro-American Imagination." In *Mass Mediations: New Approaches to Popular Culture in the Middle East and Beyond*, edited by Walter Armbrust, 146–60. Berkeley: University of California Press.

Sehaba, Mohamed. 1997. "La comédie comme une main tendue." In *Alloula ou le théâtre vivant, revue de presse 1959–1995*, 139–43. Montpellier, France: SAFA, Mediterrama–France Liberté. Originally published in *Algérie Actualité*, April 13–18, 1993.

Seigworth, Gregory J., and Melissa Gregg. 2010. "An Inventory of Shimmers." In *The Affect Theory Reader*, edited by Melissa Gregg and Gregory J. Seigworth, 1–25. Durham, NC: Duke University Press.

Senouci, Mourad. n.d. "Al-Ghul bi Usbu'a Risan." Unpublished script.

Serres, Thomas. 2019. *L'Algérie face à la catastrophe suspendue: Gérer la crise et blâmer le peuple sous Bouteflika (1999–2014)*. Tunis and Paris: IRMC/Karthala.

Shipley, Jesse Weaver. 2015. *Trickster Theater: The Poetics of Freedom in Urban Africa*. Bloomington: Indiana University Press.

Shryock, Andrew. 1998. "Mainstreaming Arabs: Filmmaking as Image Making in *Tales from Arab Detroit*." *Visual Anthropology* 10: 165–88.

Silverstein, Michael. 2003. "Translation, Transduction, Transformation: Skating 'Glossando' on Thin Semiotic Ice." In *Translating Cultures: Perspectives on Translation and Anthropology*, edited by Paula G. Rubel and Abraham Rosman, 75–105. Oxford: Berg.

Silverstein, Paul. 2011. "Masquerade Politics: Race, Islam and the Scale of Amazigh Activism in Southeastern Morocco." *Nations and Nationalism* 17, no. 1: 65–84.

———. 2013. "The Activist and the Anthropologist." In *Encountering Morocco: Fieldwork and Cultural Understanding*, edited by David Crawford and Rachel Newcomb, 116–30. Bloomington: Indiana University Press.

Slyomovics, Susan. 1987. *The Merchant of Art: An Egyptian Hilali Oral Epic Poet in Performance*. Berkeley: University of California Press.

———. 1991. "'To Put One's Finger in the Bleeding Wound': Palestinian Theater Under Israeli Censorship." *The Drama Review* 35, no. 2: 18–38.

———. 1999. "The Arabic Epic Poet as Outcast, Trickster, and Con Man." In *Epic Traditions in the Contemporary World: The Poetics of Community*, edited by Margaret Beissinger, Jane Tylus, and Susanne Wofford, 54–69. Berkeley: University of California Press.

Spolin, Viola. 1983. *Improvisation for the Theater: A Handbook of Teaching and Directing Techniques*. Evanston, IL: Northwestern University Press.

Stasch, Rupert. 2009. *Society of Others: Kinship and Mourning in a West Papuan Place*. Berkeley: University of California Press.

Stewart, Kathleen. 2010. "Afterword: Worlding Refrains." In *The Affect Theory Reader*, edited by Melissa Gregg and Gregory J. Seigworth, 339–53. Durham, NC: Duke University Press.

———. 2017. "In the World that Affect Proposed." *Cultural Anthropology* 32, no. 2: 192–98.

Stora, Benjamin. 2001. *Algeria, 1830–2000: A Short History*. Translated by Jane Marie Todd. Ithaca, NY: Cornell University Press.

Taleb-Ibrahimi, Khaoula. 1995. *Les algériens et leurs langues*. Algiers, Algeria: El Hikma.

Tang, Patricia. 2012. "The Rapper as Modern Griot: Reclaiming Ancient Traditions." In *Hip Hop Africa: New African Music in a Globalizing World*, edited by Eric S. Charry, 79–91. Bloomington: Indiana University Press.

Taylor, Diana. 2003. *The Archive and the Repertoire: Performing Cultural Memory in the Americas*. Durham, NC: Duke University Press.

Tournier, Christophe. 2003. *Manuel d'improvisation théâtrale*. Paris: Editions de l'eau vive.

Tsing, Anna Lowenhaupt. 2005. *Friction: An Ethnography of Global Connection*. Princeton, NJ: Princeton University Press.

Turino, Thomas. 2000. *Nationalists, Cosmopolitans, and Popular Music in Zimbabwe*. Chicago: University of Chicago Press.

Turner, Victor. 1974. *Dramas, Fields, and Metaphors: Symbolic Action in Human Society*. Ithaca, NY: Cornell University Press.

———. 1982. *From Ritual to Theatre: The Human Seriousness of Play*. New York: Performing Arts Journal Publications.

Urban, Greg. 1989. "The 'I' of Discourse." In *Semiotics, Self, and Society*, edited by Benjamin Lee and Greg Urban. Berlin: Mouton de Gruyter.

———. 2001. *Metaculture: How Culture Moves Through the World*. Minneapolis: University of Minnesota Press.

Venuti, Lawrence. 1998. *The Scandals of Translation: Towards an Ethic of Difference*. London: Routledge.

———. 2008. *The Translator's Invisibility: A History of Translation*. London: Routledge.

———. 2012. "Genealogies of Translation Theory." In *The Translation Studies Reader*, edited by Lawrence Venuti, 483–502. London: Routledge.

———. 2013. *Translation Changes Everything: Theory and Practice*. London: Routledge.

Venuti, Lawrence, ed. 2012. *The Translation Studies Reader*. 3rd ed. London: Routledge.

Werbner, Pnina. 2008. "Introduction: Towards a New Cosmopolitan Anthropology." In *Anthropology and the New Cosmopolitanism: Rooted, Feminist and Vernacular Perspectives*, edited by Pnina Werbner, 1–29. Oxford: Berg.

Wilk, Richard. 1995. "Learning to Be Local in Belize: Global Systems of Common Difference." In *Worlds Apart: Modernity Through the Prism of the Local*, edited by Daniel Miller, 110–33. London: Routledge.

Wolford, Lisa. 2010. "Grotowski's Vision of the Actor: The Search for Contact." In *Actor Training*, edited by Alison Hodge, 199–214. London: Routledge.

INDEX

Italicized page numbers refer to figures.

246 INDEX

Alloula, Abdelkader (playwright) (*Cont.*)
142; translation of works by, 39n7; and
unanswered questions, 227; use of MSA in
Et-Teffeh, 196; and US performances, 1
Alloula, Abdelkader (playwright), plays of:
El-Agoual (The Sayings, 1980), 76, 186–87;
El-Ajouad (The Generous Ones, 1985), 76,
176n6; *El-Lithem* (The Veil, 1989), 76; *El-
Meïda* (The Low Table), 75; *Homq Salim*
(1972), 76. See also *Apples*; *Et-Teffeh*
Alloula, Raja (playwright's spouse), 7–8
Alloula, Rihab (playwright's daughter):
on affective difference between MSA
and Shakespearean English, 197; on
Americans and *Apples*, 218; on apples
and democracy, 49, 54; author's first
meeting with, 7–8; bio of, 5–6; on cultural
exchange, 114, 115, 122; on difference
in Algerian theater, 111; on discipline,
161; on end of *Apples*, 86; on finding
resources, 139; on global economy and
power, 59–60; on interaction with
Double Edge, 132; language skills of,
17, 183; and maintenance of phatic
connections, 120–21; on message in
Apples, 148; on move from socialism,
54–55; performances of music and poetry,
82, 84; personal response to difference in
culture, 112, 113; photographs of, *4, 28, 80,
109, 114, 123, 143, 151*; and physical training,
89–90, 152–53, 158; responsibilities of,
168; *The Rumor*, 153, 154; on shadow play,
203–4, 208; and sonic atmosphere of
Caesar, 201; on street performance, 81–82;
on theatrical training, 145; use of actors'
names in *Apples*, 80; and voicing in *Apples*,
78–79, 80. See also HartBeat Ensemble;
improvisation
Amazigh (Berber) activists, 70, 176n7, 196
anthropology, research methods in, 33
Apple and Apple computers, 50–51, 66n12
apples: and democracy, 47–49; playing with
double meaning of, 49–51
Apples (Abdelkader Alloula): audience for,
2–3; compared to staging of *Et-Teffeh*,
83–84; cultural differences embedded
in, 186–87; as a dream, 84–85; ending of

the play, 84–87, 222–24; as halqa, 68; as
play of voicing, 78–80; popular Algerian
song in, 84, 95n50; references to status of
theater in Algeria, 142, 143; rehearsal in
Massachusetts, 133; setting and plot of, 35;
Shakespeare in, 79, 195–97, 199–203, 225
(*see also* tableaux developed by author);
synopsis of, 37–38; translation process for,
31–32; translation's recontextualization
of, 13, 31–32; universality in, 218, 219, 221,
227; US debut of, 1; video showings of, 213,
214. *See also* Actor; Attendant; courtroom
scene; Customer; *Et-Teffeh*; Restroom
encounter; translation of *Et-Teffeh* to
Apples
Arabic language: in *Apples*, 190–95; for
characterization and affect, 198; cultural
difference as use of, 27; use of Modern
Standard Arabic, 196
Arab Spring, 24, 124–25, 136n19, 229
Aristotelian and non-Aristotelian theater,
72, 75
artist-to-artist exchanges, 122
Ashfield, Massachusetts: conversion from
farm to theater complex in, 130; Istijmam
at apple stand in, *49*. See also Double Edge
Theatre Company
Attendant (*Apples* role): Algerian context
of, 38, 46–47; and disenfranchisement,
58, 60; reinvention of, 44, 52; role in
Apples compared to *Et-Teffeh*, 83–85; US
spectators' responses to, 219, 221, 223,
226. *See also* courtroom scene; Restroom
encounter
audiences. *See* halqa; participatory
spectatorship
author: ethnographic research by, 2; with
Istijmam, *114, 123*; as native informant,
184; as participant observer, 33; research
in Algeria, 17; role in Istijmam's US tour,
9–10; translation check and pronunciation
for *Apples*, 183
avant-garde theater, 69

Bachetarzi, Mahieddine, 71, 93nn26–27
Baffet, Roselyne, 95n51, 176n13
Bakhtin, Mikhail, 31, 77, 198

intuition in, 171; principles of, 163–65, *164*, 167, 168; readying for, 3; and reflection of uncertainty through, 160–61; techniques of, 165–67; visa difficulties incorporated into, 61–63; workshops in Algeria, 21, 119–20. *See also* Tournier, Christophe

indexical penumbras in translation: 'aṣr prayer and Arabic religious phrases in, 189–90; and "business," 188–89; concerning "deaf-mutes," 186–87; cultural contexts and, 185; and law and regulation, 187–88; occurrence of, 37; and Shakespeare, 197; use of term, 210n7

Indiana University: comments on inclusion of Arabic in *Apples*, 193; conversation with Istijmam at, 1; Living Communication at, 136n11; performance space at, 80; presentations and discussions at, 100–101, 109, 112; sonic atmosphere in *Apples* at, 201; student reactions to *Apples* at, 216–17; talk-backs at, 85–86, 91; video screenings of *Apples* at, 214, 230n1

intercultural exchange: movement to seek inspiration from, 32–33; scholar-performers' experience in, 33–34; utopian potentiality of, 34–35. *See also* cross-cultural encounters; cultural diplomacy tours

intuition, discipline of, 173–74. *See also* Lemon, Alaina

Ionesco, Eugène, 204

iPhones, 50, 66n13

Islamic discipline, 159–60

Islamic Salvation Front (FIS), 43, 229, 230

Islamism and Algerian artists, 24

Istijmam Culturelle: blog of, 178n30; choice of name, 4; development of troupe, 3, 36; difficulty in finding training and resources, 139–40; discussion of disenfranchisement, 58–59; division of responsibility in, 168; encountering their own culture anew, 31; funding for, 39n11; general assembly meeting of, 141; as laboratory theater, 9, 145; and memories of the Dark Decade, 57; on messages in plays, 148; organizational structure, funding, and touring and,

144–45; photographs of, *4, 15–16, 45, 64, 109, 114, 123, 143*; possibilities of traveling from Algeria, 23–24, 25; revisiting and interpreting Algeria in the 1990s, 44–45; self-discipline of, 162, 175; sharing music with Double Edge, 132; uncertainty and discipline of, 159–61. *See also* Algeria; Alloula, Rihab; Benhamamouch, Jamil; Boukra, Moussa; Center Stage program; disenfranchisement in neoliberalism; goual; Hadjel, Djalel; halqa; improvisation; Lakhdari, Mustapha; Living Communication; participatory spectatorship; physical training using the Grotowski sequence; plays of voicing; rehearsal discipline; rehearsal residency; Tahar Amar, Lila

Istijmam USA tour: overview of, 1–2; cultural tensions in, 102–3, 217; familiar genres of encounter in, 100; introductions to Algeria in, 215–16; metapragmatic framing during, 173–74; unrealized hopes of, 10, 21, 26, 35, 36, 100, 108, 134–35. *See also* Denmark, Maine, performance and discussions in; Double Edge Theatre Company; genres of encounter; HartBeat Ensemble; Hartford, Connecticut; Indiana University; Kennedy Center (Washington, DC); La MaMa Theater; Portland, Maine; presentations and discussions; Sarah Lawrence College students; University of New Hampshire; workshops

Jagger, Mick, 70
Jaguar Jokers, 34
Jakobson, Roman, 40n22
Jamil. *See* Benhamamouch, Jamil
Jennings, Brian, *123*, 123, 124–25, 159
Johnstone, Keith, 169
Jones, Brian, 70
Julius Caesar (William Shakespeare): *Apples'* passage from, 195–97; relationship with politics and society, 226–27; struggling with poetics of, 199–203; and 2017 controversy in US, 228–29. *See also* tableaux developed by author

phatic intuition, 173–74. *See also* Lemon, Alaina
physical theater, 88–89
physical training using the Grotowski sequence: commitment to, 69, 140, 149, 152, 156–58, 179n46; description of sequence, *150*, 151–52, 153, *154*; grueling work of, 150, *151*, 152–53; as integral to Istijmam's performance practice, 36, 89–90, 162; and Islamic discipline, 159–60; philosophy behind, 155–56; and transcendence of fear and the body's limits, 157, 158; transformation of Istijmam through, 150–51. *See also* Grotowski, Jerzy
Piscator, Erwin, 73, 146
plays of voicing, 78–80
"The Pleasure Trip of the Enamoured and the Agony of Lovers in the City of Tiryaq in Iraq," 70–71
pluralism in Algeria, 53
poetry, Arabic, 192
political and economic liberalization of Algeria, 53, 66n20
political power and human rights, 63
poor theater approach, 90, 158, 175
Portland, Maine: phatic intuition exercise in, 174; workshop exercise at, 117; workshop with modern dance company in, 99
Power, Cormac, 40n19
presentations and discussions: cultural difference in, 106; as familiar genres, 100–101, 109–10; to further develop Istijmam, 10; performance of cultural encounter in, 108–15; phatic exchange in, 107; phatic friction in, 115–16; typical questions and answers at, 110–12; unfulfilled hopes of, 36, 108, 134–35. *See also* tableaux developed by author
professionalism in Algerian theater, 144, 175, 177n20
puppet theater, 70

Raider-Ginsburg, Steven, *114*, 123, *123*, 127
rai music, 82, 84, 86, 191–92, 206, 211n11
recontextualization: of *Et-Teffeh*, 31–32; of plays in the Western canon, 32
Reed College Theater History class: and activity responding to *Apples*, 213, 214;

discussion of *Apples* by, 213; responses to end of play, 223–24
Regional Theater of Oran (TRO), 142–43, 144, 176n6, 177n14
rehearsal discipline: Istijmam and Double Edge comparing notes on, 159; Istijmam's dedication to, 155, 157–58; physical training, 149–53, 155–58; as potential cultural exchange topic, 162; Rihab on, 161–62; schedules, *170*; table reading in, *156*
rehearsal residency: description of space, 140–41; finalizing the translation during, 31–32, 181, 183. *See also* desire in neoliberalism; disappearance in neoliberalism; disenfranchisement in neoliberalism; translation of *Et-Teffeh* to *Apples*
rehearsal space: in *Apples*, 138–40, 223; finding, 176n6
remediation in staging, 84–85, 87
Restroom encounter: Actor's development of his art in, 84, 130, 138–40, 175; democracy in, 47–48; desire, disappearance and disenfranchisement in, 44–45; indexical penumbras in, 186–88; staging of *Et-Teffeh* compared with *Apples*, 82–85; start of, 42, 47–48; US spectators' responses to, 221; word play in, 193–94
revolutionary theater, 74
Rihab. *See* Alloula, Rihab
Roosevelt, Franklin D., 17
Rosenblatt, Julia, 123, *123*, 126
rough translation, 210, 225, 228, 229
Russian Academy of Theatrical Arts, 179nn45–46

Saddiki, Tayeb, 74
Sadgrove, Philip, 93n17
Sarah Lawrence College students: in improvisation workshop, 1, 97–98, 100; phatic friction in QA session with, 22; workshop exercises with, 117
scale, halqa and flexibility of, 26, 91
scaling up: in cultural exchange programs, 3, 101; of Istijmam and tour performances, 3, 13, 30; logics of, 20–21, 26

JANE E. GOODMAN is Associate Professor of Anthropology at Indiana University. She is the author of *Berber Culture on the World Stage: From Village to Video* and the coeditor of *Bourdieu in Algeria: Colonial Politics, Ethnographic Practices, Theoretical Developments*. A performer in her own right, she has appeared with the women's world music groups Libana and Kaia.

www.ingramcontent.com/pod-product-compliance
Lightning Source LLC
Chambersburg PA
CBHW030350270326
41926CB00009B/1045